Adab Al-Qadi
Imam Khassaf

Commentary By
Al Sadr Al Shahid

Translated By
Justice Dr.Munir Ahmad Mughal

Qadeem Press Edition

Breathing Life into Forgotten Pages
www.qadeempress.com

Find our titles on your favourite online bookstore using the keyword 'Qadeem Press'

This work has been selected by scholars as culturally important. This book has been reproduced from the original artefact and remains as true to the original work as possible. You may see the original copyright references, library stamps, and other notations in the work. As a reproduction of an artefact, this work may contain missing or blurred pages, poor pictures, errant marks, etc. Scholars believe, and we concur, that this work is important enough to be preserved, reproduced, and made available to the public. We appreciate the support of the preservation process and thank you for being an important part of keeping this knowledge alive and relevant.

CONTENTS

Preface

The Islamic order of this life as well as that after death is based on justice. There are numerous Qur'ānic verses ordaining maintenance of justice. For example:

"Allah enjoineth justice......."   (16:90)

......Be Just: that is next to piety......"   (5:8)

Allah has established justice in all spheres of existence. He has set up a scale to adjudge human deeds. He has prescribed a norm for distinguishing between the good and the evil and, to explain it, sent down guidance through His Apostles and His Books. He has provided for the reckoning of human deeds, good or bad. He has also designated a Day of Judgment when the quality and quantity of human deeds will be determined by Him. The following *Qur'ānic* verses point to each of these stages of justice:

"And the Firmament has He raised high, and He has set up the Balance (of Justice), in order that ye may not transgress (due) balance. So establish weight with justice and fall not short in the balance."   (55:7—9)

"We sent aforetime Our Apostles with Clear Signs and sent down with them the Book and the Balance (of right and wrong), that men may stand forth in justice."   (57:25)

The Holy Prophet Muhammad (peace and blessings of Allah be upon him) is reported to have said:

"The persons who practise justice will have their seat near Allah upon pulpits of light."   (*Muslim*)

"A single moment of justice is worth more than sixty years of worship offered on nights of vigil and days of fasting."

(Asbahani)

Judges are, of course, necessary for the administration of justice in this world. About judges, the Holy Prophet Muhammad (peace and blessings of Allah be upon him) is reported to have said:

"Allah is with a judge so long as he is not unjust. When he is unjust (purposely), He leaves and the devil takes possession of the unjust judge."   (Tirmidhi, Ibn Majah)

This is, in brief, the Islamic concept of justice and the Judge. Islam is a practical religion dealing with the warring traits of human nature and bending them to the Straight Path. It has discarded the law of jungle and the motto of 'might is right'. Islamic concept of justice is positive. It does not stop at negation of the wrong but goes forward to promote the right, so that there remains no incompatibility between the so-called justice and what is really just and equitable. The concept of Islamic justice does not permit prejudice against anyone. The Qur'ānic injunction is:

"........and let not the hatred of any people seduce you that ye deal not justly......."   (5:8)

Under Islam, justice is the sum total of life. To do injustice is sinful. To suffer injustice calls for positive remedial action on the part of Muslims. Such action might mean even the supreme sacrifice of one's life for the sake of justice.

This book is an English rendering of a popular Arabic book entitled *Adāb al-Qadi* written by the renowned Muslim Jurist Imam Khassaf. In this book the learned author has favoured us with the basic principles of the Islamic Judicial System and that of the Judiciary in the light of the Holy *Qur'ān* and the *Sunnah*.

The learned translator of this book Justice Dr. Muneer Ahmad Mughal is himself a Judge of the Lahore High Court, Lahore. He has perfect hold on the subject as well as over both the languages, the one translated from and the other translated into. The translation is therefore reliable and close to the original.

This book has been rendered into English for the benefit of those English-knowing people who are anxious to know about the Judicial System of Islam. We hope, it will serve the purpose for which it has been translated.

Muhammad Iqbal Shaikh
7th December, 1998   Advocate High Court

Adãb al-Qãdi
(ISLAMIC LEGAL & JUDICIAL SYSTEM)

Meaning of Ãdãb

Every person has control over his own self. His control over the self of any other person can be exercised on the basis of authorisation by the *Shari'ah* as the guardianship of father over his minor son is given to the father by the *Shari'ah*.

Some times two persons are in conflict about their control. If both follow the *shari'ah* there would have been no dispute. One of them exceeds his limit and the other restrains him but the later does not accept such restraint and the quarrel arises. At such an occasion conciliation is commendable. If the conciliation is not possible and they are left to remain quarrelling the dispute may even result in murder and blood shed. Hence Allah, the Almighty has given the fundamental rule in *shari'ah* that all human beings have sold their life and property to their Lord, the Almighty and cannot exercise their own control over them. When two persons fight it is in fact a deception of their self hence Allah Almighty has withdrawn their own authority and entrusted the same to a *caliph* and authorised him to command according to the *shari'ah*. Whatever is commanded according to *shari'ah* is like the personal control over an individual. A *qãdi* is entrusted with general guardianship and it is this entrustment which requires certain attributes to be possessed by a *qãdi*. These attributes are termed as "*Ãdãb*". In other words *Ãdãb al-Qãdi* means such affairs that have been defined by the *shari'ah* and are binding on the *qadi*, such as to do and show justice and to undo and remove injustice and to keep the people within the limits of *shari'ah* (the *Qur'an* and *sunnah*).

BIOGRAPHICAL SKETCH OF IMĀM ABŪ BAKR AL-KHASSAF (Allàh's mercy by on him): THE AUTHOR OF KITÁB ĀDĀB AL-QĀDÍ

Name and Profile

His name is Ahmad. His *kunniyat* (surname) is Abú Bakr. His title is al-Khassáf. His tribe is Al-Shaiban. His father s name is 'Umar and his grand father's name is Muhair. He was cobbler by profession; and due to this profession he got the title al-Khassáf.[1]

---

1. Here it seems necessary to explain that Muslim Scholars and Mashā'ikh made the teaching as their source of livelihood very rarely. They did not hasitate to do labour and to join any profession. They performed academic services as religious duty. Thus we have many such examples in the Islamic history. Allamah Shibli Nu'mani, in his book "*Al-Ghazzāli*" has mentioned that the title *al-Ghazzāli* of Abú Hamid Muhammad bin Muhammad was due to the fact that his father used to sell yarn. There after he writes that it would not be improper to state. It is mentioned about family profession of Imām Ghazzāli that during that time and even prior to it the education was so common amongst the Muslims that even the people of the lowest profession were not deprived of the education. Rather amongst such professionals people of such perfection came out whom we remember with the titles of Imām and Allamah. For example:

a. The jurist Abú al-Hasan Muhammad bin Ahmad Za'farani used to sell *Za'faran* (*saffron*).

b. Abú al-Muzaffar, Jamál al-Islam As'ad bin Muhammad bin Husain Nishapuri Karabisi.

c. Abú Ishāq, Rukn al-Islam, Ibráhim bin Ismá'il al-Ma'rúf bin Zahid, Saffar used to sell utensils made of copper.

Date of Birth and Death

The biographers are unanimous that Imám Khassáf died in 261 A.H. Kuhalah in *Mu'jam al-Mu'allifin*[2], Zarkuli in *Al-A 'lam*[3] has proved this *Hijrah* year falling in 875 A.D. ON the other hand Brockelmann[4] and Fuwãd Sezgin[5] have stated that this Hijrah year fell in 874 A.D. As Imám Khassáf had died at the age of about 80 years,[6] hence the year of his birth was 181 A.H. (797 A.D.), as is státed in *Mu'jam al-Mu'allifin*.[7]

Teachers

Imãm Khassãf got the education of jurisprudence from his father 'Umar bin Muhair[8] who was a pupil of Imãm Hasan

d. Zain al-Mashá'ikh, Muhammad bin Abú al-Qásim Khawérizmi, Baqqáli used to sell vegetables.

e. Shams al-Din, Abû Abdulláh Muhamad bin Ahmad bin Uthmán bin Qa'imaz Turkamáni Záhbi was a gold smith.

f. Abû Sahib Imám Hákim bin Mûsã bin Shairzad Baghdádi, Qantari was a cloth merchant.

g. Abû Abdullãh Ahmad bin Ibrãhim al-Baghdádi, al-Hãfiz al-Kabir al-Dawárqi used to make the Dawárqi caps.

h. Abû Bakr Muhammad bin Bashshar bin Da'rãbdi Basri was a weaver.

ı. Abú Hanifah, Imám A'zam, Nu'man bin Thãbit Kûfí was a cloth merchant.

j. Imãm Abû Ja'far Tahawi was dealer in burial cloth.

k. Abû al-Abbás Ahmad bin Muhammad bin Umar al-Natifi was a confectioner.

2. *Mu'jam al-Mu'allifin*, vol. II, p. 35.

3. *Al-A 'alam*, vol. I, p. 178.

4. *Tarikh al-Ãdãb al-'Arabi* (Arabic version), vol. III, p. 259.

5. Fuwád Sezgin, G.S. Vol. I, p. 436.

6. *Al-Fawá'id al-Bahiyyah*, p. 29.

7. Kuhalãh, vol. II, p. 35.

8. *Al-Fawã'id al-Bahiyyah*, p. 151; *Al-Jawahir al-Madiyyah*, vol. I,

bin Ziyad, while Imãm Hasan bin Ziyad was a pupil of Imãm Abû Hanifah.

The great *Muhaddithin*, on the authority of whom Imãm Khassãf transmitted the *Ahãdíth*, amongst others were:

Umar bin Muhair (father of Imam Khassãf);
Abû 'Ãsim al-Nabil (al-Dahak bin Makhlad al-Shaibani);
Hashshãm bin 'Abdul Málik;
Ibráhim bin Bashshãr al-Rimãdi.
Musaddid bin Musarhad;
Abdullãh bin Muslimah al-Qadabi;
Yahyã bin Abdul Hamid al-Hamãni;
Abdullãh bin Abí Shaibah;
Abú Mu'ãwiyah al-Darir Ali bin al-Madyani;
Mu'ãz bin Asad al-Khurasãni;
Husain bin Qãsim al-Nakhafi al-Kúfí;
'Amr bin Qãsim al-Kilãbi;
Abû 'Amir al-Aqadi;
Muhamad bin al-Fadl 'Ãrim;
Wahb bin Jarir bin Jãzim;
Hasan bin 'Anbasa al-Warrãq;
Fadl bin Dikkin Abú Na'im;
Ma'la bin Asad;
Abû 'Amr Hafs bin 'Umar al-Darir;
'Amr bin 'Aûn al-Wásiti;
Muslim bin Ibráhim al-Uzdi, and
Abû Da'ûd al-Tiyãlisy.

p. 400 under biographical note No. 1108. In both these books no date of death of Imãm Khassáf has been mentioned.

Early Life

The biographers, despite so much popularity of Imãm Khassãf, did not sate anything about his early life. However, they have stated that Imãm Khassãf possessed a high and elevated rank and position in the eye of his contemporary *caliphs* due to expansion of his learning and having perfect hold over the opinions and thought of Imãm Abú Hanifah. The *caliphs* admitted his place and rank due to which he had proximity to the *caliphs*. Despite all this his status could not remain secure from the harm attempted by his adversaries. Ill-willing courtiers became successful in their back-biting and damaged him in the matter of his rank and status. Resultantly, during the period of *caliph* Mou'taz[9], the masses also started criticising him. Later when Muhtadi Billãh became *caliph*, he again restored his earlier status and rank and granted him proximity.

Ibn Nadim stated that Imãm Khassãf was a jurist, expert in the science of compulsory duties, mathematician and well aware of the opinions and *ijtihadat* of *Hanafi* jurists and enjoyed precedence in the court of Muhtadi Billãh.[10] After the restoration of his status and rank, the ill-willing courtier's mischief also came back and they started levelling false accusations against him. The issue of Holy *Qur'ãn* being a creation which was raised by the *Mu'tazilah* and their supporters appeared and it became easy for anyone to say anything about any person. Perhaps this fact is true that Qãdi Ahmad bin Abí Dã'úd[11] had played significant role in

9. Al-Tabari, *Tarikh al-Rasul wal-Mulûk*, European edition, vol. III, p. 1684, events of the year 252 A.H.

10. *Al-Fahrist*, p. 304.

11. Abú Abdullãh Ahmad bin Abí Da'ud al-Ayãdi was the Chief Justice during the period of the caliphs al-Mu'tasim, al-Wathiq, and al-Mutawakkil. He was from among the Mu'tazilah. He died in the year 240 A.H. See *Tarikh Baghdãd*, vol. IV, pp. 141-156, biographical

Piety and Care of Imám Khassáf in Religious Affairs

Ibn Najjãr states that some of the leading jurists have reported that Imãm Khassãf was full of worship and piety. He earned his lawful earning himself. He states that he heard Abú Sahl Muhammad bin 'Umar, who narrated on the authority of a Shaikh of Balkh: "When I went to Baghdãd, I found a person standing on the bridge and declaring for three days, 'O people! about such and such problem Qãdi Ahmad bin 'Umar Khassáf was asked and he gave such reply which was incorrect and that its correct reply was such and such. May Allah be Merciful on him who conveys this solution to the person who had asked about that problem.'" (The man who was making declaration was Imãm Khassãf himself.)

Commenting on the above report Tamímí says that the same is his opinion that the scholars attitude should be such and they should exercise care in the religious affairs and should advise the people in this manner. They should not be like those people of our period who have before them to express their academic pride, arrogance and strength. When a person dominates his opponent in a debate or discussion, he does not take care as to whether he is right or wrong.

(We seek refuge with Allah, the Almighty from the mischief of our own selves.)

Status and Rank of Imãm Khassãf in Fiqh and Ijtihãd

Shams al-A'immah Imam Hulwãni states that Imãm Khassãf possessed a great status in *Fiqh*. He is one of among those to follow whom is valid.

Allamah Shams al-Dín Ahmad al-Ma'rúf ibn Kamãl Páshã has counted him in the third category of *fuqaha* and *mujtahidín*.

This category of *mujtahidin* conducts *ijtihãd* in those problems concerning which no transmission is available on the authority of any leading jurist.

Kafwi has counted Imãm Khassãf in the second category of the *fuqaha* and the *mujtahidin* and has named this category as the category of later periods great *Hanafis*. They are those who have the ability to conduct *ijtihãd* concerning those problems concerning which no transmission is available on the authority of the founder of this school of thought.

Imãm Abû bakr Khassãf has attained a great place among the eminent *Hanafi fuqaha* group as he had perfect hold on the *Fiqh* and capability to conduct *ijtihãd*. This is the reason that the *fuqaha* who came after him have mostly copied his opinions and mentioned the same in their books.

Writings

Imãm Khassãf has left behind a number of books on various scientific and legal subjects. Some of his books are listed below:

1. *Kitãb Ahkãm al-Auqãf*;
2. *Kitãb Adab al-Qãdi*;
3. *Kitãb al-Hiyal*;
4. *Kitãb al-Shurũt al-Kabir*;
5. *Kitãb al-Shurũt al-Saghir*;
6. *Kitãb al-Ridá*;
7. *Kitãb al-Iqálah*;
8. *Kitãb al-Mahadir wa al-Sijalãt*;
9. *Kitãb al-Khiráj*;
10. *Kitãb fi al-Manásik*;
11. *Kitãb al-Nafaqát*;

12. *Kitāb Iqrár al-Warathah ba'duhum li ba'din;*
13. *Kitāb al-'Asír wa Ahkāmihi;*
14. *Kitāb Zara'al-Ka'bah wa al-Masjid wa al-Qabr;*
15. *Kitāb al-Wasáya;*
16. *Kitāb Fatáwa al-Khassáf fi al-Waqf;* and
17. *Kitāb al-Kh. . . .l*

BIOGRAPHICAL SKETCH OF 'UMAR BIN 'ABDUL-'AZÍZ IBN MĀZAH AL-BUKHĀRÍ (Allah's Mercy be on him): THE COMMENTATOR OF KITĀB ĀDAB AL-QĀDI

Name and Profile

His name was 'Umar. His father's name was 'Abdul-'Azíz. His grandfather's name was 'Umar. His title was Hisām ad-Dín. His surnames were: Abú Muhammad, Abú Hafs, and Ibn Māzah. He was popular with the titles As-Sadr ash-Shahíd, Hisām, and Hisām Shahíd. Qarshí has added in his titles, the title of Burhān al-A'immah. The same is the title of his father.

Date of Birth

He was born in the month of Safar in 483 A.H. (1090 A.D.).

Family

Imām Hisām ad-Dín Sadr ash-Shahíd belonged to a family reputed in its nobility, knowledge, generosity, and governance. The lineage of this family reached upto Hadrat 'Umar bin Abd al-'Azíz (Allah's mercy be on him) Qizwíni stated: "Bukhārā has always remained the place of residence of *fuqaha* (the jurists), the treasure of *fudalā* (men of knowledge and excellence), and the centre of theoretical sciences (*nazari 'ulum*). The academic leadership of Bukhārā remained in a family whose chief was called with the title of "Khawājah Imām Ajall". The family was surviving even in the year 674 A.H.

This family, due to its superiority and excellence, was reckoned amongst the kings of Bukhārā. Qarshī stated that the grandfather of Sadr ash-Shahīd was popular with the name 'Umar Māzah, which was his title and his children were called Banī Māzah.

'Abdul-'Azíz bin 'Umar bin Māzah, the father of the commentator was popular with the titles: Burhān al-A'immah, Burhān ad-Dīn al-Kabír, Sirāj al-A'immah, Sadr al-Mādí, and al-Sadr al-Kabír. When Sultān Sanjar sent him to Bukhārā in the year 495 A.H., he gave him the title "Sadr". He was the Imām of the people of Bukhārā and was reckoned among the chiefs and elite of Bukhārā. He had two sons. One was the commentator of this book and the other was Tāj ad-Dīn Ahmad, whose title was as-Sadr as-Sa'íd,, who was the teacher of the author of the *Hidayah*.

Ahmad had two sons. One was Burhān ad-Dín Mahmúd, who was the author of *Muhít Burhani* and *Zakhirah Burhaniyyah*. His tittle was Sadr ad-Dín. Ibn Kamāl Pāshā has reckoned him among the *Mujtahidín*. A son of Burhān ad-Dín Mahmud was Sadr al-Islām Tāhir, which was counted among the chiefs of *Hanafi fuqaha* and had full expertise in the matter of the roots and branches of jurisprudence (*fiqh*).

The second son of as-Sadr as-Sa'íd al-Ahmad was by the name Mas'úd. His son was Burhān al-Islām 'Umar, who had died in 615 A.H. The son of 'Umar was Nizām ad-Dín Muhammad (bin 'Umar).

The son of Imām Hisām ad-Dín 'Umar bin 'Abdul-'Azíz as-Sadr ash-Shahíd, the commentator of the book, had a son Shams ad-Dín Muhammad Abú Ja'far, who died in 560 A.H. and was reckoned among the great jurists and elite of Bukhãrã and he was very popular among the kings. The son of Muhammad was 'Abdul-'Azíz, who was also reckoned as one of the *Hanafi* jurists. And he was regarded as one of the chiefs of 'Al-Burhan (family of Burhãn). 'Abdul-'Azíz had a son by the name Muhammad popularly called Sadr Jahán and Jahán Fársí. He was considered a great and the most famous personality of Baní Mãzah. He was considered an Imãm with no parallel in the matter of debates. About six thousand jurists lived under his patronage. Iftikhãr Jahãn was brother of Muhammad (Sadr Jahãn), who had two sons, viz., Malik al-Islãm and 'Azíz al-Islãm.

Early Life

Imãm Sadr Shahíd Hisám ad-Dín was born in the year 483 A.H. (1090 A.D.) He was brought up and educated alongwith his brother Sadr Sa'id Tãj al-Dín Ahmad by his father Burhãn al-A'immah Sadr Ajall 'Abdul-'Azíz with so much attention that both the sons got superiority over their contemporary jurists.

Burhãn ad-Dín Zamauji (died in 620 A.H.) has narrated in his book *Ta'lim al-Muta'allam*, on the authority of his teacher Burhãn ad-Dín Marghinani (died in 593 A.H.), the author of *Hidayah* and the pupil of Hisám, that Sadr Ajall *Burhán al-A'immah* had fixed the time to give lesson to his sons Sadr Shahíd and Sadr Sa'íd after giving lessons to all the other pupils at about sunrise. When the said sons of the teacher felt restlessness waiting for such a long time, complained of it to their father, he replied that to him the sons of the rich and the poor come from far off places, hence I would prefer them in the matter of giving lessons to you. Thus the blessings of the father resulted in the excellence of his sons in the matter of *'ilm al-fiqh* over the contemporary jurists.

Both the brothers worked very hard in seeking knowledge. Especially Imăm Hisám worked so hard that he excelled in the expertise of the school of thought of Imám Abú Hanífah (Allah's mercy be on him) and his greatness went on increasing. He had obtained a distinct status among the men of knowledge of Khurasán even during the lifetime of his father. He held many open discussions and debates on many issues with the '*ulama* and always remained dominant and successful as has been mentioned by al-Zahabi. Imám Hisám used to give lessons to the jurists and he was the Shaikh of his period. Rather he was a unique personality and a genius. The judges, the parties, the adversaries, and the followers all admitted his superiority and excellence. His greatness became popular even uptill Mawara al-Nahr. So much so that even the king and other big people respected and honoured him and used to decide matters in accordance with the opinions given by him. Thus, he lived his life in a state of respect and honour.

Qarshí stated that the author of *Hidāyah*, in his book *Mu'jam al-Shuyúkh*, has stated: "I had learnt the theoretical sciences and '*ilm al-Fiqh* from Hisám and got great guidance from his academic and theoretical sessions. He respected me the most and reckoned me among his special pupils in all his significant lessons. But I could not get permission to transmit on his authority. However, through the chain of several *Mashá'ikh*, I have received his transmissions."

He was martyred in the battle of Qatwán on 5 Safar, 536 AH (1141 A.D.)

Introduction

ADMINISTRATION OF JUSTICE

What is Needed for Knowing the Manners of Justice

1. *Hadrat Ali* (Allah's pleasure be on him) said: "For Knowing the manners of justice, the knowledge of the meaning of the word *al-Qādā*, both literal and legal is necessary. Besides this, it is also necessary to know as to who is competent to be appointed as a *qādi* and to whose appointment is permissible or not permissible. Similarly it is also necessary to know as to whether entry into it is lawful."[12]

Meaning of Qadā

2. Literally the word *Qādā* has got three shades of meaning:

a. *To bind others*:

It is for this reason that a ruler is named as a Qādi as he binds the people with the orders.

b. *To fix*:

It is for this reason that is said that such and such person has

---

12. Regarding Hadrat Ali (Allah's pleasure be on him), the Messenger of Allah (peace and blessings of Allah be on him) said, "Ali is excelling in the matter of doing justice." (Hadrat 'Umar Farûq (Allah's pleasure be on him) said, "Had there not been Ali, 'Umar would have been lost." It had become a proverb during the period of the companions: "This is a dispute for which there is no Abul Hasan." In other words, this is such a difficult dispute which could be resolved only by a person who possesses perfectness like Ali.

fixed maintenance for such and such person, i.e., he fixed the amount and the quantity of the maintenance.

c. *To give a command*:

Allah, the Almighty says: "Thy Lord hath decreed
That ye worship none but Him......." (17:23)

Legal (Shar'i) Meanings of Justice (al-Qadã)

According to the *Shara 'i* sciences. the technical meanings of *qadã* is to settle and decide the disputes.

Competency for Qadã

3. The most significant thing in the matter of *qadã* is the competency of *qãdi*. Only such person is competent for his appointment as a *qãdi* who possesses knowledge of *Kitãb-o-Sunnah* and is also competent to conduct *ijtihãd* according to his opinion. Hence a person should not be appointed as *qãdi* who does not possess knowledge of Kitáb and *sunnah* and is unable to conduct *ijtihãd* by his personal judgement (*ijtihãd*). This is proved both on the authority of the text and is also valid according to reason.

Proof on the Authority of Text

4. Its Proof on the authority of text of *hadith* is this that the Holy Prophet (peace and blessings of Allah be on him) while appointing and sending Mu'ãz bin Jabal as *qãdi* of Yemen asked:

"O Mu'ãz! according to what you will decide?"

Mu'ãz submitted: "According to the Book of Allah."

The Holy Prophet (peace and blessings of Allah be on him) asked: "If you do not find in it, then?"

Mu'āz submitted: "According to the *sunnah* of the Messenger of Allah."

The Holy Prophet (peace and blessings of Allah be on him) asked: "If you find no solution in it, then?"

Mu'āz submitted: "I will exercise my personal judgment to decide that case."

The Holy Prophet (peace and blessings of Allah be on him) said: "Thanks be to Allah who granted such *tawfiq* to the messenger of the Messenger of Allah whereby His Messenger is pleased."[13]

Proof on the Authority of Reason

5. The *qādi* has been commanded to decide according to the truth.

The Holy Qur'ān says:
"O Dā'úd! We did indeed

---

13. *Sunan Abū Dā'ūd*, Kitāb al-Aqdiah, vol. III, p. 303, *Hadith* No. 3592; *Sunan al-Tirmizi*, Kitāb al-Ahkām, vol. II, p. 394, *Hadith* No. 1348; *Sunan al-Darimi al-Muqaddimah*, vol. I, p. 55, *Hadith* No. 170; *Musnad Ahmad bin Hambal*, vol. I, p. 37, vol. V, pp. 230, 236, 242; *Jami' al-Usūl*, vol. X, p. 552, *Hadith* No. 7651; *Jam'ul Fawā'id*, vol. I, p. 685, Hadith No. 4923.

Mu'āz bin Jabal (Alla's pleasure be upon him) was an eminent companion, who participated in all the *Mashāhid* along with the Messenger of Allah (peace and blessings of Allah be on him). He died in 18 A.H., in Amwās, a city of Jordan, due to plague. At the time of his death, his age was 33 years.

Al-Ma'ārif. Ukkāshah, p. 254; *Mashāhir Ulama al-Amsār*, No. 321; *Al-Isti'āb*; vol. III, pp. 335-341; *Usud al-Ghābah (al-Sh'ub)*, vol. V, pp. 194-197, No. 4953: *Tazkarah al-Huffāz*, vol. I, p. 19, No. 8; *Al-Isabāh*, vol. III, pp. 406-7, NO. 8039; *Tahzib al-Asmā al-Lughāt*, Vol. I, p. 98.

> Make thee a vicegerent
> On earth: so judge thou
> Between men in truth (and justice)."   (38:26)

To judge between men in truth (and justice) is possible only when a *qādi* is learned in the Holy *Qur'ān* and *sunnah* and has the ability to make personal judgement (*ijtihād*) in the light of these two.

The reason is that the events are unlimited while the texts are limited in number. As a *qādi* can not have a text concerning every matter coming before him for decision hence he is in need of deducing meanings from the texts. Further, deduction of meaning from the text will be possible for a *qādi* when he is able to make personal judgement (*ijtihād*) and the personal judgement (*ijtihād*) is an authority (*hujjat*) only when it is not contrary to the Holy *Qur'ān* and the *sunnah,* and it is possible only when a *qādi* is learned in the Holy *Qur'ān* and *sunnah.* For this reason it became a condition precedent for a *qādi* to be learned in the Holy *Qur'ān* and *sunnah* for his appointment as a *qādi.*[14]

14. Shaikh Burhānn ad-Dín Marghinani says that a Qādi mus be a *mujtahid* and learned in *hadith* or a *muhaddith* and learned in *fiqh* (jurisprudence). He has also declared a *qādi* who intentionally gives wrongful decisions and a *mufti* who intentionally gives wrongful *fatwas* (Majin) as a guilty person liable to be punished with confinement.

    Qadi is the name of the power to give decision while *mufti* is the name of power who determines the issues under the fundamentals of *shari'ah.*

    Imam Khassaf also adds the condition of being just (*'adil*) for appointment of a person as a *qadi.*

    Imam Mawardi (Abul Hasan 'Ali bin Muhammad bin Habib al-Basri, al-Baghdadi) has mentioned in his book titled as *Ahkam al-Sultaniyyah* that the appointment of a person to the office of *qadā* (judgeship) is permissible if he possesses the following seven qualifications:-

View Point of Imam Shafi'i

Imam Shafi'i declares it a mandatory condition precedent for the appointment of a person to the office of judgeship that he should be *'adil* (of an unimpeachable integrity). According to him if a person who is *gher 'adil* (that is who is not just) shall not be accepted as a judge and if he gives any decision in any matter his decision shall not be enforceable. The difference between the view point of Imām Shāfi'i and the view point of Imām Khassāf is as under:

Imām Khassāf has declared the condition of *'adl* as a preferential condition while Imām Shāfi'i declared such condition as a mandatory condition. Imām Khassāf stated that it is better that a judge should be *'adil*. As it is better and preferential that a judge should not give decision based on the evidence of a *fāsiq*

a. He should be a male adult;

b. He should be sane, that is, he should be of sound mind, intellectually fit, secure from mistakes and ignorance and able to solve hard and difficult problems;

c. He should be a free man;

d. He should be a Muslim;

e. He should be *'adil*, that is, true in his words, trustworthy, pious in conduct, secure from doubts, equally satisfactory in a state of joy and grief and exercising courtesy for people of equal status. Similar are the qualities of a just witness (*shahid 'adil*);

f. He should possess soundness of hearing and sight; and

g. He should possess complete knowledge of the four sources of Islamic Law (*usul 'arb'ah*) and high expertise in the branches of Islamic Law (*fru'at*).

The four sources of Islamic Law are:

i. *Kitabullah* (The Holy Qur'an);

ii. *Sunnah Rasulullah* (The *Ahadith* of the Messenger of Allah (peace and blessings of Allah be on him);

iii. *Ijma'* (consensus); and

iv. *Qiyas* (analogical deduction).

(transgressor) but if he gives decision on the basis of the evidence of a transgressor his decision shall even then be enforceable. Similarly here it is better that office of judgeship is not entrusted to transgressor but in case a transgressor is appointment as a judge he shall be deemed to be a judge and if he pronounces a judgement his judgement shall be enforceable.

Authority Competent to Appoint a Judge

6. A group of the learned is of the view that the head of the state (*sultán*), irrespective of his being *'adil* or *ja'ir*, has the right to appoint a person as a judge (*qãdi*).

Imãm Shãfi'i said, "If the truth becomes manifest according to the statement of my adversary in a moot and he is declared as successful I will prefer my defeat over my success and feel more happy.[15]

During the period of an *'adil* head of the state, the appointment of Mu'ãz bin Jabal (Allah's pleasure be on him) as the governor and judge of Yemen[16] and the appointment of 'Itãb bin Asid (Allah's

---

15. *Kitãb al-Umm*, vol. VI, p. 207; *al-Mukhtasar* Vol. V, p. 242; *Adãb al-Qãdi*, Imãm Mawardi, Vol. I, p. 618, No. 1503.

16. His name is Mu'ãz. His father's name is Jabel. His *kuniyyat* (surname) is Abû Abdullãh. He is from Ansãr and belongs to the tribe of Khazrãj. He was one of the seventy persons who were present at the Bai'at uqba thaniah. He embraced Islãm while he was 18 years old. He participated in *ghazwah* Badr and other *ghazwãt*. The Holy Prophet (peace and blessings of Allah be on him) had appointed him as *qãdi* and *mu'allim* of Yemen. Hazrat Umar (Allah's pleasure be upon him) had appointed him the governor of Syria after Abú 'Ubaidah bin Jarrãh (Allah's pleasure be on him). Umar bin Abbãs and Ibn Umar have transmitted Ahadíth on his authority. He died in 18 A.H., while he was 38 during the year of plague of Amwãs. *Al-Ma'arif* (Ukkãshah) p. 254; *Mashahir Ulama al Amsãr*, No. 321; *Al-Isti'ãb* Vol. III; pp. 241, 335; *Usud al-Ghábah* Vol. V, pp. 194-197, No. 4953; *Tazkarah al-Huffaz*, vol. I, p. 19; *Ikmal Asmã' al-Rijal*, Shaikh

pleasure be on him) as the governor of Makkah[17] by the Holy Prophet (peace and blessings of Allah be on him) are the examples.

The acceptance of the offices by the companions (Allah's pleasure be on all of them) given by Amír Mu'āwiyah (Allah's pleasure be on him) after his differences with Hadrat 'Alí (Allah's pleasure be on him) while he knew that the later was right is the example of otherwise.

However, the acceptance of an offer made by a *sultān ja'ir* of an office of judgeship will be permissible for a person who feels that he can dispense justice even during such *sultān*. If it is not possible for a person to do justice, then he should not accept the offer. The basis of this is the incident of Hakam bin 'Amr al-Ghifāri (Allah's pleasure be on him), the governor of Khurasān. who

Waliyyuddín Abí Abdullāh Muhammad bin Abdul Khātib, *Mishkāt al-Masābih*, vol. III, p. 394, No. 6793.

17. His name is 'Itāb. His father's name is Asid and grandfather's name is Abū al-'Ais. His grand great father is 'Umayyah bin Abd Shams. His *kunniyat* (surname) is Abú Muhammad. He is an eminent *sahābi*. He embraced Islām on the day of conquer of Makkah al-Mukarramah. The Holy Prophet (peace and blessings of Allah be on him) appointed him the governor of Makkah al-Mukarramah in the year of *Fath Makkah* on return from Hunayn or at the time of proceeding towards Hunayn. Hadrat Abū Bakr Siddíq (Allah's pleasure be on him) also maintained him on that post. According to the statement of the children of 'Itāb (Allah's pleasure be on him) and Waqidi, he died on the same day when Hadrat Abū Bakr Siddíq (Allah's pleasure be on him) died. The statement of Muhammad bin Salām etc., is that 'Itāb (Allah's pleasure be on him) was buried and at that moment the *janāzah* of Hadrat Abū Bakr Siddíq (Allah's pleasure be on him) arrived for burial. 'Itāb was the most pious companion of the Messenger of Allah (peace and blessings of Allah be on him). [*Al-Isti'āb*, 3/153-154; *Usud al-Ghābah*, 3/556, No. 3533; *Al-Isabāh*, 2/444, No. 5393; *Nasab Quraish*, al-Mus'ab al-Zubairi, p. 187; *Tahzíb alAsmā' wa al-Lughāt*, part I, vol. I, p. 318; *Al-Ma'arif*, Ukkāshah, p. 383; *Talkhis al-Habir*, vol. II, p. 25, Hadíth No. 1202; *al-Sunan al-Kubra*, al-Bayhaqi, Vol. V, p. 313.]

received an order in writing from Hadrat Mu'āwiyah (Allah's pleasure be on him), the *Amir al-Mu'minin* that he should separate the yellow and white (gold and silver) and despatch the same to him. On that, Hakam bin 'Amr (Allah's pleasure be on him) proclaimed that the Book of Allah (the Holy *Qur'ān*) has precedence over the words of Amir al-Mu'minin and recited the following verse of the Holy *Qur'ān*:

> "And know that out of
> All the booty that ye
> May acquire (in war),
> A fifth share is assigned
> To Allah,-and to the Apostle,
> And to near relatives,
> Orphans, the needy,
> And the wayfarer,—
> If ye do believe in Allah
> And in the revelation
> We sent down to Our Servant
> On the Day of Testing,—
> The Day of the meeting
> Of the two forces:
> For Allah hath power
> Over all things."   (8:41)

Then he came to the pulpit (*minbar*) and addressed the people as under:

"O people! Verily I have received a communication from the *Amir al-Mu'minin* in which he has ordered me to select the yellow and the white things. The Book of Allah has got superiority over the letter of *Amir al-Mu'minin*. I hereby divide the booty amongst you. Let every one of you stand up and receive his right."

Thereafter, he said, "O Allah! Take away my life into Thy possession."

After some time of this incident, Hakam Ghifārī (Allah's pleasure be on him) died.[18]

7. There is difference of opinion between the jurists in the matter of acceptance of the office of judgeship voluntarily.

According to some jurists this office can be accepted voluntarily as the prophets and messengers of Allah and the righteous *caliphs* had accepted this office voluntarly.[19]

According to some others, if there is compulsion to accept it then it may be accepted. They base this view on the authority of the transmission according to which Imām Abú Hanifah (Allah's mercy be on him) was thrice offered the office of chief judgeship and he did not accept that offer and was punished with thirty stripes each time. When it happened thrice, he asked some time to consult his companions. Imām Abú Yúsuf (Allah's mercy be on him) advised that his joining the offered office would be beneficial for the public. On that Imām Abú Hanifah (Allah's mercy be on him) looked towards him and said, "Do you consider that in case I am commanded to cross the ocean by swimming I would be able to do so? It seems to me that one day you would definitely become a judge.[20]

18. *Al-Isti'āb*, vol. I, pp. 314-315; *Tabaqāt Ibn Sa'd*, part 7, vol. I, p. 18

19. The prophet Yúsuf (peace be on him) had said to the King of Egypt: "Set me over the storehouse of land: I will indeed guard them, as one that knows (their importance)."   (al-Qur'ān, XII:55)

20. *Manāqib al-Imām al-A'zam*, al-Maufaq, vol. I, pp. 162, 202-205; *Manāqib al-Imām al-A'zam*, Imām Kurdari, vol. I, pp. 78, 204, 231, 234; *Manāqib al-Imām al-A'zam*, Imām Zahabí, pp. 16-17; *Jami' al-Imām Abí Hanifah*, vol. I, p. 38; *Talkhís al-Habír*, vol. IV, p. 186;

Similarly, it is transmitted that Imām Muhammad (Allah's mercy be on him) was offered the office of chief judgeship and he refused on which he was kept under confinement and ultimately accepted it under compulsion.[21]

The correct view is that to join the office of judgeship with one's free consent is in the category of *rukhsat* (concession) and to join such office under compulsion is in the category of *azimat* (resolution). To accept the office of judgeship voluntarily is permissible but to avoid its acceptance is better. The proof of voluntarily accepting this office has already been referred to above. There are two proofs concerning its avoidance.

The first proof is that a judge is commanded to decide the matter before him according to the truth. May be that in the beginning he is sure that he will be able to do justice according to the truth and yet the decision given by him might be against the truth.

The second proof is that for a judge to decide according to the truth is not possible without the help of others. He may be able to get the chance of joining others in coming to the just decision and may be that the others so joined may or may not help him in this behalf.

After knowing these preliminaries we revert to the matter mentioned by the author in the beginning of this book.

Nasb al-Ra'iyah, vol. IV, p. 65; *Al-Darāya*, vol. II, p. 166; *Akhbār al-Qudāt*, vol. I, p. 26; *al-Mabsūt*, vol. XVI, p. 69; *Fatāwa Hindiya*, vol. III, p. 311; *Fath al-Qadir*, vol. V, p. 460; *Tahzib al-Asmā' wa al-Lughāt*, vol. II, p. 218; *al-Mustatrif*, vol. I, p. 97; *Fatāwa Bazāziyah*, Vol. V, p. 132; *Bidā'i al-Sanā'i* vol. IX. p. 408.

21. *Manāqib al-Imam Abi Hanifah wa Sāhibayh Abi Yūsuf wa Muhammad bin al-Hasan*, Imām Zahabi, p. 55; *al-Jawāhir al-Bahiyah*, vol. II, p. 44; *Nasb al-Ra'iyah*, vol. IV, p. 65; *al-Darāya*, vol. II, p. 166; *al-Fatāwa al-Hindiyah*, vol. III, p. 311; *Fath al-Qadir*, vol. V, p. 460.

CHAPTER 1

Entry into Office of Judgeship

8. Imām Khassāf (Allah's mercy be on him) has begun this chapter with the *hadith* of 'Ā'ishah (Allah's pleasure be on her). She said:

"A judge of unimpeachable integrity will be brought on the Day of Resurrection and due to the severity of accountability he will wish that alas he would not have decided between two persons."[22]

The *muhaddithin* (Allah's mercy be on them) have narrated this *hadith* as a warning against seeking and joining the office of judgeship.[23]

---

22. *Musnad,* Imām Ahmad. vol. VI, p. 75; al-Bayhaqi, *al-Sunan al-Kubra,* vol. X, p. 96; Ibn Habbān and Uqailí, *Talkhis al-Habir,* vol. IV, p. 184, *Hadith* No. 179; Tabrāní, *al-Ausat,* vol. IV, p. 192; al-Zayla'i, *Nasb al-Ra'iyah fi takhrij Ahadith al-Hidayah,* vol. IV, p. 65; Ibn Hajr al-'Asqalani, *al-Dara'iyah fi Takhrij Ahadith al-Hidayah,* vol. II, p. 166; Waki', *Akhbār al-Qudāt,* vol. I, pp. 20-21.

23. The example of a judge of an unimpeachable integrity is like the rich, pious and generous persons about whom it is mentioned in the *hadith* that such persons shall enter paradise five hundred years after the entrance of the poor and the destitute persons. This will be due to engagement of the rich in their accountability. Likewise, the judges of unimpeachable integrity will be engaged in accountability of their conduct in deciding the cases. After successful clearance

It is worth consideration that when this is the state of affairs of a judge having unimpeachable integrity on the Day of Resurrection then what will be state of affair of a court judge.

When the severity of accountability and punishment is for all judges then you should know that a judge with unimpeachable integrity will get salvation due to his doing justice and a corrupt judge will be condemned forever.

9. Sa'sa'ah bin Sûhãn (Allah's mercy be on him) said, "Hadrat 'Alí (Allah's pleasure be on him) addressed to us from the top of Zarb[24], a mountain of the town of Zi-Qar[25]. At that time

their ranks in paradise will be elevated. It is mentioned in the *hadith* that the poor *sahabah* submitted to the Messenger of Allah (peace and blessings of Allah be on him) that they would lag behind the rich *sahabah* in the matter of charitable deeds. The Messenger of Allah (peace and blessings of Allah be on him) told them to recite *Subhãnallah* 33 times, *Alhamdulillãh* 33 times, and *Allahu Akbar* 34 times counting on their fingers and thus there ranks will become equal to the rich *sahãbah*. When this advice reached to the ears of the rich *sahabah* they also started reciting the aforesaid *kalimãt* (formulae). On that the poor *sahãbah* again approached the Messenger of Allah (peace and blessings of Allah be on him) and submitted that their rich colleagues have also started acting according to them and their ranks will remain higher than the poor due to their charities. On this the Messenger of Allah (peace and blessings of Allah be on him) said, "This is the special blessings of Allah which he grants to whom so ever He wills."

Its reason is stated in the Holy Qur'ãn in the following verse:-

"They feed the needy, the orphan and the prisoners for the sake of love of Allah and they prefer others as against their own selves although they themselves are in severe need of it." (76:8)

These two matters are the cause of elevation of their ranks with which the poor have not been confronted.

24. *Zarab* starting with the Arabic alphabet "*za*" is top of a mountain and it is also written with the Arabic alphabet "*dad*" which means a mound. The Arabs used to address the people standing over the

Hadrat 'Alí ('Allah's pleasure be on him) had tied a black turban following the example of the Messenger of Allah (peace and blessings of Allah be on him) who had black turban with red ribbon on his head on the sacred day of conquer of Makkah.[26] Hadrat 'Alí (Allah's pleasure be on him) said in his sermon:

"O people! verily I have heard the Messenger of Allah (peace and blessings of Allah be on him) saying: 'Verily there will not be a judge or governor, irrespective of his being *'adil* or *ja'ir*, brought on the day of judgement and made to stand before Allah Almighty and thereafter in presence of his subjects and subordinates the angels will open the sheet of deed and read it. That is, it will be read in presence of the witnesses as Allah Almighty says in the Holy Qur'ãn:

.....The day when the witnesses will stand forth."   (40:51)

mountains or mounds. So that their voice may reach far and may spread. For this purpose it had become usual to address from the "*minbars*". The Messenger of Allah (peace and blessings of Allah be on him) had also got prepared for him a wooden pulpit (*minbar*). The "*Mú'zzanín Nabawí*' namely, Hadrat Bilãl (Allah's pleasure be on him) and Hadrat Abdullãh ibn Umm Maktúm (Allah's pleasure be on him) were directed by the Messenger of Allah (peace and blessings of Allah be on him) to pronounce the call for prayer (*azãn*) from the roof of the house and for this purpose minarets of the mosque were also constructed and *mihrab* (the central arch in the prayer halls) were constructed to transmit the voice of Imãm (leader of congregation prayer) to the *muqtadis* (the persons following the Imãm while offering prayers in congregation) to the maximum distance.

25. Zi Qar is the name of a place.

26. *Sahíh Muslim*, Vol. II, p. 990, *Hadíth* Nos. 451-452; *Sunan*, Abu Dãúd, Kitãb al-Libãs, vol. IV, p. 54, *Hadíth* Nos. 4076-4077; Sunan, Ibn Mãjah, Kitãb al-Jihãd, vol. II, p. 942, *Hadíth* No. 2822; *Sunan*, Ibn Mãjah, Kitãb al-Libãs, vol. II, p. 1186, *Hadíth* Nos. 3585-3586; *Sunan*, al-Tirmizi, Kitãb al-Libãs, vol. III, pp. 138-139 *Hadíth* No. 1789; *Musnad*, Imãm Ahmad bin Hanbal, vol. III, pp. 363, 387 & vol. IV, p. 307.

If the judge will be *'adil* (of just conduct), Allah Almighty will grant him salvation due to his just conduct. And if he wil be *ja'ir* (corrupt), the Bridge Path shall shiver so forcefully that there will become a distance of a hundred years between each one of his limbs.

This *hadith* has been interpreted in two ways. Some interpreters state that his limbs will be made so fat that the fatness of each limb will be equal to a hundred years distance.

The Messenger of Allah (peace and blessings of Allah be on him) said: "The skin of a disbeliever shall become fat to the extent of 40 yards."[27]

The Messenger of Allah (peace and blessings of Allah be on him) also said: "The grinder of a disbeliever shall become like the Uhad mountain."[28]

Thus the limbs shall become big to the extent of the punishment to be given to such person.

The other interpretation of this *hadith* is given that the limbs shall be thrown away to such a distance that it will be a distance of 100 years in between them.

Thereafter he stated:

"Then the Path Bridge shall burst."

In another transmission, the words are:

"The Path Bridge shall move away i.e., it shall bow."

The first transmission is more correct than the second.

"And he will fall down in the pit of Fire and will go down leaving his face and forehead."

27. *Sunan*, al-Tirmizi, vol. IV. p. 105.

28. *Sahih* Muslim, Kitab al-Jannah, No. 44.

This portion of *hadith* has also been interpreted in two ways. One is the 1ˢᵗ thing to be punished with the fire of Hell shall be the face. Allah, the Almighty says:

"The days they will be dragged and put into the Fire faced downwards." (54:48)

Such treatment will be met to him as the judge had given wrong decision to secure his face hence 1ˢᵗ of all his face shall be punished with Fire. The 2ⁿᵈ interpretation is that such a person will be made to fall into the Fire had downward and this is the severest punishment that a person is made to fall in the Fire with his head downward.

Thus the unjust judge shall be in the lowest portion of the Hell along with the hypocrites. It will be so as he showed that he had done justice but in fact he did injustice. Thus he acted like the hypocrites and will be in the lowest valley in the hell along with the hypocrites.

The object to mention this *hadith* is to warn against seeking the office of judgeship.

10. Hadrat Sufyān bin 'Uyainah (Allah's mercy be on him) on the authority of Majālid bin Sa'íd and he on the authority of Masruq (Allah's mercy be on him) transmitted:

"There will not be any judge (or any ruler) who decided a case between two persons who shall not be brought on the day of resurrection held by an ángel from his neck and he will look towards Allah, the Almighty and regarding him it will be ordered that he should be thrown down into a pit the depth of which shall be equal to 70 years distance."[29]

29. *Musnad* Ahmad bin Hanbal, vol. I, p. 430; *Sunan Daraqutni*, kitāb al-ahkām, vol. IV, p. 205, *hadīth* No. 9; *Sunan al-Kubra*, Al-Bayhaqí, vol. X, pp. 96-97; *Al-Mabsút*, al-Sarakhsi, vol. XVI, p. 72; *Majma' al-*

This hadíth is equal in rank of a *marfu 'hadíth*. The reason is that a warning concerning an event of the Hereafter cannot be known by personal opinion rather it can only be known by hearing it from the Messenger of Allah (peace and blessings of Allah be on him) hence this *hadith* is like a *hadíth Marfu 'Ilar-Rasúlullah*.

This *hadíth* is also a proof that the warning to the judges is also warning to the rulers. This warning is much more for a person who is not eligible to become a judge.

After election of Abú Bakr Siddíq (Allah's pleasure be on him) as the First righteous *caliph*, he delivered a sermon in which he said:

> "You people have elected me but I am not of higher status than you. You people have put heavy load on my shoulders and you have to help me in carrying it.'"

It shows that Hadrat Abú Bakr Siddíq (Allah's pleasure be on him) had accepted the office of *caliphate* under compelling circumstances and thus he was not a seeker of such office.

The words: "He (the *qãdi*) will intend to see towards Allah," have also been interpreted in two ways.

One interpretation is that here real seeing is not meant. Rather he will wait for the command of Allah to act accordingly.

The other interpretation is that here real seeing is meant.

The scholars have different opinions concerning the seeing of Allah, the Almighty. Some say that the seeing will be for the human beings and not for the angels while the others say that it will be for the human beings as well as angels. However, the care demands that such a matter should not be over probed.

Zawã'id, vol. IV, p. 193; *Al-Matalib al-'Aliyah*, vol. II, p. 202, *hadith* No. 2049; *Sunan*, Ibn Majah, vol. II, p. 775, *hadith* No. 2311.

The words of the Messenger of Allah (peace and blessings of Allah be on him): "Seventy years distance in the pit" do not refer to actual seventy years, but to show a longer distance and period. It is usual with the Arabs that when they intend to mention a very long period or distance, they use the word forty or seventy.

The object of this *hadith* is also to warn against seeking the office of judgeship.

It is transmitted on the authority of Masrúq (Allah's mercy be on him) that he said: "It is more favourite to me to do justice in accordance with the truth than to fight the whole year (participate in *jihád fi sahílillāh*).[30]

Hadrat Masrúq (Allah's mercy be on him) has narrated the excellence of judgeship as he was put on this trial. A person states the good points of a job to which he is made responsible and undergoes its trial. It is exactly according to the human habit. Whatever he had stated is based on reason as in participation of *jihād*, there is the benefit of *'amr bil ma'rúf* (commanding good), while doing justice in accordance with the truth (the devine law) there are three fold benefits, viz., *'amr bil ma'rúf* (commanding good), *izhār al-haqq* (manifestation of the right), and *nusrah al-mazlúm* (helping the oppressed). Thus the benefits of judgeship are general and a thing having general benefits is, obviously superior.

12. Abú Hurairah (Allah's pleasure be on him) narrated that the Messenger of Allah (peace and blessings of Allah be on him) said, "Whosoever is made a judge, it is as if he has been slaughtered without a knife."[31]

30. *Akhbār al-Qudāt*, Waki', vol. II, p. 398; *Sunan* Dar Qutani, *kitāb al-Aqdiah wa al-Ahkām, hadith* No. 9, Vol. IV, p. 205; *Al-Sunan al-Kubra*, Al-Bayhaqi, vol. X, p. 89; *Al-Mabsút*, al-Sarakhsi, vol. XVI, p. 72.

31. *Sunan Ibn Mājah*, kitāb al-ahkām, vol. II, p. 447, *hadith* No. 3308; *Sunan* Abú Dã'úd, kitāb al-'aqdiah, vol. III, pp. 298-299; *Sunan*

In another transmission, the words are, "Whosoever is made (entrusted the office of) a judge, it is as if he has been slaughtered without a knife."[32] This is so because a knife has its effect both outward as well as inward. A slaughter without knife is either by suffocation or grief or such like other method which effects only inwardly. Similarly, the decision does not effect outwardly and appears to be life but inwardly it is destruction.

al-Tirmizí, kitāb al-ahkām, vol. II, p. 393, *hadith* No. 1340; *Jami' al-Usúl*, Ibn Athir, vol. X, p. 545, *hadith* No. 7632; *Musnad* Ahmad bin Hanbal, vol. II, pp. 230 & 365; *Al-Mustadrak* Hākim, vol. IV, p. 91.

32. *Sunan al-Kubra*, Al-Bayhaqi, vol. X, p. 96. Imām Bayhaqi has transmitted it with three different versions:

i) Whosoever is made a judge, it is as if he has been slaughtered without a knife;

ii) Whosoever sits between two Muslims as a judge, it is as if he has been slaughtered without a knife.

iii) Whosoever is entrusted with judgeship, it is as if he has been slaughtered without a knife.

See also *Talkhis al-Habir*, al-'Asqalani, vol. IV, p. 184, hadith No. 2078; *Subul al-Salām Sharh Bulugh al-Marām al-San'ani*, vol. IV, p. 116; *Nail al-Awtār*, al-Shawkani, vol. VIII, p. 269; *Akhbār al-Qudāt*, vol. I, pp. 7-13; *Jam'ul Fawā'id min Jami'al Usúl*, vol. II, p. 682, *hadith* No. 4902; *Al-Mu'jam al-Saghir*, al-Tabrāni, vol. II, p. 176.

Abú Sulaimān al-Khattābi has in his book *Ma'alim al-Sunan*, stated that this *hadith* is a warning against being greedy for seeking the office of judgeship. Whosoever insisted to get that office, as if he offered to slaughter himself. Hence, such a person is made to fear from it so that he may be saved. The words "without a knife" have two shades of meaning. One meaning is that according to the general custom slaughter is made with a knife, and here the Messenger of Allah (peace and blessings of Allah be on him) has stated a thing against the general custom and habit so that whosoever intends to seek judgeship should know that there is apprehension that destruction both bodily and spiritually. The other meaning is that slaughter, when conducted with a knife, is such a shock whereby the soul goes off the body and the slaughtered feels comfort and is

13. Hãrith (in another narration, Hasan) Basrí (Allah's mercy be on him) stated, Whenever Banú Isrã'il appointed a person as a judge they lost all hope of such a person being selected by Allah as a prophet. The object of this *hadith* is also to warn against inculcating a longing for the office of judgeship and to make a seeker fearful of its acceptance. The reason is that the rank of prophethood is the highest rank and when hope is lost concerning it in the matter of a person, then the appointment to the rank of judgeship is to lower the status of a man and not increasing it. It was so because in Banú Isrã'il, whosoever reserved himself for worship for sixty years. the people used to become hopeful of his being blessed with the office of prophethood. but if such a person had accepted the office of judgeship then they lost the said hope about him.

14. Abû Qulãbah (Allah's mercy be on him) was called for to be appointed as a judge but he ran towards Syria. During those days. the judge of Syria had also withdrawn himself from his office and had gone to Yamamah. Abû Qulãbah (Allah's mercy be on him) said, "The example of a judge is like a person who is to swim in the ocean [Tell me] for how much period such a person can swim. Ultimately, he will be drowned into the ocean."[33]

This is so because a person swimming in the ocean is often met with the consequence of being drowned into it and his escape is rare. Similarly, in joining the office of judgeship the destruction is probable while the escape is rare.

released of pain and its severity. On the other hand, if it is otherwise than slaughtering with a knife, there is suffocation and severe pain. Hence this example is more communicative for warning and keeping a person away from seeking judgeship.

33. *Sunan al-Kubra,* Al-Bayhaqi, vol. X, p. 97; *Akhbãr al-Qudãt,* al-Waki', vol. I, pp. 23 & 206; *Al-'Iqd al-Farid,* Ibn 'Abd Rabbihi, on the authority of alSakhtiani, vol. I, p. 23.

Thus when the *hadith* of Abû Qulābah (Allah's mercy be on him) reached Abû Hanifah (Allah's mercy be on him), he said to Abû Yûsuf (Allah's mercy be on him), "Do you command me to cross the ocean by swimming? Do I possess such power?"[34]

This *hadith* is also a warning agaisnt seeking judgeship.

15. It is stated that al-Hâkim bin Ayyûb had written a letter to a group of people whom he intended to appoint as judges and Abû ash-Sha'thâ' Jâbir bin Zaid bin 'Amr, wrote back, as far as I remember, "I do not possess anything in this world besides this ass of mine. If I am called to ride it and it runs away from me, what can I do?"

This *hadith* is also a warning against the acceptance of the office of judgeship.

16. It is stated that Shuraih (Allah's mercy be on him) said, "The judgement is an ember (live coal), remove it with two sticks, i.e., with two witnesses."[35]

---

34. *Fath al-Qadir*, vol. V, p. 460. Al-Kamal bin al-Hammam stated that Abú Hanifah (Allah's mercy be on him) had said to Abû Yûsuf (Allah's mercy be on him), "The ocean is deep. How can I cross it by swimming?" Abû Yûsuf (Allah's mercy be on him) submitted, "The ocean is deep, the ship is strong, and the captain is well versed." On that, Abû Hanifah (Allah's mercy be on him) remarked, "It seems to me that you shall accept judgeship."

35. *Akhbâr al-Qudāt*, al-Waki', vol. II, p. 287. This *hadith* of Shuraih (Allah's mercy be on him) has been transmitted by al-Waki' on the authority of 'Abdullâh bin Ahmad bin Hanbal, who said that it was narrated to him by his father, who said it was narrated to us by al-Waki', who said it was narrated to us by Mis'ar on the authority of Abí Hasin on the authority of Shuraih, who said, "Verily, the judgment is an ember and remove the ember from yourself by two sticks, i.e., basing your judgement on the evidence of two witnesses." Al-Sarakhsi (Allah's mercty be on him) has stated that it is one of the *ahadith* of the Messenger of Allah (peace and blessings of Allah be on him).   [Al-Mabsút, vol. XVI, p. 64]

The interpretation of this *hadith* is that when two litigants appear before judge, they are burning Fire and at that time it is incumbent upon him to save himself from being burnt by the aid of the two witnesses. If he decides a case on the evidence of two witnesses, he saves his soul from Fire, otherwise he would be burning himself.

17. Sulaimān bin Junaid al-Madani (Allah's mercy be on him) repoted that he was narrated by a person who had heard Abú Huriarah (Allah's pleasure be on him) that he said, "By God, Allah, the Almighty shall make the bodies of the judges the target of the embers (live coals) bigger than the mount Hidab of Hisma."

In the Holy *Qur 'ān* Allah Almighty says:

"Indeed it throws about sparks huge as forts."

(77:32)

Here sparks mean the Fire, Al-Hidāb means mounds, and Hisma is the name of a place. Al-Hidbah is the singular of al-Hidāb which is the name of a small mountain in Hisma. It is also stated that Hisma, on the scale of Kisra, is the most accurate and it is the name of a great mountain. If it is argued that here in this *hadith* the reference is towards a corrupt judge the answer is that the manifest words of the *hadith* cover all kinds of judges whether just or corrupt. This *hadith* is also a warning against the seeking and acceeptance of the office of judgeship.

18. It is mentioned that 'Abd ar-Rahmān bin Ghanamal-Ash'arí said:

Woe to the *dayyān ahl al-Ard* (earthly judges) from the *Dayyān ahl as-Samā* (Judge of the Heavens) on the Day they will meet Him, except those who intend justice, decide according to law (*al-haqq*) and do not decide by the whims and for the sake of any kinship or for any temptation or under any fear and keep the book of Allah before their eyes as a mirror.

Dayyān ahl al-Ard means a ruler and *Dayyān ahl al-samā* means Allah, the Almighty. One of the attributes of Allah Almighty is *al-Dayyān*.

In other words, on the Day of Judgement there shall be curse of Allah for a ruler who rules against law (*haqq*).

The words: *amma bil 'adl* signify intends to do justice.[36]

19. Imrān bin al-Hasīn decided a matter and one of the parties said to him: "By God, you have done injustice to me to the maximum".

Allah, the Almighty says: "....They will not fail to corrupt you....."   (3:118)

Imrān asked: "How was it so?"

The man said: "The evidence given against me was false."

Imrān said: "The decision I gave shall be recovered from my property. By God, I shall not sit as a judge from now onward."[37]

The statement of Imrān that whatever is the decreed amount the same shall be recovered from the property of Imran was a penalty as an act of righteousness (*tabarru)* and not as an obligation (*wājib*).

The statement of Imrān that By God he shall not sit as a judge thereafter was to show that a judge who delivers his judgement relying upon the evidence of two witnesses and after full probe of the matter in issue is not responsible any more and if after such reliance and probe the remarks are adverse as in this

36. Woe be to worldly judges from God on the Day of Judgement, except such judges who decide justly and according to the truth and not according to their whims nor on account of any fear or favour, and keep the book of Allah before them as a guide.

37. *Akhbār al-Qudāt*, al-Waki', vol. I, p. 291.

case then it is better to avoid the holding of such an office."[38]

38. It is stated that after this event Imrān approached Ziyād and tendered his resignation from the office of judgeship.

CHAPTER 2

Appointment to Office of Judgeship under Coercion

20. *Anas* bin Mālik (Allah's pleasure be on him) reported that the Messenger of Allah (peace and blessings of Allah be on him) said: "Whosoever seeks the office of judgeship he is entrusted to his own self and whosoever is coerced to accept this office an angel is sent down upon him to help him."[39]

21. Anas bin Mālik (Allah's pleasure be on him) reported that the Messenger of Allah (peace and blessings of Allah be on him) said: "Who seeks the office of judgeship and seeks recommendations in his behalf is entrusted to his own self and who is coerced to hold such office an angel is appointed on him to help him."[40]

39. *Sunan* Ibn Mājah, kitāb al-ahkām, Voi. II, p. 774, *Hadith* No. 2309; *Sunan* al-Tirmizí, kitāb al-ahkām, Vol. II, p. 392, *Hadith* No. 1338; *Jami' al-Usúl*, Vol. X, p. 547, *Hadith* No. 7636; *Jam 'al-Fawā'id*, vol. II, p. 683, *Hadith* No. 4906; *Nasb al-Ra'iyah fi takhrij Ahadith al-Hidayah*, Al-Zayla'i, vol. IV, pp. 68-69; *Al-Dira'iyah fi Takhrij Ahādith al-Hidayah*, Ibn Hajar al-'Asqalani, vol. II, p. 168, *Hadith* No. 818; *Sunan al-Kubra*, Al-Bayhaqi, Vol. X, p. 100; *Nailul-Awtār*, vol. VIII, p. 266; *Sunan* Abú Dāwûd, kitāb al-'aqdiah, vol. III, p. 300, *Hadith* No. 3578.

40. *Sunan* Ibn Majah, kitāb al-ahkām, vol. II, p. 774, *Hadith* No. 2309;

The reason is that a person who seeks the office of judgeship of his own accord he relies upon his own wisdom, piety and purity and thus becomes a victim of self appreciation and is deprived of guidance and *tawfiq*. It is impossible that a person who seeks an office and gets it is not entrusted to his own self. However a person who is coerced to accept the office of judgeship surely holds the rope of Allah and trusts in Him.

Allah, the Almighty says:

"....And if any one puts his trust in Allah, sufficient is Allah for him...." (65:3)

In other words one who trusts in Allah he is inspired with guidance and helped to follow the right path.

The words of the Messenger of Allah (peace and blessings of Allah be on him): "An angel is sent down upon him to save him" means that such a person is inspired to follow the guidance and is granted courage and fortitude (*tawfiq*) as the Messenger of Allah (peace and blessings of Allah be on him) said: "The angel speaks on the tongue of 'Umar."[41]

Sunan al-Tirmizi, Kitāb al-Ahkām, vol. II, p. 392; *Jami' al-Usûl*, Ibn Athir, vol. X, p. 547, *Hadith* No. 7636; *Jami' al-Fawā'id min Jami'al-Usûl wa Majma' al-Fawā'id*, edited by Al-Yamani, vol. II, p. 683, *Hadith* No. 4906; *Nasb al-Ra'iyah fi Takhrij Ahadith al-Hidayah*, Al-Zayla'i, vol. IV, pp. 68-69; *Al-Dira'iyah fi Takhrij Ahadith al-Hidayah*, Ibn Hajar al-'Asqalani, vol. II, p. 168, *Hadith* No. 818; *Musnad* Ahmad bin Hanbal, vol. III, pp. 118-220; *Sunan al-Kubra*, Al-Bayhaqi, vol. X, p. 100 and on its margin *Nail al-Awtār*, Al-Shawkani, vol. VIII, p. 266.

41. Seerat Umar, Ibn al-Jawzi, p. 170.

Ibn al-Jawzi transmitted this *Hadith* from the chain of Tāriq bin Shahab on the authority of 'Ali (Allah's pleasure be on him) *Mawqufan* and its words are: "We used to state that an angel speaks on the tongue of Umar," that is he is blessed with *tawfiq* (courage and fortitude) to say the correct thing.

CHAPTER 3

Permissibility of Entry to Office of Judgeship

22. **Hasan** (Allah's mercy be on him) transmitted that they said: "The compensation of a just ruler is superior than the compensation of a person who offers prayers in his house for seventy years" or he stated, "for sixty years."[42]

It was the habit of Hasan (Allah's mercy be on him) that when he transmitted on the authority of a single transmitter, he

---

42. Al-Zayla'i stated that Ishāq bin Rāhwayh has transmitted in his *Musnad* that Ja'far bin 'Awn al-harith informed that Affan bin Habír informed him that Ikramah informed him that Ibn Abbās reported that the Messenger of Allah (peace and blessings of Allah be on him) said:

"A day of justice by a ruler is superior than sixty years worship and implementation of a *hadd* of Allah on the earth is more purifying than forty days rain."

Nasb al-Ra'iyuah fi Takhrij Ahadith al-Hidayah, Al-Zayla'i, vol. IV, p. 67.

Al-Dira'iyah fi Takhrij Ahadith al-Hidayah, Ibn Hajar al-'Asqalani, vol. II, p. 167, hadith No. 817, where it is also mentioned that Abú 'Ubaid in his *Kitāb al-Amwāl* has mentioned on the authority of Abú Hurairah who reported that the Messenger of Allah (peace and blessings of Allah be on him) said: "A day's justice of a ruler among his subjects is superior than the one hundred and fifty years worship of a worshipper among his family."

named such transmitter, but when he transmitted on the authority of more than a single transmitter, he used to say, "They said."

Hasan (Allah's mercy be on him) had held the office of judgeship and a person who is engaged in a profession, he definitely mentions the goodness in it.

The statement, "A day's justice of a ruler is superior than sixty years prayers offered by another person in his house" indicates, as already mentioned by us, that in Banú Isrã'il, a person who worshipped God for sixty years, the people had been hopeful of his being blessed with the office of the prophethood and he used to become very eminent among them. In our *shari'ah* (al-Islãm) no prophet or messenger shall come after the Messenger of Allah Muhammad (*Sallallahu Alaihi wa Sallam*). Hence to do justice according to law is equal to sixty years worship. This superiority of doing justice is being told by this *hadith*.

As we have earlier mentioned that to do justice according to law (*al-qadã bi al-haqq*) is superior than struggle in the way of Allah (*jihãd fi sabilillãh*) and the struggle in the way of Allah is superior than supererogatory worship (*nafl 'ibãdat*) in solitude. Therefore, to do justice according to law is much more superior than supererogatory worship in solitude.

Thereafter, Hasan (Allah's mercy be on him) stated: "Yes, due to a day's justice of a ruler brings excellence to every member of Muslim families. Due to doing of justice the rain falls and due to injustice they are confronted with the famine.

In other words, doing justice according to law causes blessings and benefits to all Muslims.

23. Abú 'Ubaidah said, "A ruler who does justice according to law silences all noise of criticism against Allah and a ruler who does injustice (or is an oppressor) adds in the complaints against Allah.

It is so because when justice is done in accordance with law, the parties go back to their homes satisfactorily having no doubt in their minds. The one who wins the case he goes back to his house with a heart full of gratitude and having no complaint against the judge and the one who loses the case he goes back to his house knowing that no cause is left to agitate any further.

On the other hand, when justice is not done according to law, both the parties return to their homes having doubts in their minds. The reason is that a person whom justice has been denied has no doubt about it and the person who succeeds through such injustice gets a thing unlawfully (*harām*) and is not secure of being confronted with injustice to him by the hands of some other unjust person.

24. Hasan (Allah's mercy be on him) said, "Verily, Allah Almighty has made the people bound to obey three things (and these three things cannot be of the knowledge of Hasan himself. Evidently, he might have heard a hadíth concerning them or committed them to his memory as he studied the books of earlier *muhaddithín* and committed them into his memory and then used to narrate it further):

i. Do not follow the desires...

In it is the proof that the thing forbidden is the following of the desires and not the desires itself. It is because a man is forbidden from a thing which is within his power. Not to have the desires itself is not within the power of a man. Therefore, when two litigants appear before a judge, it is inevitable to come to his mind that the issue between them should be determined in such and such manner. It is impossible for him to avoid it. Hence it is not ordained that he should avoid it. What he is said to do is to restrain himself from following the self, which is within his power.

Allah, the Almighty says:

> "O David! We did indeed
> Make thee a vicegerent
> On earth: so judge thou
> Between men in truth (and justice):
> Nor follow thou the lusts
> (Of thy heart). for they will
> Mislead thee from the Path
> Of Allah for those who
> Wander astray from the Path
> Of Allah, is a Penalty Grievous,
> For that they forget
> The Day of Account."   (38:26)

II. And fear Him (Allah, the Almighty) and do not fear people

It is so because Allah, the Almighty says:

> "Therefore fear not men, but fear Me,......"   (5:44)

The Messenger of Allah (peace and blessings of Allah be on him) said: "Whoever fears Allah, everything fears him; and whosoever fears people, Allah makes him afraid of everything."[43]

The reason is that when a person fears people, it is not possible for him to seek the pleasure of Allah. On the other hand, when a person fears Allah, he gets the pleasure of Allah and also pleases the people.

---

43. *Al-Maqāsid al-Hasanah,* Al-Sakhahwi, pp. 411-412, *hadith* No. 1119; *Kashf al-Khifā'*, al-'Ajluni al-Jarrahi, vol. II, p. 244, *hadith* No. 2479; *al-Bayān wa al-Tabyin,* al-Jahiz, vol. III, 146.

iii. And do not sell His Signs for a miserable price

Allah, the Almighty says:

"And sell not My Signs for a miserable price...." (5:44)

Here the giving and taking of bribe (illegal gratification) is forbidden. Allah, the Almighty says:

"(They are fond of) listening to falsehood of devouring anything forbidden...." (5:42)

In this verse, the word *al-suht* (anything forbidden) refers to the giving and taking of the bribe. It is so because if a person receives bribe to do injustice, it is unlawful for him to receive it. And if he accepts or demands and receives bribe to remove injustice, then it was obligatory for him to remove injustice without accepting or demanding or receiving bribe.

25. Besides the above quoted *ahadith*, there are many other *ahadith* in which there is caution (*karāhiyyat*) against acceptance and entrance upon office of judgeship.

26. Imām Khassāf said: "The good people have joined the office of judgeship and the good people have avoided and abandoned entry into it. The abandonment of it is much better both materially and spiritually as we have already stated in the beginning of this book with reasons. It is so because when in a city there are good people, fit and qualified for the office of a judge and if anyone amongst them does not accept that office, he does not render himself as sinful. However, if there is none to hold that office and he is the only person fit and qualified for that assignment then his refusal will render him sinful. When in a city, there are good people and they all restrain themselves from accepting the office of a judge lying vacant and the head of the state also does not decide the cases then all the good people denying to join such office will become sinful jointly as by their such act the injunctions of Allah remain un-enforced (and the rights of the people go waste). However, where the head of the state decides the cases between the litigants himself, then the said good people do not render themselves sinful as the injunctions of Allah, the Almighty remain enforced. Similarly when all the good people restrain themselves from joining the office of a judge and an ignorant (who is neither fit nor qualified for holding such office) person is appointed to such office, even then all the good people who restrain themselves from joining such office will be considered jointly sinful as their silence in the matter or withdrawal from acceptance of responsibility of the said office will not be lawful as it will become a cause of suspension of the injunctions of Allah. (Allah knows the best)

CHAPTER 4

Decision by Exercise of Personal Judgement (Ijtihād)

27. *Ibn Buraidah* transmitted on the authority of his father that the Messenger of Allah (peace and blessings of Allah be on him) said: "Judges are of three kinds; two will go into the Fire and one will go to the Paradise.

A man who has knowledge and decides according to his knowledge, he shall go to the Paradise."[44]

44. *Sunan* Abû Dâ'ûd Kitâb al-aqdiah, vol. III, p. 299, *Hadith* No. 3573; *Sunan* Ibn Mâjah, kitâb al-ahkâm, vol. II, p. 776, *Hadith* No. 2315; *Al-Mustadrak al-Hākim*, kitâb al-ahkâm, vol. IV, p. 90; *Al-Talkhis 'alal-Mustadrak*, al-Zahabi, vol. IV, p. 90; *Majma al-Zawā'id*, al-'Iraqi wa ibn Hajar, vol. II, p. 682, *Hadith* No. 4903; *A'zab al-Mawarid*, al-Yamani, vol. II, p. 682; *Nail al-Awtār*, Al-Shawkani, vol. VII, p. 274; *Subul al-Salām, Sharh Bulugh al-Maram*, al-San'ani, vol. IV, p. 116; *Nasb al-Ra'iyah fiTakhrij Ahadith al-Hidayah*, Al-Zayla'i, vol. IV, p. 65; *Al-Dirā'iyah fi Takhrij Ahadith al-Hidayah*, Ibn Hajar al-'Asqalani, vol. II, p. 166, hadith No. 816; *Talkhis al-Habir*, vol. IV, p. 185, *Hadith* No. 2082; *Sunan al-Kubra*, Al-Bayhaqi, vol. X, p. 117; *Akhbār al-Qudāt*, al-Waki', vol. I, pp. 13-14; *Jami' Masanid al-Imām Abi Hanifah*, al-Khawarizmi, vol. II, p. 280; *Musnad*, al-Imām Abi Hanifah, p. 218; *Jami' Bayān al-'Ilm*, Ibn Abd al-barr, vol. II, pp. 70-71.

It is so because he manifested the truth by exercising his knowledge and delivered justice to the oppressed by getting his right from his opponent. Hence he will go to the Paradise.

The *'ulamā* have then discussed as to whether such a person can be termed as *khalifatullāh*? The majority of them agrees on it that such a person shall be titled as *Khalifatur Rasūlillāh* or *Warithur Rasūlillāh* but he shall not be titled as *Khalifatullāhi* as this term or title is specific for the prophets of Allah.

The words of the Messenger of Allah (peace and blessings of Allah be on him). "And a man who is ignorant and decides the matter ignorantly, he shall go to the Fire."

It is so because he is ignorant and acts recklessly.

The words of the Messenger of Allah (peace and blessings of Allah be on him). "And a man who is knowing but does not decide by exercise of his knowledge, he will go to the Fire."

It is so because he is intentionally, wrong doer. So, he will go to the fire.

28. Ibn Buraidah also narrated on the authority of his father that the Messenger of Allah (peace and blessings of Allah be on him) said, "The judges are of three kinds: two of them shall go to the Fire and one of them shall enter into Paradise. A man who has knowledge and exercises such knowledge at the time of deciding a case shall enter Paradise; and a man who is ignorant and decides a case ignorantly shall go to the Hell. And a man who has no knowledge and decides without knowledge and feels ashamed in asking another the solution of the problem before him, shall go to the Hell.

Thus it is befitting a judge not to hesitate in asking solution of the problem when he does not know the answer. Similarly, he should not feel ashamed in admitting that he does not know when actually he is not knowing the solution. It is narrated on the authority of **Abdullāh** bin 'Umar that he was asked about the solution of some problem. He replied that he did not know and then he turned to his own-self and said, "It is strange that Abdullāh, the son of 'Umar, does not know the solution of the problem put to him."[45]

It is so because when a judge does not know the solution, it is compulsory (*fard*) for him to ask for it. In case he does not ask for the solution, he is guilty of non-performance of an act the performance of which was compulsory for him.

29. It is narrated on the authority of Alī (Allah's pleasure be on him) that he said, "Rulers are of three kinds: two shall go into the Fire and one shall go to the Paradise. A man who leaves the truth knowingly will go to the Hell and a man who exercised *ijtihād* and reached the correct decision shall go to the Paradise and a man who exercised *ijtihād* and reached incorrect decision shall go to the Hell."[46]

This *hadith* is *mawquf* at 'Alī (Allah's pleasure be on him). The *hadith* which is *marfū ila Rasūlillāh* [the chain of narration of which is continuous from the first narrator to the Messenger of Allah (peace and blessings of Allah be on him)] says that a judge who exercises his personal judgement (*ijtihād*) and does not reach correct decision will get one reward, while a guide who exercises his personal judgement (*ijtihād*) and reaches the correct decision will get two fold reward.[47]

45. *Sunan* Al-Darimi, vol. I, p. 57, *Hadith* No. 187; *Jami' al-Bayān al-'ilm*, Ibn Abd al-Barr, vol. II, p. 52.

46. *Sunan al-Kubra*, Al-Bayhaqi, vol. X, p. 117; *Al-Mabsūt*, al-Sarakhsi, vol. XVI, p. 72; *Jami' Bayān al-'Ilm*, Ibn 'Abd al-Barr, vol. II, p. 71.

47. *Sahih al-Bukhāri*, kitāb al-I'tisām, vol. IV, p. 181; *Sahih Muslim*, kitāb al-aqdiah, vol. III, p. 1342, hadith No. 1716; *Sunan* Abū Dā'ūd, kitāb al-Aqdiah, vol. III, p. 299, hadith No. 3574; *Sunan* al-Tirmizi, kitāb al-Ahkām, vol. II, p. 393, hadith No. 1341; *Jami' al-Usūl*, Ibn Athir, vol. X, p. 548, hadith Nos. 7640 & 7641; *Al-Mustadrak*, al-

It is inevitable to reconcile this *marfu hadith* with the *hadith mauquf* at 'Ali (Allah's pleasure be on him).

The reconciliation is by two ways. One is interpretation that we have stated under the *marfû' hadith*, i.e., the judge exercised personal judgement (*ijtihãd*) while he was one of those competent to exercise personal judgement (*ahl-al-ijtihãd*).

And the interpretation that we have stated under the *hadith* of 'Ali (Allah's pleasure be on him), i.e., the judge exercised personal judgement (*ijtihãd*) while he was not one of those competent to exercise personal judgement (*ijtihãd*) (*lam yakun min ahl al-ijtihãd*). In such a case it was not lawful for him to exercise personal judgement (*ijtihãd*) and as he did exercise it, he will go to the Hell.

Hadrat 'Ali (Allah's pleasure be on him) has pointed out towards it and said, "He is a *hurûri* who exercised personal judgement (*ijtihãd*) and made a mistake and will go to the Hell."

Hurûris were the people from among *al-Khawãrij* who did not accept the *sunnah* of the Messenger of Allah (peace and blessings of Allah be on him) and argued, "We will act upon only that which we find in the Book of Allah. We will not act upon anything not found in the Book of Allah." It is for this stand of their that they did not find *rajm* stoning to death for offence of *zina* and the *nisab al-sariqah*.

The second way of reconciliation of the two *ahadith* (*maufuq* and *marfû'*) is the interpretation that has been mentioned under

Hãkim, vol. IV, p. 88; *al-Musnad*, Abû 'Awanah, vol. IV, p. 12; *Sunan* Daraqutni, vol. IV, p. 203; *Sunan* Ibn Mãjah, kitãb al-ahkãm, vol. II, p. 776, *Hadith* No. 2314; *Al-Muntaqi*, Ibn al-Jarud, pp. 331-332, *Hadith* No. 996; *Kitãb al-Umm*, al-Shafi'i, vol. VI, p. 203 and vol. VII, p. 85; *Musnad* al-Shafi'i, vol. VI, p. 263; *Mukhtasar al-Muzani*, p. 242; *Musnad* Ahmad bin Hanbal, vol. IV, pp. 198, 204 & 205; *Jami' Bayãn al-'Ilm*, Ibn 'Abd al-Barr, vol. II, p. 71.

the *hadith marfu* that he exercised personal judgement (*ijtihād*) at an occasion where personal judgement (*ijtihād*) was to be exercised.

The interpretation that is mentioned in the *hadith* of 'Ali (Allah's pleasure be on him) is that he had exercised personal judgement (*ijtihād*) at a place which was not the place of such exercise as the said place was a place where a text (*nass*) was available.

The proof of it is the report about Hasan Basri (Allah's mercy be on him).[48] He went to Ayas bin Mu'awiyah (Allah's mercy be on him) after the later was appointed to the office of a judge and found him weeping and full of grief.[49] Hasan asked him, "What is

48. His name is Hasan. His father's name is Yasar. His *kuniyyat* (surname) is Abu Sa'id, he was a *tabi'i*, he was from Ansar. He lived in Basrah. He was an eminent Imam having full expertise in every subject. He has the honour to have listened *hadith* from the companions, viz., Ibn 'Umr, Anas. and Abu Bakr (Allah's pleasure be on all of them). He also listened *hadith* from the *tabi'in* (Allah's mercy be on all of them). Ibn Sa'id says that Hasan Basari was a person who was exhaustive and high ranking scholar, a jurist, authentic and secure in his transmissions. He was a person who worshipped in humility and performed all *manasik*. He had versatile knowledge, eloquent in speech and handsome in appearance. He died in the year 110 A.H. [See *Akhbar ul-Qudat*, al-Waki' vol. II, pp. 3-15; *al-Huliyah*, Abu Nu'aim vol. II. p. 131; *Tabaqat*, al-Sha'rani vol. I. p. 39; *Mizan al-I'tidal*, al-Zahabi, *Hadith* no. 1948; *Tabaqat*, Ibn Sa'd, vol. VII, p. 114; *Asma al-Rijal*, *Mishkāt al-Masābih*, Imam Waliyyuddin Muhammad bin Abdullah al-Khatib al-Umari, Tabi'i, *Hadith* No. 193. p. 314].

49. His name is Ayas. His father's name is Mu'awiyah. His grand father's name is Qurrah. His *kunniyat* (surname) is Abu Wa'ilah. The name of his tribe is Muzani. He held the judgeship of Basrah. He was unique in his intellect and quick in understanding and solving the problems. His wisdom was proverbial. Jahiz says that Ayas was one of those people of the tribe of Mudar of which the tribe felt elevated in the eyes of others. He excelled among the judges and was very truthful and full of wisdom and

the wrong with you?" He replied, "I   pondering upon the words
of Hadrat 'Ali (Allah's pleasure be on him) that whosoever
exercised personal judgement (*ijtihad*) and made a mistake shall
go to the Hell." Hasan recited the following verses of the Qur'ān:

> "And remember David
> and Solomon. when they
> gave judgement in the matter
> of the field into which
> the sheep of certain people
> had strayed by the night:
> We did witness their judgement.
> To Solomon We inspired
> the (right) understanding
> of the matter: to each
> (of them) We gave judgement
> and knowledge; it was
> Our power that made
> the hills and the birds
> celebrate Our praises,
> with David: it was We
> Who did (all these things)."   (21:78-79)

It is so because Hadrat Dã'ûd (peace be upon him) was fully
competent to exercise personal judgement (*ijtihād*) while Hadrat
Sulaimãn (peace be on him) had exercised personal judgement
(*ijtihād*) and reached the correct decision and Allah, the Almighty
appreciated both of them in the following words: "To each of

understanding. The contemporary *caliphs* respected him very
much. Mada'ini wrote a book titled as *Zakan Ayas*. He died in
Wasit in the year 122 A.H. [Akhbar al-Qudat, al-Waki', vol. I, pp.
312-374].

them We gave the power of judgement and knowledge."[50]

Hasan Basrí (Allah's mercy be on him) explained to Ayas bin Mu'āwiyah (Allah's mercy be on him) that Hadrat 'Alí (Allah's pleasure be on him) was referring to a judge who was not competent to exercise personal judgement (*ijtihād*) or who exercised it at a place which was not the place of the exercise of personal judgement (*ijtihād*).

So this is the reconciliation between the two *ahadith*.

30. Qatādah reported on the authority of Abū Mūsā al-Ash'arí (Allah's pleasure be on him) who said:

"A judge should not give decision till the truth becomes as clear as the night becomes clear and distinct from the day." When this transmission reached 'Umar bin al-Khattāb (Allah's pleasure be on him). he remarked, "He spoke the truth."

It is so because the Messenger of Allah (peace and blessing of Allah be on him) had criticised a particular witness and said to him, "When you see a thing like the sun, only then give evidence

50.   David and Solomon (peace be on both of them) were given authority in the land. When sheep of a people trespassed in the cultivated field of an join other and thereby damaged the crop, the matter came to David (peace be upon him) and after hearing the parties gave the decision that all the sheep shall be handed over to the owner of the produce in lieu of the damage caused by the sheep. At that time Solomon (peace be upon him) was only 11 years old. Allah, the Almighty blessed him with the understanding of the matter in dispute. He decided that the loss can be made good by paying compensation as such he ordered that the sheep shall remain in the custody of the owner of the produce and he will utilise their milk, wool and issues till the loss is fully compensated. On receiving full compensation the owner of produce shall return the custody of the sheep and the issues to the owner of sheep.

about it, otherwise withdraw yourself."[51]

The responsibility of a judge is higher than the responsibility of a witness. The reason is that the decree or order of a judge is binding itself while the evidence is not binding as such unless a decree or order is passed according to such evidence. Thus when it is so much essential for a witness to be extremely careful in the matter of bearing and giving of evidence concerning any matter, the responsibility of a judge who is to base his decision on the evidence of a witness is, therefore, much more heavy.

In the presence of an absolute text (*nass qat'i*), the right becomes clear and distinct as the day becomes clear and bright as against the night. In the absence of an absolute text, one has to exercise personal judgement (*ijtihād*). As a personal judgement (*ijtihād*) is not an absolute proof, hence the right does not become as clear as a day becomes distinct and clear against night.

31. It is narrated about Sha'bi (Allah's mercy be on him) that someone asked him: "Decide between us according to that which Allah has shown you." He replied: "*lasta tarani qādiyan*."

The *'ulamā* have interpreted the reply of Sha'bi in three ways.

One interpretation is, "I am of those *mujtahidín* whose *ijtihād* is based on the truth. Those were the prophets (peace be on all of them). I am only a judge and not a prophet. What you have stated is as if I am a prophet and not a judge?" This is the proof that a *mujtahid* sometimes comes to a correct personal judgement (*ijtihād*) and sometimes to an incorrect personal judgement (*ijtihād*).

The second interpretation is, "You are demanding such a thing from me to which I cannot have an access, i.e., my having an access to the truth definitely is not possible."

51. *Al-Mustadrak* al-Hākim, vol. IV, pp. 98-99; *Sunan al-Kubra*, Al-Bayhaqi, vol. X, p. 156.

The third interpretation is, "I shall not sit as a judge as I know that the parties to a litigation demand definite right and justice."

This *hadith* shows that a *mujtahid* may be right or wrong in his *ijtihād*.

32. Abdullāh bin 'Amr bin al-'Ās (Allah's pleasure be on them) who heard the Messenger of Allah (peace and blessings of Allah be on him) saying: "When a judge gives a decision exercising his personal judgement (*ijtihād*), he will get two rewards if his personal judgement (*ijtihād*) is correct and he will get single reward if his personal judgement (*ijtihād*) is incorrect."

The reason is that if he reached correct conclusion in his personal judgement (*ijtihād*) he got one reward for the exercise of personal judgement (*ijtihād*) and the other reward for exposing the verity (*haqq*). If on the other hand, he committed a mistake, then he got only one reward for the exercise of personal judgement (*ijtihād*) as by this he did not expose the verity (*haqq*).

The reward will be only when the personal judgement (*ijtihād*) is exercised at the place and occasion of personal judgement. If a judge exercised his personal judgement (*ijtihād*) without an occasion for it or without a place for it, and he committed mistake, he would not get any reward as in such a case he was negligent. It is like a person who offered prayer in a direction which he considered in his heart most probably the correct direction of *qiblah*, which, in fact, was not the correct direction but the method of knowing the direction was valid as the signs and proofs of direction were not available, his prayer would be considered valid. But if the method of knowing the direction was incorrect, i.e., he was at a place where there were signs and arches etc., showing the direction of *qiblah* then it was not an occasion or place of acting upon probability. In such a case, his prayer shall not be considered valid and he shall have to offer it again in the correct direction of *qiblah*.

This *hadith* also shows that a *mujtahid* is not infallible.

33. The author then mentioned the *hadith* narrated by Abû Hurairah (Allah's pleasure be on him).[52]

34. A report says that Hadrat 'Umar (Allah's pleasure be on him) announced judgement in a case. On that a man stated, "By God, this judgement is based on verity." Hadrat 'Umar (Allah's pleasure be on him) remained silent. Thereafter Hadrat 'Umar again announced the judgement. The said man again repeated the same remark. Hadrat 'Umar (Allah's pleasure be on him) again announced the judgement. The said man repeated the same remark third time. On that Hadrat 'Umar (Allah's pleasure be on him) said: "How do you know? By God, 'Umar does not know himself as to whether he decided with verity or committed mistake. However, he did not commit any negligence in the decision (i.e., he strained every nerve in that *ijtihãd*).[53]

In this incident is the proof that when any person hears the remark of any person that are irrelevant and out of place, he should not reply to it as there is possibility of committing a mistake, but when the same remark is repeated with certainty of heart by another then it should be replied.

This *hadith* shows that a *mujtahid* can commit a mistake and can also come to the correct finding in his judgement.

35. It is narrated on the authority of Shuraih (Allah's mercy be on him) that he gave a decision and thereafter one of the parties remarked, "You have given a decision against me wrongfully." He replied: "By God, I cannot split a hair into two, i.e., I am not of those *mujtahidin* who find the truth by their *ijtihãd*. Similarly, I

---

52. It is the same *hadith* that has already been referred to in para 29 on the authority of 'Amr bin al-'Ãs (Allah's pleasure be on him).

53. *Muo'tta*, Imãm Mãlik with commentary of al-Zarqani, vol. IV, p. 372; *Jami' al-Usûl*, Ibn Athir, Vol. X, p. 547, *hadith* No. 7638.

cannot split a hair into two.[54] My function is to rely upon the proof and to decide accordingly. In this way the objective is achieved for which I am commanded to achieve. After this your remark that I have committed a mistake is of no harm to me."

This shows that a judge should remain tolerant in the matter of the litigants and should not feel irritated on any adverse remarks. Similarly, a *mufti* should also not feel aggrieved if any remark is passed against him concerning his *fatwa*.

36. Ibn Sirín (Allah's mercy be on him) reported that Hadrat 'Umar (Allah's pleasure be on him) said, "I have delivered different kinds of judgements in the matter of inheritance of grand father, but I have not deviated from verity and justice by committing any sort of negligence."[55]

This *hadith* also shows that a *mujtahid* can be correct as well as mistaken.

This *hadith* further shows that a decision based on personal judgement (*ijtihād*) is not set aside by a similar personal judgement (*ijtihād*).

According to what a Judge should Adjudicate a Case

37. Ahmad bin 'Umar (Allah's mercy be on him) the author of the book said: "A judge should adjudicate in accordance with the injunctions of the Book of Allah, which have not been abrogated. It is so because the Book of Allah is the leader of the righteous and the leader of all the proofs. If he does not find anything

---

54. *Akhbār al-Qudāt*, al-Waki', vol. II, pp. 213, 214 & 256.

55. *Sunan* al-Darimi, kitāb al-fara'id, vol. II, p. 254, *Hadith* No. 2903; *Sunan al-Kubra*, Al-Bayhaqi, vol. VI, p. 245; *Al-Mabsūt*, al-Sarakhsi, vol. XVI, p. 84; *Akhbār al-Qudāt*, al-Waki', vol. II, p. 400; *Tabaqāt*, Ibn Sa'd, part 2, vol. II, p. 100.

in the Book of Allah, then he should adjudicate in accordance with the *ahadith* of the Messenger of Allah (peace and blessings of Allah be on him). It is so because we have been enjoined to follow the Messenger of Allah (peace and blessings of Allah be on him).

> Allah, the Almighty says:
>
> ".....So take what the Apostle
> Assigns to you, and deny
> Yourselves that which he
> Withholds from you...." (597)

If he does not find any text (*nass*) in the *ahadith*, then he should adjudicate in accordance with the consensus of the companions (Allah's pleasure be on all of them).

The Messenger of Allah (peace and blessings of Allah be on him) said, "It is obligatory upon you to follow my *sunnah* and the *sunnah* of the *caliphs* after me and hold it fast."[56]

If there is difference of opinion on any problem between the Companions (Allah's pleasure be on all of them) and the judge is of those who are men of discernment and judgement (*ahl al-tamyiz wa'l-nazar*). He should distinguish between their statements and prefer one over the other and the one he finds the best and the nearest to verity, he should decide the matter according to such opinion.

---

56. *Sunan* al-Darimi, vol. I, pp, 44-45, *hadith* No. 96; *Sunan* Abú Dā'úd, vol. IV, pp. 200-201, *hadith* No. 4607; *Sunan* Ibn Mājah, vol. I, p. 15, *hadith* No. 42; *Musnad* Ahmad bin Hanbal, vol. IV, pp. 126-127; *Al-Mustadrak* al-Hākim, vol. I, pp. 95-98; *Talkhis al-Mustadrak*, al-Zahabi, vol. I, p. 96; *Talkhis al-Habir*, al-'Asqalani, vol. II, p. 190, *hadith* No. 2097; *Takhrij Ahadith 'Usul*, al-Bazdawi, p. 238.

The Messenger of Allah (peace and blessings of Allah be on him) said, "My companions are (luminous) like the stars. To whomsoever you will follow, you will get guidance."[57]

If a judge does not find anything in the statements of the companions (Allah's pleasure be on all of them), then he should decide the matter in accordance with the consensus of *tabi'in* as the consensus of each period becomes a proof (*hujjat*) as when all the people agree concerning a problem, then such an agreement becomes the collective way of the Muslims (*sabil al-mu'min*) and no one has the scope to deviate from it.

If there is difference of opinion in any matter between the *tabi'in* then the judge should thoroughly probe into the matter and exercise his personal judgement and prefer an opinion which is better and nearest to verity and decide the case accordingly.

If the judge dos not find any thing in the statements of the *tabi'in*, then, in case he is a *mujtahid*, he should make analogical deductions from similar *shari'ah* values (*ahkām*) and exercise his personal judgement (*ijtihād*) and decide accordingly. In case he is not a *mujtahid*, he should consult a *mufti*. He should not decide a case if he is not having the knowledge. He should not feel any hesitation or shame in asking the solution of the problem lest he should become liable to the consequence stated in the *hadith* quoted above.

38. To know the juristic way the knowledge of three things is necessary, which are stated in three sections below:

Section I: *Following of Companions and their statements.*

Section II: *Following of Tabi'in and their statements.*

Section III: *To exercise personal judgement after thorough probe of the problem.*

---

57. *Talkhis al-Habir*, al-'Asqalani, vol. IV, pp. 190-191, *Hadith* No. 2098.

In the Matter of Following the Opinions of the Companions

39. In this behalf. there are. in all. three transmissions on the authority of Imām Abú Hanifah (Allah's mercy be on him).[58]

40. The first transmission is that Imām Abû Hanifah (Allah's mercy be on him) said:

The companions who possess the rank of *qādi* and *mufti*, I follow them as the Messenger of Allah (peace and blessings of Allah be on him) said, "Follow who come after me, viz.. Abû Bakr and 'Umar (Allah's pleasure be on them)."[59] All agree that they were of the rank of *qādi* and *mufti*. Besides them other companions who are equal in rank with them which include 'Uthmān 'Alí, *'Ibadalāh thalathah*,[60] Zaid bin Thābit, Mu'āz bin

58. *Al-Manaqib*. Al-Mawfaq. vol. I, p. 77.

59. *Sunan* al-Tirmizí, vol. V, pp. 271-272, *Hadith* Nos. 3742-44; *Sunan*, Ibn Mājah, vol. I, p. 37, *Hadith* No. 97; *Musnad* Ahmad bin Hanbal, vol. V, pp. 382, 385, 399 and 402; *Al-Jami' al-Saghir*, al-Manawi, vol. I, p. 51; *Al-Taisir bi Sharh al-Jami' al-Saghir*. al-Manawi, vol. I, p. 191; *Talkhis al-Habir*, al-'Asqalani, vol. IV, p. 190, *Hadith* No. 2096; *Al-Mustadrak* al-Hākim, vol. III, p. 75; *Zakha'ir al-Mawarith fi al-dalalah 'ala Mawadi' al-hadith*, al-Nablasi, vol. I, p. 189. *Hadith* No. 1708; *Takhrij Ahadith Usūl*, al-Bazdawi, p. 237.

60. *'Ibādalah thalāthah* (the three companions whose name is Abdullāh). They are Abdullāh bin 'Umar, Abdullāh bin 'Abbās, and Abdullāh bin Zubair. Imām Nawāwi has added Abdullāh bin 'Amr bin al-'Ās and named them *'ibadalah arba'ah* (i.e., the four companions whose names are Abdullāh). Imām Ahmad bin Hanbal and all other *muhaddithin* have named them so. It was asked from Ahmad (bin Hanbal) as to whether Abdullāh bin Mas'úd was one of them? He said, "No, he is not one of them." Al-Bayhaqi stated it was

Jabal, and every other companion who possesses a rank equal to them. I follow all of them. I do not consider it permissible to act against their opinions, but some companions are not equal to their rank which include Abû Amamah, Sahl bin Sa'd as-Sa'idi, Abû Hamid as-Sa'idi, and Barā' bin 'Āzib, etc.. (Allah's pleasure be on all of them).

41. The second transmission is that Imām Abû Hanifah said, "I follow companions and do not consider it permissible to differ with them. However three companions. viz.. Anas bin Mālik, Abû Hurairah. and Samurah bin Jundab are such to differ with them is considered by me as permissible."

When Imām Abû Hanifah was asked for what reason he considered it permissible to differ with them. He replied: "So far as Anas bin Mālik is concerned. his memory has become weak in his old age and he used to ask solution of problems from 'Alqamah (a *tabi'i*). When I do not follow 'Alqamah, how can I follow him who asks solution of problems from 'Alqamah.

So far as Abû Hurairah is concerned. he used to transmit everything he heard without pondering into its meanings. He also does not know the repealing and the repealed (*ahadíth*).

So far as Samurah bin Jundab is concerned, I felt worried in my heart when a transmission on his authority reached that he considered intoxicating drinks other than wine (*khamr*) as permissible. Hence I do not follow his *fatwas*.

> so because he died earlier while they lived long when they were needed by the people for seeking knowledge from them and when they agreed on any matter, it was said that it was the opinion or the practice of the *'ibādalah*. The companions including Ibn Mas'úd whose name was Abdullāh were 220 in number. Al-Jauhari has stated in his *Sihah* that Ibn Mas'úd was one of the *al-'ibādalah al-arba'a*. He excluded the name of Ibn 'Amr bin al-Ās from them which is manifestly incorrect. [*Tahzib al-Asmā wa al-Lughat*, al-Nawawi. part 1, vol. I. p. 267.]

However. the narrations of the companions (Allah's pleasure be on all of them) narrating the *ahadith* of the Messenger of Allah (peace and blessings of Allah be on him) shall be accepted because every companion is authentic in that which he narrates."

42. The third transmission is that Imãm Abû Hanifah said. "If any companion has given any *fatwa* in any problem. I shall follow him and shall not differ with him. i.e., I follow all such companions (Allah's pleasure be on all of them). [This is the manifest *maslak* of Imãm Abû Hanifah (Allah's mercy be on him)]. The reason is that whatever the said companions stated would either be on the basis of *zann* and *takhmin* or would have stated after hearing it from the Messenger of Allah (peace and blessings of Allah be on him) or would have exercised personal judgement (*ijtihãd*). So far as their saying anything merely on surmises is concerned it cannot be even imagined about them. If they have stated anything after hearing the same from the Messenger of Allah (peace and blessings of Allah be on him) then to follow them is necessary. If they have exercised personal judgement (*ijtihãd*) then their personal judgement (*ijtihãd*) is superior and better than the personal judgement (*ijtihãd*) of the people other than them. The reason is that the degree of conformity with verity available to their personal judgement (*ijtihãd*) cannot be available to that extent to any other personal judgement (*ijtihãd*).

SECTION II

In the Matter of Following the Opinions of the Successors of the Companions

43. Regarding following the opinions of the successors of the companions. there are two transmissions on the authority of

Imām Abû Hanifah (Allah's mercy be on him).

One transmission is that Imām Abû Hanifah (Allah's mercy be on him) said, "I do not follow successors of the companions because they were human beings like us who exercised personal judgement (*ijtihād*) and we are also human beings like them who exercise personal judgement (*ijtihād*).

[According to the manifest narration (*zahir al-riwayat*), this is the *maslak* of Imām Abû Hanifāh (Allah's mercy be on him)].

The other transmission, which is mentioned in *al-Nawādir*, is that Imām Abû Hanifah (Allah's mercy be on him) said, "The successors of the companions who are considered *a 'immah* (the leading ones) and who gave *fatawa* (opinions) during the period of companions and their opinions became popular and the companions (Allah's pleasure be on all of them) gave them permission to exercise personal judgement (*ijtihād*). I follow them. Such successors include Shuraih,[61] al-Hasan,[62] Masrûq bin al-

---

61. Abû Umayyah Shuraih bin Hārith Kindi, *tābi'i*. He got the period of the Messenger of Allah (peace and blessings of Allah be on him) but had not seen him. According to some, he had the honour to see the Messenger of Allah (peace and blessings of Allah be on him). Most of the historians state that Hadrat 'Umar (Allah's pleasure be on him) had appointed him the Judge of Kûfah. He held that post for sixty years, i.e., uptil the period of Hajjāj. He died in 80 A.H. According to *Tārikh al-Bukhārí*, at the time of his death, he was 120 years old. He was well versed in the science of tracking (*qa'if*) and also a poet (*sha'ir*). [*Akhbār al-Qudāt*, al-Waki', vol. II, p. 189; *Tabaqāt Ibn Sa'd*, vol. VI, pp. 50-56; *Al-Bidāyah wa al-Nahāya*, Ibn al-Kathír, vol. III, p. 77 and vol. II, p. 562; *Al-Huliyah*, Abû Nu'aim, vol. IV, p. 132; *Tahzib al-Asmā' wa al-Lughāt*, al-Nawāwi, part I, vol. I, p. 243-249; *Taqrib al-Tahzib*, al-'Asqalani, vol. I, p. 349, No. 51; *Tazkara al-Huffāz*, vol. I, p. 59, No. 44.

62. Al-Hasan Basarí, his biographical details have been given under para 29 above.

Ajza'[63] and 'Alqamah.[64]

The reason is that these successors had attained the status of *muftis* during the period of the companions and the later had granted permission to them to give *fatawa*, hence the status of their statements is like the statements of companions.

If anyone objects that why Imãm Abû Hanifah (Allah's mercy be on him) has mentioned the statement of the successors of the companions in his book, there is no need to answer him in the light of the second transmission.

As against this, according to the first transmission (*zahir al-riwayat*) the object needs to be answered. The answer is that Imãm Abû Hanifah (Allah's mercy be on him) did not mention the opinions of successors as proofs rather his objective was to show that he was not alone in the opinions adopted by him. And that the same opinions have been expressed by those who were before

63. Abû 'Ã'isha Masrûq bin Ajza', *tābi'i*. He is considered among Kûfî *'ulama* and *qurrã'*. He transmitted *ahadith* on the authorities of Abû Bakr Siddíq, 'Uthmãn, 'Alí, 'Umar, and Ibn Mas'ûd (Allah's pleasure be on all of them). All agree on his eminence, superiority and authenticity. he is called Masrûq as he was taken away by someone in his childhood. He died in 62 or 63 A.H. (*Tahzib al-Asmã' wa al-Lughãt*, al-Nawãwí, part1, vol. II, p. 88, No. 128; *Mizãn al-I'tidal*, (8463); *Mashahir 'Ulama al-Amsãr*, p. 101; *Tabaqãt*, Ibn Khayyat, 149; *Tazkarah al-Huffãz*, vol. I, p. 49, No. 26; *Taqrib al-Tahzib*, vol. II, p. 242, No. 1055.]

64. Abû Shibal, 'Alqamah bin Qays Abdullãh Nakh'i, Kûfi, *tābi'i*. He was an eminent jurist. He heard *hadith* from 'Umar, 'Uthmãn, 'Alí, Ibn Mas'ûd, Salmãn Farsí etc. (Allah's pleasure be on all of them) while Abû Wa'il, Ibrãhim Nakh'i, Sha'bi, and Ibn Sirín (Allah's mercy be on all of them) transmitted *hadith* on his authority. All agree on his greatness. He died in the year 62 A.H. or 72 A.H. [*Tabaqãt*, Ibn al-Khayyãt, 147; *Taqrib al-Tahzib*, vol. II, p. 31, 286; *Tahzib al-Asmã' wa al-Lughãt*, al-Nawãwí, vol. I, pp. 342-343, No. 425; *Tabaqãt*, Ibn Sa'd, vol. VI, pp. 57-62.]

him. Therefore, whatever he said himself in it, he was a follower (*muttabi'*) and not an innovator (*mubtadi'*).

SECTION III

To exercise Personal Judgement (Ijtihād) after thorough probe of the Problem

44. To discuss this matter it is necessary to first know the meaning of personal judgement (*ijtihād*) and to see who are qualified and competent to exercise personal judgement (*ijtihād*).

Meaning of Ijtihād

45. *Ijtihād* means to struggle hard to seek the objective (*hazl u'l-majhūd fi talab i'l-maqsūd*).

Competency for Ijtihād

46. The *Mashā'ikh* are of different opinion regarding the competency for *ijtihād*. According to some *mashā'ikh* only such a person is competent to exercise *ijtihād* who is expert in the science of *hadith* (*'ilm al-hadith*) and also knows its meanings and interpretation or who is expert in *'ilm al-hadith* along with being a jurist (*faqih*).

According to some others, only such a person is competent to exercise *ijtihād* who is intelligent, psychologist, and knows the states (*ahwāl*), habits (*'adāt*), and customs (*a'rāf*) of the people. It is so because the custom (*'urf*) dominates the analogical deduction (*qiyās*), as you know *al-istisnā'* is permissible as a custom as against *qiyās*.

Al-Shaikh, al-Imām, Shams al-A'immah Abū Bakr

Muhammad (bin Ahmad) bin Abí Sahl al-Sarakhsi (Allah's mercy be on him) said that a person will be declared competent for *ijtihād* if he has learnt by heart *al-Mabsūt*[65] and also committed to his memory the way of the earlier jurists (*madhab al-mutaqaddamin*).[66]

65. Hāji Khalifah says that there are many books titled as *Al-Mabsūt* in the matter of branches concerning Hanafi school of thought, such as the book titled as *Al-Asl*, written by Imām Abū Yūsuf Ya'qūb bin Ibrāhim, the chief justice, Hanafi jurist and pupil of Imām Abū Hanifah (Allah's mercy be on him). He died in 182 A.H. Similarly, Imām Muhammad bin al-Hasan al-Shaibani, who died in 189 A.H. and was a pupil of Imām Abū Hanifah (Allah's mercy be on him) wrote *Kitāb al-Salāt*, then *Kitāb al-Buyū'*, and *Kitāb al-'Aymān* and *Kitāb al-Ikrāh*, and then collected them as a *Mabsūt* and whenever it is mentioned in the other books, it is referred to as that Imām Muhammad has said this or that in *Kitāb Al-Mabsūt*. It should also be known that there are many persons who have transmitted *Al-Mabsūt* on the authority of Imām Muhammad, but the most manifest of them is that of Abū Sulaimān al-Juzjani. The later leading jurists have written commentaries on *Al-Mabsūt* like Shaikh al-Islām Abū Bakr al-Ma'rūf bin Khawāhar Zādah and Shams al-A'immah al-Hulwāni. It is narrated that Imām Shafi'i appreciated this work and had committed it to his memory. A wise man of the people of the book studied it and embraced Islām and had remarked, "When such is the book of Imām Muhammad (the pupil of Imām Abū Hanifah), how great will be the Book of Muhammad, the Messenger of Allah (peace and blessings of Allah be on him), i.e., al-Qur'ān. [*Kashf al-Zunūn*, vol. II, p. 1581; *Mu'jam al-Musannifīn*, al-Taunki, vol. I, p. 167; *Miftāh al-Sa'adah*, Tash Kubra Zādah, vol. II, pp. 262-263].

66. *Al-Jawāhir al-Mudi'ah*, al-Qarashi, vol. II, pp. 28-29, No. 85; *Taj al-Tarajum fī Tabaqāt al-Hanafiyyah*, Ibn Qatlubagha, pp. 52-53, No. 157; *Tabaqāt al-Fuqaha al-Hanafiyyah*, Tash Kubra Zadah, p. 75; *Mu'jam al-Musannifīn*, al-Taunki, vol. I, pp. 155, 157; *Al-Fikr al-Sami fī Tārikh al-Fiqh al-Islāmi al-Rub' al-Rabi*, Al-Hajwi al-Tha'alibi, p. 19, No. 529; *Miftāh al-Sa'adah*, Tash Kubra Zādah, vol. II, pp. 186, 263, 272.

The Knowledge of the Conflict and Agreement between Imãm Abû Hanifah (Allah's mercy be on him) and His Pupil

47. It is inevitable for a *mujtahid* to know the following two situations of the Hanafi *madhab* (school of thought).

a. On which point all the three leading jurists (namely, Imãm Hanifah, Imãm Yûsuf, and Imãm Muhammad have consensus of opinion).

b. On what point they three have conflict of opinion.

48. In the first situation, a judge has no right to differ with them on account of his own personal judgement (*ijtihãd*). The reason is that the verity (*haqq*) is not beyond their statements. Imãm Abû Yûsuf was a great *muhaddith*. It is narrated about him that he said, "I remember by heart 20,000 repealed *ahadith*." When he had in his memory so great number of repealed *ahadith*, how much repealing *ahadith* would be in his memory. Besides this, he was a great jurist (*faqih*).

Imãm Muhammad was very intelligent, a psychologist of high calibre and a great jurist. He was a forerunner in jurisprudence and a pioneer in the science of diction and grammar. He was an expert in the knowledge of *hadith*.

Imãm Abû Hanifah was superior in all these affairs. However, he transmitted a very few number of *ahadith*. The reason was that he had his own point of view in the matter of transmission of *ahadith*, i.e., according to him the transmitter must be remembering by heart the hadith from the point of its transmission.

49. In the matter of the second situation, the '*ulamā* have difference of opinion. According to Abdullāh bin Mubārik (Allah's mercy be on him),[67] the statement of Imām Abû Hanifah (Allah's mercy be on him) shall be accepted because he is counted amongst the *tābi'in* and he used to contest in the matter of *fatawa* with the *tābi'in*.[68]

According to the *shuyukh* of the later time when two *a'imma* agree on a point and one of them is Abû Hanifah, their statement shall be accepted. If the opinion of Abû Hanifah is on one side and the two pupils are on the other side and the judge is *mujtahid* and possesses the insight, he has the option to adopt any one of such opinion and if the judge is not *mujtahid*, then he should ask *fatwa* from some other scholar.

67. Abdullāh bin Mubārak bin Wādih, Hanzali, Tamimi was a *tābi'i*. He heard *hadith* from Sufiyān Thauri and Sufiyān bin 'Uyainah. Imām Muhammad bin Hasan Shaibani has transmitted *hadith* on his authority. He was well-known of his piety and abstinence. He was an eminent *muhaddith*. He was an expert in the '*ulum* of *rijal hadith*. He died in 81 A.H., and was buried in the city of Hayt. He has written many books. *Tārikh Baghdād*, al-Khatib al-Baghdādi, vol. X, p. 153; *Tazkarah al-Huffāz*, al-Zahabi, vol. I, p. 273; *Tahzib al-Asmā' wa al-Lughāt*, al-Nawāwi, vol. I, p. 285; *Wafiyāt al-A'yān*, Ibn Khalkān, vol. II, p. 237; *Al-Nujūm al-Zāhirah*, Ibn Taghri Burdi, vol. II, p. 203; *Tahzib al-Tahzib*, al-'Asqalani, vol. V, p. 283; *Al-Bidāyah wa al-Nahāyah*, Ibn al-Kathir, vol. X, p. 177; *Al-Jāwahir al-Mudi'ah*, al-Qarashi, vol. I, p. 281; *Mir'ah al-Janān*, al-Yafi'i, vol. I, p. 379; *Kitāb Abdullāh bin Mubārik al-Imām al-Qudwah*, Muhammad 'Uthmān Jamāl.]

68. *Al-Manāqib*, al-Kurdari, vol. I, p. 41; *Tārikh al-Baghdād*, al-Khatib al-Baghdādi, vol. XIII, p. 343; *Al-Khairāt al-Hisān fi Manāqib al-Imām al-A'zam Abi Hanifah al-Nu'mān*, p. 41; *Kitāb Abdullāh bin Mubārik*, Muhammad 'Uthmān Jamāl, p. 100; *Al-Fatawa Hindiyyah*, vol. III, p. 312.

To Counsel Along with Competency to Exercise Personal Judgement (Ijtihād) and Knowledge of the Juristicway (Fiqhi Maslak)

50. Imām Khassāf said: "If the *fuqaha* (jurist consultants) are available in the city, the judge should consult them.

Allah, the Almighty says: "....And consult them in the affairs....."   (3:159)

It is evident that a judge cannot be more intelligent than the Messenger of Allah (peace and blessings of Allah be on him). Further consultation opens the mind.

51. If a judge consults such jurist consultants and they all have one and the same opinion concerning the problem or issues and the judge is also of the same opinion, he should decide accordingly. If there is disagreement between the jurist consultants, then in case the judge is a *mujtahid*, he should adopt such opinion which appears to him the nearest to the verity (*haqq*).

52. In the matter of consultation, the age or number of persons are not to be kept in view. The reason is that at times a young person knows correctly about a problem before a judge than an old person. As it is narrated about Hadrat 'Umar (Allah's pleasure be on him) that he used to consult Hadrat Ibn 'Abbās (Allah's pleasure be on him) and used to say to him, "O deep diver in the ocean of knowledge have a dive (concerning this issue)." Thereafter, when Hadrat Ibn 'Abbās (Allah's pleasure be on him) expressed his opinion in the matter, Hadrat 'Umar (Allah's pleasure be on him) used to say, "It is the same opinion which I find in my son Akhzam."[69]

---

69. *Al-Nahāya*, vol. I, p. 504 and vol. V, p. 60; *Al-Bayān wa'l Tabyīn*, vol. I, p. 231; vol. II, p. 171; *Al-Iqd al-Farid*, vol. II, p. 63.

It was proverbial amongst Arabs that in case a son resembled his father, the above remarks were made by them. Hadrat 'Umar (Allah's pleasure be on him) was much older in age than Hadrat Ibn 'Abbās (Allah's pleasure be on him).

The multiplicity of numbers of the persons to be consulted is not to be taken into considereation as at times only a single person may be on verity (*haqq*), and it is not necessary that the whole group of such persons might be knowing the verity. For example, when the sky is cloudy a single person's testimony is accepted in the matter of sight of crescent. The reason is that the crescent was seen by that single person and none else.

53. If the jurists of the city have consensus of opinion concerning an issue, but the judge, who is to adjudicate upon the issue has a different opinion, the judge should not make haste in deciding the said issue and should get the opinion from other jurists in writing. Thereafter, as per the opinion of the jurists which is approximately the best and the nearest to the verity in his mind, he should adopt the same and decide the matter in issue. To get consultation through a written letter is like consulting a man face to face.

Hadrat 'Umar bin al-Khattāb (Allah's pleasure be on him) used to send his advice to Hadrat Abû Mûsā al-Ash'arí[70] (Allah's

---

70. His name was Abdullāh bin Qays. He was an eminent companion of the Messenger of Allah (peace and blessings of Allah be on him). He had undergone three migrations, the first, from Yemen to Makkah al-Mukarramah when he visited the Messenger of Allah (peace and blessings of Allah be on him) and embraced Islām. The second, from Makkah al-Mukarramah to Habsha (Avecena), and the third, from Makkah al-Mukarramah to al-Madínah al-Munawwarah. The Messenger of Allah (peace and blessings of Allah be on him) had appointed him the governor of Zabid, Aden, and territory of Yemen. Hadrat 'Umar (Allah's pleasure be on him) had appointed him the governor of Kûfah. A number of traditions

pleasure be on him) in writing and the later used to ask advice from the former in writing. Hence, if the opinion of the judge is in accordance with the opinion of the jurists, he should decide accordingly, but if the opinion of the judge himself is different then he should decide according to his own opinion as he considers his opinion valid and does not consider the opinion of others as valid. It is for this reason that he should decide according to his own opinion and not according to the opinions of others to which he does not consider valid.

54. If a judge feels any difficulty in a matter before him and he consults some other person who is a jurist consult, it may be of two forms.

   a. If the judge is not *ahl al-rā'i* or *mujtahid*, he should adopt the opinion of the other person who is *faqih*. The reason is when a judge is not himself *ahl al-rā'i*, it is obligatory on him to get *fatwa* of a *mufti* and decide in the light of it.

   b. If a judge is himself *ahl al-rā'i* and *mujtahid* and his own opinion in the matter before him is opposite to the opinion of the other person who is *faqih*, the judge should decide only according to his own opinion as he considers his own opinion still correct and valid. The consultation with another

(*ahadith*) of the Messenger of Allah (peace and blessings of Allah be on him) have been transmitted on his authority. Five *ahadith* are mentioned in the *Sahihain* (the two authentic books compiled by Imām Bukhāri and Imām Muslim containing the *ahadith* of the Messenger of Allah (peace and blessings of Allah be on him). Fifteen *ahadith* are mentioned in *Sahih Bukhari*, fifteen *ahadith* are mentioned in *Sahih Muslim*. He died in 50 A.H. in Makkah al-Mukarramah. A report is that he died in Kûfah. [See *Tahzib al-Asmā' wa al-Lughāt*, al-Nawāwi, p. 268; *Al-Mustadrak* al-Hākim, vol. III, p. 464; *Sunan al-Tirmizi*, vol. V, p. 355; *Sirat 'Umar bin al-Khattāb*, al-Jawzi, p. 91; *Majma' al-Zawā'id*, vol. IX, p. 358; *Akhbār al-Qudāt*, al-Waki', vol. I, p. 283].

person who is a *faqih* is made obligatory on the judge to see perhaps the opinion of another person who is jurist is also according to the opinion of the judge. When the opinion of the other person is not in accordance with the opinion of the judge, the later should not discard his own opinion.

If a judge pronounces a judgement according to his own opinion, his judgement shall be enforced. If a judge pronounces a judgement according to the opinion of another person who is *faqih*, then, according to Imām Abû Hanifah (Allah's mercy be on him), the judgement shall be enforced but according to Imām Abû Yûsuf and Imām Muhammad (Allah's mercy be on them) shall not be enforced. The reason is that if any such judgement is brought to the notice of the *sultān* (the highest court), he can set it aside.

The argument of *sāhibain* (Imām Abû Yûsuf and Imām Muhammad) is that the judge, while pronouncing the judgement, considers his own opinion as valid and the opinion of the jurists consultants as invalid. In such a case, if a judge announces his judgement according to the opinion of the other person, he considers that he is giving a wrong judgement. Hence his judgement shall not be enforced. Its example is like the example of a person who deeply pondered upon to find out the direction of *qiblah* and when he determined it, he acted upon the advice of some other person and offered prayer according to that advice. His prayer shall not be considered as validly offered, even if actually the *Ka'batullāh* is in the same direction. Similarly, if some property is given in custody of some person as a trust and the owner of property forgets it and the custodian intends to give the *zakāt* of his own property to the said person, of whose property he is the custodian, it will not be permissible as according to the knowledge of the custodian. the said person is *ghani* (affluent *sāhib nisāb*) and not entitled to receive the *zakāt*.

Similarly, a person who is to offer a *qadā* prayer, which he forgets to offer and begins the *adā* prayer in time and some other person comes and stands behind him to offer prayer knowingly that a *qadā* prayer is still due upon the said person, the prayer of the Imām will be valid but the prayer of the *muqtadi* shall become *fasid* (invalid) as he knows fully well that his Imām is wrong.

The above examples make it clear that such a judgement which is based on an opinion which the giver of the judgement considers in his heart and mind as incorrect, shall not be enforced.

The argument of Imām Abū Hanifah (Allah's mercy be on him) is that the judge has given judgement in a matter which is *ijtihādi*. Hence. his judgement shall be enforced. It is as if he has given the judgement according to his own opinion. The reason is that the judge is not shower that the personal judgement (*ijtihād*) of the jurists is necessarily wrong as a *mujtahid* cannot declare his own opinion as absolutely valid. Rather there is possibility of both validity and invalidity in his own opinion. Hence when the judge accepted·the personal judgement (*ijtihād*) of another and decided the matter according to it, then the said personal judgement (*ijtihād*) got preference. Hence, such judgement shall be enforced.

The above said form is in the circumstance when the *qādi* has his own opinion concerning the matter and he had adopted the opinion of another person who is a *faqih* and had delivered judgement in accordance with such opinion.

In case, at the time of delivery of judgement, the judge has no opinion of his own and delivered the judgement accepting the opinion of another person who is a *faqih* and thereafter the said judge formed an opinion against the opinion of the said *faqih*, whether such judgement will be valid or not?

There is conflict of opinion between Imām Abū Yûsuf and Imām Muhammad. According to Imām Abū Yûsuf, such a decision shall not be void, while according to Imãm Muhammad, such a decision shall be void.

Imãm Muhammad says that after the pronouncement of the decision, the formulation of any opinion by the judge himself is like a *nass* and where a judge gives a decision according to his own opinion and later on a *nass* comes to his knowledge, his pronounced decision becomes void. Similarly. in the present circumstance, the decision will become void.

Imãm Abû Yûsuf says that where the judge has no opinion of his own, the opinion of the other person becomes like his own opinion. His decision in the absence of his own opinion and basing the decision on the opinion of another person is like giving decision with his own opinion. However, if, later on. the said judge formulates a different opinion, this will not render the decision void.

The same is the situation here.

[Allah knows the best]

CHAPTER 5

Permissibility of Exercising Ijtihãd and other Proper Directions for a Judge

55. *Imãm Khassãf* (Allah's mercy be on him) has begun this chapter with the *hadith* of Hadrat Mu'ãz (Allah's pleasure be on him).[71] There are many advantages of this *hadith*. Some of them are as under.

The appointing authority, before appointment of a person to any post should test the ability and competence of such person regarding the responsibility to be assigned to him as the Messenger of Allah (peace and blessings of Allah be on him) had asked Mu'ãz (Allah's pleasure be on him) to test his ability as according to what he shall decide the cases.

❖ This *hadith* also shows that all the problems are not mentioned in the *Kitabullah* as such the Messenger of Allah (peace and blessings of Allah be on him) had asked Mu'ãz further as according to what he shall decide the cases if

71. The *takhrij* (the chain of authorities) of this *hadith* **has already been** mentioned in para 4 above.

nothing is found in the *Kitabullāh* concerning the matter before him. Hadrat Mu'āz (Allah's pleasure be on him) had replied that according to the *sunnah* of *Rasūl Allāh*. This reply refutes the viewpoint of the *ahl al-zāhir*, who consider that *Kitabullāh* encompasses all things. Their viewpoint is based on the following Qur'ānic verse:

"All wet and dry things are mentioned in the Open Book."

(6:59)

According to them. *Kitāb Mubin* referred to here in this verse is the Holy *Qur'ān* while according to us the reference is to the Sacred Tablet (*lauh mahfūz*).[72]

❖ Further all the problems are not present in the *sunnah* of the Messenger of Allah (peace and blessings of Allah be on him). Hence, he had asked Mu'az (Allah's pleasure be on him) as with what will he decide the matters if he does not find the solution in the *sunnah* of the Messenger of Allah (peace and blessings of Allah be on him).

This *hadith* also shows the superiority of Hadrat Mu'āz (Allah's pleasure be on him), who had given the reply, "I will exercise my personal judgement (*ijtihād*) and the Messenger of Allah (peace and blessings of Allah be on him) allowed him to exercise his personal judgement (*ijtihād*) and did not direct him to turn towards him in such a case.

72. *Tafsir* al-Tabari, vol. XI, p. 402: *Mukhtasar Tafsir al-Tabari*, vol. I, p. 170; *Tafsir al-Khāzim*, vol. II, p. 117; *Tafsir al-Baghawi*, on the margin of *Tafsir al-Khāzim*. vol. II, p. 117; *Tafsir Ibn Kathir*, vol. II, p. 137.

Can a Companion Exercise Personal Judgement (Ijtihād) during the Period of the Messenger of Allah
(peace and blessings of Allah be on him)

56. As to whether a companion can exercise personal judgement (*ijtihād*) during the period of the Messenger of Allah (peace and blessings of Allah be on him), there are three different views of the '*ulamā*.

* According to some '*ulamā*, a companion, cannot exercise personal judgement (*ijtihād*) during the period of Messenger of Allah (peace and blessings of Allah be on him) as it was possible to turn to the messenger of Allah (peace and blessings of Allah be on him) to get solution of the problem. As the access to the text (*nass*) was possible, therefore, during the presence of the text (*nass*) an *ijtihād* would be void.

* According to some others, if the companion is away (or far off) from the Messenger of Allah (peace and blessings of Allah be on him) then exercise of *ijtihād* is permissible for him, but in case he is at a near (or close distance) to the Messenger of Allah (peace and blessings of Allah be on him) then to exercise *ijtihād* is not permissible for him.

* According to still some others, for a companion to exercise *ijtihād* is permissible as Hadrat Mu'āz (Allah's pleasure be on him) had said, "I shall exercise personal judgement (*ijtihād*)" and the Messenger of Allah (peace and blessings of Allah be on him) had allowed him to do so. Likewise, the proof of this is the *hadith* in which the Messenger of Allah (peace and blessings of Allah be on him) had said to

Hadrat Abû Bakr Siddíq (Allah's pleasure be on him) and Hadrat 'Umar (Allah's pleasure be on him), "You both make your statement as the things in which no revelations come to me, I am like you both."[73]

This shows that a companion can exercise personal judgement (*ijtihād*) during the life of the Messenger of Allah (peace and blessings of Allah be on him).

The Ijtihād of the Messenger of Allah
(peace and blessings of Allah be on him)

57. The basis of it is another principle in which there is difference of opinion of men of knowledge, i.e., an affair in which there was no revelation can the Messenger of Allah (peace and blessings of Allah be on him) exercise personal judgement (*ijtihād*) and decide the matter.

- According to some *'ulamā*, the Messenger of Allah (peace and blessings of Allah be on him) did not exercise personal judgment (*ijtihād*). Rather he awaited for the revelation.

- According to some other *'ulamā*, the Messenger of Allah (peace and blessings of Allah be on him) used to turn to the past prophets, *shari'ats* as the past *shari'ats* are considered our *shari'at* till their repeal is not known.

- According to still some other *'ulamā*, the Messenger of Allah (peace and blessings of Allah be on him) did not exercise personal judgement (*ijtihād*) till he had the hope of arrival of revelation. When there remained no such hope, then he exercised personal judgement (*ijtihād*) and

---

73. *Al-Mabsût*, vol. XVI, p. 70; *Badā'i al-Sanā'i*, vol. IX, p. 1400.

whatever had been his personal judgement (*ijtihād*) the same would have become for us the *shari'ah*, but if, later on, the revelation came otherwise, it repealed the earlier command.

❖ According to us *Kitābullāh* can repeal the *sunnah* of *Rasūl Allāh*. However, the command under the *ijtihād* that had been enforced did not become void and only the future decisions were to be made according to the new command (that came under revelation).[74]

Other Useful Commands that come to light from the Hadith of Mu'az (Allah's pleasure be on him)

58. Thereafter the Messenger of Allah (peace and blessings of Allah be on him) said to Mu'āz (Allah's pleasure be on him):

"All praise is for Allah who granted courage and fortitude to the representative of His messenger of an affair, which is liked by His Messenger (peace and blessings of Allah be on him)."

The Messenger of Allah (peace and blessings of Allah be on him) considered this affair as one of the favours bestowed upon him by Allah, the Almighty as he began the statement with the words *alhamdulillāh* (All praise is for Allah). This shows that the head of the state should consider it among the favours of Allah, the Almighty on him if any of his agent (representative, public servant) is righteous (of good conduct). Likewise, a

---

74. In other words the repealing law and prospective effect and not retrospective. All acted upon and closed transactions under the repealed law prior to the enforcement of the repealing law remained valid.

husband should consider it a favour of Allah, the Almighty on him if his wife is righteous and should offer thanks to Allah, the Almighty. Similarly, a master having a servant of good conduct and a father having children of good conduct should consider them as favour of Allah upon them.

59. Imãm Khassãf has again quoted the hadíth of Mu'ãz (Allah's pleasure be on him) which is transmitted through another chain of authorities with the following additional words:

> "If a matter comes before you is such for which no solution is available in the Book of Allah and you do not find any decision of the Messenger of Allah (peace and blessings of Allah be on him) and of the *sãlihín* (the righteous)."[75]

The word *sãlihín* occurring in this *hadíth* has been variously interpreted by the *'ulamã*.

- ❖ According to some *'ulamã*, this word refers to the prophets and the Messenger of Allah (peace and blessings of Allah be on him).

- ❖ According to some others, this word refers to Hadrat Abû Bakr Siddíq and Hadrat 'Umar (Allah's pleasure be on both of them).

- ❖ According to a report on the authority of Abdullãh bin Mas'ûd, the Messenger of Allah (peace and blessings of Allah be on him) said, "Whenever the *sãlihûn* (righteous) are mentioned, then first of all mention the name of Hadrat 'Umar (Allah's pleasure be on him)."[76]

75. *Al-Mabsût*, al-Sarakhsi, vol. VI, p. 69.

76. *Al-Mustadrak* al-Hãkim, vol. III, p. 93; *Musnad Ahmad bin Hanbal*, vol. VI, p. 148; *Majma' al-Zawã'id*, al-'Irãqi wa ibn Hajar vol. IX, p. 67; *Al-Mabsût* al-Sarakhsi, vol. XVI, p. 69; *Al-Nahãyah fi Gharib al-Hadíth*, Ibn al-Athir, vol. I, p. 472.

Hadrat 'Umar's (Allah's pleasure be on him) Framing of Principles and Rules through Memorandums and Letters Regarding Administration of Justice by the Judges

60. *Hadrat 'Umar* (Allah's pleasure be on him) had written a letter to *qādi* Shuraih with the following contents:

❖ When you find a thing in the *Kitābullāh*, decide according to it. The reverence of any person or any other thing should not make you inattentive to decide according to verity and justice. (In some narations, the words are, "Due to the people, your attention should not be diverted from it"). If a matter comes before you regarding which you do not find anything in *Kitbābullāh* and *sunnah* of *Rasûl Allah* (peace and blessings of Allah be upon him), then see on what is the consensus of the people.

It is so because the consensus of the people (*ijmā' al-nās*) is also an authoritative proof (*hujjat*). Thereafter, he wrote:

❖ If you do not find anything in *Kitābullāh* and *sunnah* of *Rasûl Allah* (peace and blessings of Allah be upon him) and anyone before you has also not stated anything regarding that problem then you have the choice to adopt any of the two ways, viz., if you want to step-forward yourself by exercise of personal judgement (*ijtihād*), do exercise it.

In other words, if you step-forward exercising your personal judgement (*ijtihãd*) on the hope that your personal judgement (*ijtihãd*) will be according to the verity and justice, you will get double reward.

❖ And if you opt not to step-forward, then you should not step-forward.

In other words, if you do not step-forward apprehending that you may not commit mistake in the exercise of personal judgement (*ijtihãd*), then avoid it.

Thereafter he wrote:

❖ But I consider it better for you that in such a matter you should not step-forward.[77]

In other words, you should secure your faith (*din*) as it is not necessary that a *mujtahid* in every circumstance reaches that thing which is the truth in the sight of Allah.

The '*ulamã* state that the period of Hadrat 'Umar (Allah's pleasure be on him) was a period when the *mujtahidin* were many in numbers. Hence, if any *mujtahid* restrained from exercising *ijtihãd*, the Divine Commandments did not go waste. In our period, there is dearth of *mujtahidin*. If a *mujtahid* stops the process of *ijtihãd*, there is apprehension of going waste of the Divine Commandments.

61. After that, Imãm Khassãf has mentioned the narration of the *qãdi* Shuraih in which there is additional word, "Verily" he, the Messenger of Allah (peace and blessings of Allah be upon

---

77. *Sunan* al-Darimi, vol. I, p. 55 (*muqaddimah*), *Hadith* No. 169; *Jãmi' al-Usûl*, Ibn Athir, vol. X, p. 552, No. 7653; *Jãmi' Bayãn al-'Ilm wa Fadlihi*, vol. II, p. 56; *Jami' al-Fawã'id min Jãmi' al-Usûl wa Majma' al-Fawã'id*, edited by Al-yamani, vol. I, p. 685, No. 4925; *Sunan al-Kubra*, Al-Bayhaqi, vol. X, pp. 110-115; *Al-Mabsût* al-Sarakhsi, vol. XVI, p. 69; *Akhbãr al-Qudãt*, al-Waki', vol. II, p. 189.

him) said, "If nothing becomes clear to you from *Kitābullāh* and *sunnah* of *Rasūl Allah* (peace be upon him) then exercise personal judgement (*ijtihād*) and do not commit any negligence.

That is, leave no stone unturned in the matter of exercise of *ijtihād* and seeking of the verity (correct thing).

62. It is transmitted on the authority of 'Atā bin al-Sā'ib, who on the authority of Abū al-Bakhtarí reported that Hadrat 'Umar appointed a person who was called Hābis bin Sa'd Tā'i[78] as a judge and asked him:

"O Hābis! How shall you decide cases?"

He replied: "In the light of the Book of Allah."

He further asked: "If you do not find any command in the Book of Allah?"

He replied: "In that case I shall turn to the *sunnah* of the Messenger of Allah (peace and blessings of Allah be upon him)."

He again asked: "If you do not find in the *sunnah* of the Messenger of Allah (peace and blessings of Allah be upon him)?"

He replied: "In that case I shall exercise personal judgement (*ijtihād*) and will also consult my colleagues."

On that, Hadrat 'Umar (Allah's pleasure be on him) said:

. 78. Hābis bin Sa'd bin Munzar bin Rabi'ah bin Yathrabi, al-Tā'i was a
companion of the Messenger of Allah (peace and blessings of Allah
be upon him). The historians have counted him among those
companions who had come to Syria. He became famous in Syria as
a Yamani. Hadrat 'Umar bin Khattāb (Allah's pleasure be on him)
had appointed him the judge of Hims. He was the son-in-law of 'Adí
bin Hātim and his son was the maternal uncle of Zaid bin 'Adí. He
participated in the battle of Siffin from the side of Hadrat Amír
Mu'āwiyah (Allah's pleasure be on him). [See *Al-Isti'āb fi Asmā al-
Ashāb*, Ibn Abd al-Barr, vol. I, pp. 358-359; *al-Isābah fi Tamyiz al-
Sahābah*, al-'Askalani, vol. I, pp. 271-272, No. 1356; *Usud al-
Ghābah*, Ibn al-Athir, vol. I, pp. 375-376, No. 836; *Tārikh*, Khalífah
bin Khayyāt, ed. Dr. Akrām al-'Umarí, vol. I, pp. 176-178].

"You have answered correctly and excellently."

The said person did not join the assignment. Later on, when he met Hadrat 'Umar (Allah's pleasure be on him) he asked: "Why you did not join the post of judgeship."

He replied: "O *Amir al-Mu'minin*! I saw a dream which made me fearful."

He asked: "What was that dream?"

He replied: "I saw the sun and the moon fighting with each other."

Ibn Fudayl says that Hābis had said: "I saw the sun coming from the East with a great crowd and I saw the moon coming from the West with a great crowd and thereafter they collided with each other and they all started fighting with each other."

Hadrat 'Umar (Allah's pleasure be on him) asked: "With whom were you?"

He replied: "With the moon."

On that Hadrat 'Umar (Allah's pleasure be on him) recited the following verse of the Holy *Qur'ān*:

"And we made the night and the day two signs. So we dimmed the sign of the night and brightened the sign of the day."   (17:12)

After that he said: "You were with the moon, which was in the West of the sun. Give us back our command whereby we had appointed you as a judge."

'Atā says, "I learnt that Hābis was with Hadrat Amîr Mu'āwiyah (Allah's pleasure be on him) in the battle of Siffin and he was martyred in the battle."[79]

This *hadith* bestows the following benefits:

79. *Seerat,* Ibn al-Jawzi, pp. 83-84; *Al-Isti'āb.* Ibn Abd al-Barr, vol. I, page 359.

❖ Whenever a responsibility is entrusted to a person, he should not make delay in its acceptance and should immediately proceed straight to the place of his posting. The reason is that Hadrat 'Umar (Allah's pleasure be on him) had expressed his displeasure to the aforesaid person who had not gone to the place of his posting. It was so that when a person accepted the trust of an assignment, it is binding upon him to fulfil that trust and the fulfilment of the trust is possible only when he goes to the place of his assignment and joins the duty and looks after the affairs of the people.

❖ There is no harm in taking good omen. It has no connection with bad omen.

❖ Hadrat 'Umar (Allah's pleasure be on him) knew the science of interpretation of dreams but Hadrat Abû Bakr Siddíq (Allah's pleasure be on him) was ahead of him in the matter of interpretation of dreams. Once the Messenger of Allah (peace and blessings of Allah be upon him) had asked the interpretation of a dream from Hadrat Abû Bakr Siddíq (Allah's pleasure be on him).

The Messenger of Allah (peace and blessings of Allah be upon him) said, "I saw that I am driving goats which were followed by dust."

Hadrat Abû Bakr Siddíq (Allah's pleasure be on him) interpreted it and submitted, "Firstly, the Arabs shall follow thee and then the non-Arabs."[80]

❖ According to the dream that had seen by Hābis, Hadrat Mu'āwiyah (Allah's pleasure be on him) was fortunate as

---

80. *Al-Mustadrak* al-Hākim, vol. IV, p. 3951; *Musnad* Ahmad bin Hanbal, vol. V, p. 455; *Majma' al-Zawā'id*, al-'Irāqi wa ibn Hajar, vol. VII, p. 183.

Hābis was with the moon which was coming from the western side of the sun. The moon is a sign from amongst the sign of Allah, the Almighty as the sun is a sign from amongst the signs of Allah, the Almighty, but the sun is brighter than the moon. With reference to this, Hadrat Mu'āwiyah (Allah's pleasure be on him) also stood fortunate although the turn of *caliphate* was of Hadrat 'Alí (Allah's pleasure be on him). Further, the good fortune of Hadrat Mu'āwiyah (Allah's pleasure be on him) was in the capacity of a king and not in the capacity of a *caliph*. The Messenger of Allah (peace and blessings of Allah be upon him) said, "After me the *caliphate* shall remain established for thirty years and thereafter there will be kingship and emirate."[81]

The *caliphate* had come to an end with the death of Hadrat 'Alí (Allah's pleasure be on him), but the stand of Hadrat Mu'āwiyah (Allah's pleasure be on him) was based on an interpretation of a saying of the Messenger of Allah (peace and blessings of Allah be upon him) in which he had remarked about Hadrat Mu'āwiyah (Allah's pleasure be on him), "At the time when you will become the king of my *'Ummah* deal with them goodly."[82]

81. *Sunan* Abû Dā'ûd, kitāb al-sunnah, vol. IV, p. 211, *Hadíth* Nos. 4646-47; *Sunan* al-Tirmizi, kitāb al-fitān, vol. II, p. 341, *Hadíth* No. 2326; *Musnad* Ahmad bin Hanbal, vol. IV, p. 373; vol. V, pp. 44, 50, 220, 221, 404; *al-Mustadrak* al-Hākim, vol. III, p. 71; *Mawarid al-Zam'ān ila Zawā'id Ibn Habbān*, al-Haithimi, p. 369, *Hadíth* Nos. 1534-35; *Al-Kashshāf*, al-Zamakhshari, vol. III, p. 82; *Al-Kāfí al-Shāffi takhrij Ahadith al-Kashshāf*, Ibn Hajar, vol. IV, p. 120, *Hadíth* No. 87.

82. *Majma' al-Zāwa'id*, Al-'Irāqi *wa* Ibn Hajar, vol. IX, pp. 355-356; *Musnad* Ahmad bin Hanbal, vol. IV, p. 101.

But the interepretation of Hadrat Mu'āwiyah (Allah's pleasure be on him) was not valid as he got the share from kingship and not from *caliphate* as the Messenger of Allah (peace and blessings of Allah be upon him) had said, "At the time when you become the king of my '*Ummah*...". This proves that the stand of Hadrat Mu'āwiyah (Allah's pleasure be on him) was based on his interpretation of this *hadith*. Hence silence should be observed from making any comment on him.

Memorandum of Hadrat 'Umar' Fārûq (Allah's pleasure be on him) to Hadrat Abû Mûsā al-Ash'ari (Allah's pleasure be on him) regarding the Administration of Justice

63. *It* is narrated that Hadrat 'Umar Fārûq (Allah's pleasure be on him) had written a letter to Hadrat Abû Mûsā al-Ash'arí (Allah's pleasure be on him).... *al-hadith.*[83]

83. The *hadith* that Hadrat 'Umar Fārûq (Allah's pleasure be on him) had written a letter to Hadrat Abû Mûsā al-Ash'arí (Allah's pleasure be on him) which was called the judicial policy or the constitution of administration of justice is being explained by the compiler. *Darāqutni*, has transmitted this *hadith* [in his *al-Sunan*] in Kitāb al-Aqdiah, with the words, "to us Abû Ja'far Muhammad bin Sulaimān bin Muhammad al-Nu'māni, to whom Abdullāh bin abd al-Samad bin Abí Khaddash, to whom 'Ísā bin Yûnus. to whom 'Ubaidullāh bin Abû Hāmid, to whom Abí al-Mālih al-Hazali, stated: 'Umar bin al-Khattāb (Allah's pleasure be on him) wrote a letter to Abû Mûsā al-Ash'arí (Allah's pleasure be on him): That administration of justice is a decisive ordinance of Allah and his Rasul (*Sallallahu Alaihi wa Sallam*), which must be followed..." [*Sunan al-Darāqutni*, vol. IV, pp. 206-207, *Hadith* No. 15]. He has transmitted it with another chain of authorities with the words, "To us Muhammad to whom Abdullāh bin Ahmad bin Hanbal, to whom his father, to whom Sufian Ibn 'Uyainah, to whom Idrís al-Udi, to whom Sa'íd bin Abí Bardah who narrated the letter and said. "This is the letter of Hadrat 'Umar Fārûq (Allah's pleasure be on him). Thereafter, he read it over to Sufyān "From here to Abû Mûsā al-Ash'arí, "That administration of justice is a decisive ordinance of Allah and his Rasul (*Sallallahu Alaihi wa Sallam*)..." with a little difference, Al-Abbās Muhammad bin Yaqûb, to whom Muhammad bin Ishāq al-San'ani, to whom

Ja'far bin Barqãn, to whom Ma'mar al-Basrí, to whom Abi al-'Awãm al-Basri who stated: "Umar wrôte to Abû Mûsã al-Ash'arí (Allah's pleasure be on both of them), 'that administration of justice is a decisive ordinance of Allah and his Rasul (*Sallallahu Alaihi wa Sallam*)...." [*Sunan al-Kubra*, Al-Bayhaqi, vol. X. p. 150], and from him copies were made with other chains. [See *Sabil al-Mathãl*, vol. X, pp. 115, 119, 135, 155-56]. Ibn Hazm has objected to the proof of this letter of Hadrat 'Umar Farûq (Allah's pleasure be on him) in his *Kitãb al-Ahkãm*, but the earlier leading jurists have consensus that it is reliable. They have taken quotations from it and depended upon it. Imãm Khassãf (Allah's mercy be on him) has transmitted it here and the commentator Imãm Hisãm ad-Dín (Allah's mercy be on him) has written a commentary on it. Imãm Jassãs (Allah's mercy bé on him) has also written a commentary on it. [See *Adãb al-Qãdi li 'l-Khassãf bi ta'líq al-Jassãs*, manuscript, p. 7a]. Imãm Muhammad bin Hasan al-Shaibãni (Allah's mercy be on him) has begun his book *Adãb al-Qãdi* with this letter. Imãm Sarakhsi (Allah's mercy be on him) has pointed out this fact in his book *al-Mabsút* and has also written a commentary on it. [See *al-Mabsút*, vol. XVI, pp. 60-65]. Allamah Ibn al-Qayyim has compiled his book titled *I'lam al-Mu'waqqi'in* only to explain this letter. In many old and new books, this letter has been edited, discussed upon and many of its sentences have been thoroughly explained. Some books have been written to refute the stand of Ibn Hazm (Allah's mercy be on him). [See *I'lam al-Muwaqqi'in*, vol. I, p. 99 and vol. II, p. 2; *I'jãz al-Qur'ãn*, pp. 214-216; *Sharh Nahj al-Balãghah*, Ibn Abí Hadíd, vol. III, p. 116; *Al-Tabsarah*, Ibn Farhûn, vol. I, pp. 43-45; *Tãrikh al-Qadã fi al-Islãm*, 'Arif al-Kindi, p. 21; *Kitãb al-Kharãj*, Abû Yûsuf, p. 140; *Al-Bayãn wa al-Tabyin*, al-Jahiz vol. II, pp. 48-50; *Al-'Iqd al-Farid*, vol. I, p. 98; *Akhbãr al-Qudãt*, al-Waki, vol. I, p. 70; *Al-Kãmil*, al-Mubarrad, vol. I, p. 14; *Nihãyah al-Arab fi Funûn Adab*, al-Nûwayri; *Subh al-A'shah fi Sin'ah al-Inshã*, al-Qalqashandi, vol. X, p. 193; *Talabah al-Talabah*, al-Nasafi, p. 129; *Mu'in al-Ahkãm*, al-Trablasi, p. 14; *Jãmi' Bayãn al-'Ilm*, Ibn' 'abd al-Barr, vol. II, pp. 82, 108; *Kitãb Adãb al-Qudãt* (manuscript Berlin), pp. 9a & 9b; *Al-Muhallah*, Ibn Hazm, vol. IX, p. 393; *Kitãb Adãb al-Qadã*, (manuscript), pp. 6a & 7b; *Adãb al-qãdi min al-Hãwi al-Kabir*, al-mawardi, vol. I, p. 250; sec. 396, p. 570; sec. 1347; p. 688, sec. 1772; vol. II, p. 8, sec. 1840; p. 93, sec. 2210; p; 241, sec. 2938; *Muqaddimah*, Ibn Khaldún, vol. I, p. 221; *Nasb al-Ra'iyah fi Takhrij Ahadith al-Hidãyah*, al-Zayla'i, vol. IV, pp. 81-82; *Al-Dirãyah*

64. Imām Muhammad (Allah's mercy be on him)[84] has mentioned this hadíth in his book *Adāb al-Qādi*[85] and has begun the said book with it. Imām Khassāf (Allah's mercy be on him) has also mentioned the hadith but with different words at some places. Despite this, the meanings are the same in all books. He has given this letter the title of "*Siyāsah al-Qudāt*" (judicial policy for the judges).

65. Hadrat 'Umar Fārûq (Allah's pleasure be on him) said:

"*Bismillāhir-Rahmānir-Rahím*"

(In the name of Allah, the Beneficent, the Merciful).

"*Ammā ba 'du...*"

(As for...)

These words are used to keep distance between the speech. Those were used for the first time by Hadrat Dāwûd (peace be upon him).

Allah, the Almighty says:

".....And We gave him (Dāwûd) wisdom and sound

fí Takhrij Ahadíth al-Hidāyah, Ibn Hajar al-'Asqalani, vol. II, p. 171, *hadíth* No. 892; *Talkhis al-Habír*, al-'Asqalani, vol. IV, p. 196, *hadíth* No. 2106; *Nasihah al-Mulûk*, al-Māwardi, (manuscript), p. 61a; *Badā'i al-Sana'i*, al-Kasani, vol. IX, p. 4093

84. Muhammad bin al-Hasan al-Shaibani, companior. and pupil of Imām Abû Hanifah (Allah's mercy be on him).

85. According to the preferred statement, this book, *Adāb al-Qādi* is a part of *al-Mabsût* as the biographers of Imām Muhammad (Allah's mercy be on him) have not mentioned any permanent book of Imām Muhammad (Allah's mercy be on him) with the title of *Adāb al-Qādi* [See *Al-Fahrist*, Ibn Nadím, pp. 301-302; *Kāshf al-Zunûn*, Hāji Khalífah, vol. I, p. 44; *Miftāh al-Sa'adah*, Tash Kubrah Zadah, vol. II, pp. 262-263]. Imām Sarakhsi has stated that Muhammad bin al-Hasan has begun his book with this letter and has also written a commentary on it. [*Al-Mabsût*, vol. XVI, p. 60].

judgement in speech and decision."   (38:20)

According to some interpreters, the words "*fasl al-khitāb*" refer here to the words "*ammā ba'd*".

Here the words "*ammā ba'd*" mean: that listen to that carefully which I am going to say.

66. Hadrat 'Umar Fārūq (Allah's pleasure be on him) said:

"*fa inna 'l-qadā'a farīdatun muhkamatun*"

[and verily, the administration of justice is a decisive ordinance (of God)].

In other words. to decide according to law (verity) and justice is a solid duty, which was present in the earlier *shari'ahs* and also in our *shari'ah*. This ordinance has not been repealed nor there has occurred any amendment in it.

67. He further said:

"*wa sunnatun muttaba'atun*"

(and it is a practice of the Holy Prophet (peace and blessings of Allah be on him) which has always been followed, i.e., it is a *sunnah* which has never been abandoned).

68. Thereafter, he said:

"*fā afham izā adla 'l-khasmān*"

(and when the parties bring their case before you grasp all its aspects fully).

That is when the parties put their case before you, you should clear your heart and mind from all other things so that you may listen to their statements well. In this manner, you will reach to the correct and true decision.

69. Thereafter, he said:

"fã innahu la yanfa'u takallumun bi haqqin lã nafãza lahu"

(and verily, a right which is not to be enforced is useless).

That is, sometimes a plaintiff makes such an admission whereby his right claimed in the plaint becomes void or the defendant makes such a confession whereby payment of something becomes necessary on him and in such cases, you are not in need of enforcement of the decree. Therefore, a matter which you will not hear for the sake of enforcement to talk about it is of no use.

69 (a). Thereafter, he said:

"asi baynan nãs"

(maintain equality between the people).

That is equally treat both the parties to a suit. The word *asa* is not derived from the word *al-taswiyah*. Had it been derived from the word *taswiyah* then the sentence would have been: *sawwi baynan nãs*. It is derived from the word *al-tã'si*. The proof of it are the following verses of poetess Khansã[86] (that are in long metre):

---

86. She was Tamãdar bint 'Amr bin al-Sharîd al-Salmiyah. She was a famous poetess both during the period of *Jãhiliyyah* and *Islãm*. She visited, along with her people, the Holy Prophet (peace and blessings of Allah be upon him) and embraced Islam. It is the statement of the companions (Allah's pleasure be on all of them) that the Messenger of Allah (peace and blessings of Allah be upon him) listened to her verses and appreciated them. When she recited her poetry, the Holy Prophet (peace and blessings of Allah be upon him) used to say, *"Hayyah ya khannãs"* (O! once again) and also indicated it by his hand. Her sons had been martyred in the battle of Qãdsiyah. [See *Al-Isti'ãb fi Asmã al-Ashab*, Ibn 'Abd al-barr, vol. IV, pp. 287-290; *Al-Isabãh fi Tamyiz al-Sahãbah*, al-'Asqalani, vol. IV, p. 279-281; *Tabaqãt*, Ibn Sa'd, vol. III, part 2, p. 67; *Tabaqãt al-Shu'rã*, al-Jamhi, pp. 78-82; *Kitãb al-Khansã'*, Ismã'il al-Qãdi, two volumes; *Tãrikh al-Adãb al-'Arabi*, Brockelmann, vol. I, pp. 164-166].

"wa lau lā kathratul bākinah haulī
'ala ikhwāni him la qataltu nafsī;

wa mā yabqûna misla akhī wa la kin
a'azzin nafsa 'anhu bit-tā'ssī;

yazkurunī tulû'sh shamsi Sakhrān
wa azkuruhu li kulli ghûrubi shamsi."

(Had there not been a crowd of mourners on the death of my brothers, I would have killed myself.

People have not wept as I have wept on my brother, but I console my heart keeping equality with them.

I remember my brother Sakhr every day and night).

Here the poetess Khansa' has used the word "*al-ta'si*" in the sense of "equality".

70. Thereafter, he said:

"*fi wajhi ka*"

(in facing you).

That is, you should maintain equality in looking towards both the parties. If you will look more towards one of them, the other will feel hurt and will leave seeking right and justice from you and thus will waste his right.

71. Thereafter, he said:

"*wa majlisi ka*"

(in your sitting).

That is, you should maintain equality between the parties when you sit among them.

72. Thereafter, he said:

"wa adli ka"

(and in your adjudication).

A report on the authority of Hadrat Abû Bakr Siddíq (Allah's pleasure be on him) says that when he was addressing on the pulpit and asked the meaning of *al-'adl*, he spontaneously replied in the following iambic poetical verse:

"al 'adlu an ta'ti ila akhíka

ma mithluhu min nafsihi yardíkã"

[The justice is your liking for your brother whatever you like for your own-self].

It has been counted amongst the eloquence of Hadrat Abû Bakr Siddíq (Allah's pleasure be on him) as he had given that reply spontaneously.

73. Thereafter, he said:

"hatta lã yatma'u sharífun fi haifíka"

(so that no influential person may have hope of your inclination towards him).

Haif means inclination (towards injustice). That is, no one should hope that your inclination will become towards him.

Allah, the Almighty says:

"....Or are they in fear,

That Allah and His Apostle

Will deal unjustly with them...." (24:50)

74. Thereafter, he said:

"wa lã yai'ãsa da'ifun min 'adlika"

(no weak person should become hopeless in the matter of getting justice from you).

In his book *Adāb al-Qādi*, Imām Muhammad (Allah's mercy be on him) has quoted the following words:

"wa lā yakhāfu da'ifun jaurūka"

(no weak person should apprehend any in join justice from you).[87]

The meaning of both the sentences is the same.

75. Thereafter, he said:

"al bayyinatu 'alal-mudda'iyyi wal-yaminu 'ala man ankara"

(the proof is on the plaintiff while the oath is on the one who denies the claim).[88]

This is a *marfū' hadith*[89] (the chain of authorities who

87. This sentence is present in *Al-Mabsūt*, vol. XVI, p. 61 and Imām Sarakhsi has given its commentary.

88. It is a *marfū hadith* as stated by the author, but here the statement of Hadrat 'Umar Fārūq (Allah's pleasure be on him) has been mentioned as *mauqūf*. According to the majority of the *'ulamā*, a *mauqūf hadith* is like a *marfū hadith*.

89. *Sunan al-Kubra*, Al-Bayhaqi, vol. X, p. 252; *Nasb al-Rā'iyah fi Takhrij Ahadith al-Hidāyah*, al-Zayla'i, vol. IV, pp. 95-96; *Al-Dirāyah fi Takhrij Ahadith al-Hidāyah*, Ibn Hajar al-'Asqalani, Vol. II, p. 175, *hadith* No. 740; *Talkhis al-Habir*, al-'Asqalani, vol. IV, p. 208, *hadith* No. 2135; *Takhrij Ahadith Usūl al-buzdawi*, Ibn Qatlūbaghā, pp. 175-176; *Sunan* al-Tirmizi, vol. II, p. 399, *Hadith* No. 1356; *Jāmi' al-Usūl* Ibn Athir, Vol. X, p. 554, *Hadith* No. 7157; *Sunan al-Kubra*, Al-Bayhaqi, vol. VIII, p. 123; *Sunan, Dāraqutni*, vol. III, p. 111 and vol. IV, pp. 217-218; *Al-Jāmi' al-Saghir*, al-Suyūti, vol. I, p. 128; *Al-Taisir bi Sharh al-Jāmi' al-Saghir*, al-Manāwi, vol. I, p. 444; *Sahih* al-Bukhārī, Kitāb al-Rahn. vol. II, p. 52; *Sahih* Muslim, Kitāb al-Aqdiah, vol. III, p. 1336, *Hadith* No. 1711; *Sahih Muslim bi Sharh al-Nawawi*, vol. XII, p. 3; *Sunan* al-Nisā'i, vol. VIII, p. 248; *Sahih* al-Bukhārī, Tafsir Surah Al-Imrān, vol. III, p. 73; *Musnad*, Imām Abū Hanifah, p. 220, *Hadith* No. 494; Jāmi' Masanid, al-Imām Abī Hanifah, vol. II, pp. 270-271.

transmitted it reaches uptil the Messenger of Allah (peace and blessings of Allah be upon him). It is counted amongst the *jawāmi' al-kalim* (all exhaustive statements). From these two sentences the *'ulamā* have deduced the solution of so many problems that there are volumes of books containing them. Every sentence is based on an indication available in the *Kitābullāh*.

The indication of the sentence, "*al-bayyinatu 'alal-mudda 'ī*" is indicated in the following verse of the Holy *Qur 'ān*:

"*Qul hatū burhānakum inkuntum sādiqin.*"

"....Say: Produce your proof if ye are truthful...."

(2:111)

The indication of the sentence, "*al-yaminu 'ala man ankara*" is found in the following *Qur 'ānic* verse:

"*wallāhi rabbinā mā kunnā mushrikin*"

"By Allah, Our Lord, we were not those who joined gods with Allah." (6:23)

76. Thereafter, he said:

"*was-sulhu jā 'izun baynan-nās*"

(and the reconciliation is permissible between the people).

In his book *Adāb al-Qādi*, Imām Muhammad (Allah's mercy be on him) has written the words, "*was-sulhu jā 'zun baynal-muslimīn*" (and the reconciliation is permissible between the Muslims).[90] But the interpretation of Imām Khassāf (Allah's mercy be on him) is general inclusive of the Muslims and non-Muslims.

---

90. *Al-Mabsūt*, al-Sarakhsi, vol. XVI, p. 61. Imām Sarakhsi (Allah's pleasure be on him) says that it is also transmitted on the authority of the Messenger of Allah (peace and blessings of Allah be upon him). [See *Sunan* Abú Dā'ūd, Kitāb al-Aqdiyah, vol. III, p. 304, *Hadith* No. 3594; *Sunan* al-Tirmizi, Kitāb al-Ahkām, vol. II. p. 403,

77. Thereafter, he (Allah's pleasure be on him) made an exception to the special kind of reconciliation and said:

"illā sulhan harrama halālan au ahalla harāman"

(except a reconciliation that renders a lawful as un-lawful or that renders an unlawful as lawful).

This is a proof (*hujjat*) in favour of the argument of Imām Shafi'i (Allah's mercy be on him) against us. We (Ahnaf) interpret this *hadith* as where the reconciliation renders such a thing unlawful which, in itself, is lawful (*halāl li 'ainihi*) as where two wives of a person enter into a compromise that their husband shall not have sexual intercourse with anyone of them or where the reconciliation renders such thing lawful which is in itself unlawful (*harām li 'ainihi*) as where someone may compromise over drinking of wine (*khamr*) or eating porch (*lahm khinzir*). Besides it, compromise or reconciliation is permissible in other affairs.

78. Thereafter, he said:

"wa lā yamna'uka min qadā'i qadiātihi bil amsi wa rajā'at fihi nafsuka wa hadiyat fihi li rushdika an tarāja'a fihi haqq; fā innalhaqqa qadimun lā yabtilu wa marāji'atul haqqi khairum-minat-tamādi fil bātil"

(There is no prohibition to recall your earlier decision if you come to know of the true facts later on as the truth does not become void and remains established and it is better to return towards the truth than to remain in the falsity).

Hadith No. 1363; *Sunan* Ibn Mājah, Kitāb al-Ahkām, vol. II, p. 788, *Hadith* No. 2353; *Musnad Ahmad bin Hanbal*, vol. II, p. 366; *Al-Mustadrak* al-Hākim, vol. II, p. 49; *Mawarid al-Zam'ān ila Zawā'id Ibn Habbān*, al-Haithami, p. 291, *Hadith* No. 199, *Talkhis al-Habir*, al-'Asqalani, vol. III, p. 44, *Hadith* No. 1246.]

The reason is that Hadrat Abú Músã al-Ash'arî (Allah's pleasure be on him) was not higher in rank and status than Hadrat 'Umar Fãrûq (Allah's pleasure be on him). Even Hadrat 'Umar Fãrûq (Allah's pleasure be on him) had set aside his own decisions where he found them against the proved authentic text.

Likewise, Hadrat Abdullãh bin Mas'ûd[91] (Allah's pleasure be on him) had withdrawn his opinions which he found against the proved authentic text.

It is only when a decision is made by the exercise of personal judgement (*ijtihãd*) and later on, it transpires that the said decision is against an authentic (proved) text. If another personal judgement (*ijtihãd*) is found against the decision based on an earlier personal judgement (*ijtihãd*) then the decision will not be set aside because one *ijtihãd* is not set aside by another *ijtihãd*.

91. Abû Abdur-Rahmãn Abdullãh bin Umm 'Abd al-Hazli was a companion and remained in the service of the Messenger of Allah (peace and blessings of Allah be upon him). He is counted amongst *al-sãhiqunal-awwalun* (the first and the foremost), and the eminent companions who participated in the battle of Badr and the great jurists and *qurrã*. He had learnt the Holy Qur'ãn directly from the Messenger of Allah (peace and blessings of Allah be upon him) and the Messenger of Allah (peace and blessings of Allah be upon him) had said about him, "A person who wants to recite the Holy Qur'ãn as it was revealed, he should recite it on the pattern of recitation of Ibn Umm 'Abd (Allah's pleasure be on him). Hadrat 'Umar Fãrûq (Allah's pleasure be on him) had appointed him the judge, the director-general of education, and a minister in Kûfah. He had enriched the land of Kûfah with knowledge. He died in 32 A.H. For his biography, see *Al-Tabaqãt al-Kubrah*, Ibn Sa'd, vol. II, p. 104; vol. VI, p. 7; *Akhbãr al-Qudãt*, al-Waki', vol. II, p. 188; *Tahzib al-Asmã' wa al-Lughãt*, al-Nawãwi, part 1, vol. 1, pp. 288-290, biographical note No. 333; *Tazkarah al-Huffãz*, al-Zahabi, vol. I, pp. 13-16, biographical note No. 5, *Al-Mustadrak* al-Hãkim, vol. III, pp. 312-320; *Al-Isabah fi Tamyiz al-Sahãbah*, Ibn Hajar al-'Asqalani, vol. II, pp. 390-392, note 3177.

79. Thereafter, he said:

"al-fahmu! al-fahmu!"

(Thorough probe and under-standing, thorough probe and understanding).

This repetition is to give stress as every repetition is made to give stress.

Allah, the Almighty says:

"aula laka fa aula; thumma aula laka fa aula."

> "Woe to thee, (O man!), yea, woe!
>
> Again, woe to thee, (O man!), yea, woe!"   (75:34-35)

Here also there has been a stress by way of repetition. The meaning is that you should fully understand your objective.

80. Thereafter, he said:

"fī mā yakhtaliju fī sadrika."

(Regarding which you feel some perturbation in your heart).

In some manuscripts, the words are *"yatakhallaju fī sadrika"*; in some others, the word is *"yatakhaliju"*; in some still others, the word is *"talajlaju"* and in some manuscripts, the word is *"yatalajlaju"*.

Thereafter, he said:

"mimmā laisa fī qur'ānin walā sunnatin"

(The solution of which is neither in the Holy *Qur'an* nor in the *sunnah* of *Rasûlullāh* (peace and blessings of Allah be upon him).

In other words, the matter concerning which you feel some perturbation then thoroughly ponder upon it and make all efforts to understand it. By doing so, you will be able to decide it with an insight.

81. Thereafter, he said;

"thumma a'rifil-ashbāha wal amthāla"

(Then find out the similar and resembling precedents.)

That is, make an effort to understand such problems which have some cause of resemblance and which are mutually similar problems. It is necessary to know them with regard to the matters before you as the problems concerning which there is no proof of any *hukm* or *shari'ah* value. The ascertainment of a legal rule for a new case or problem by deduction from a rule laid down in the *nass* (text of the Holy *Qur'ān* and *sunnah* or even in an *ijma'* verdict), by means of establishing a common link (*'illā mushtarikah*), between the original case and the new case sought to be overed by the same *hukm* (or *shari'ah* value), is necessary to apply it to the recent problem.

82. Thereafter, he said:

"fa qisil-umûra 'inda zalik wa'mad ila aqrabihā ilallāhi wa ashbahihā bil haqqi wāj'al liman yatlubu ghā'iban au shahidan amadan yantahi 'ilaihi"

(So evaluate the affairs through analogy and adopt the judgement which is most pleasant to Allah, the Almighty and most in conformity with the truth and justice. To every person, whether present or absent, who seeks an adjournment, grant him the same).

That is, when a plaintiff seeks an adjournment to bring proof (to establish his claim), the judge should grant it. Likewise, when the plaintiff completes his evidence to prove his case and the defendant makes a request for an adjournment to bring his defence, the judge should grant him the adjournment and should not make haste in deciding the matter.

83. Thereafter, he said:

"fā in ahdara bayyinatan ukhiza bihaqqihi fā in 'ajiza 'anhā istahallalat 'alaihil-qadiah"

(If the plaintiff presents the proof, he will get his right and if he fails you can decide the case against him).

84. Thereafter, he said:

"fā innahu ablaghu fil- 'uzri wā ajla lil 'amyi"

(It would be more proper to do so when there is any just excuse available with a party and it would serve as a light in, the darkness).

It would be proper where just excuse is available as if the judge decides hastily, the party having the proof can say that he had the proof or he could defend himself but the judge did not provide me an opportunity to do so.

It would be a light in the darkness as, when, after providing full opportunity to both the parties, the judge decides the case, it would be based upon an insight having no scope for entertainment of any doubt.

85. Thereafter, he said:

"al muslimūna 'udūlun ba'duhum 'ala ba'dihim"

(All Muslims are '*adil* (credit worthy) witness against each other).[92]

---

92. Imām Sarakhsi (Allah's mercy be on him) says that these words are transmitted on the authority of the Messenger of Allah (peace and blessings of Allah be upon him). [See *Al-Mabsût*, al-Sarakhsi, vol. XVI, p. 63]. These words are also included in the *Hadith* of Abdullāh bin 'Amr bin al-'Ās (Allah's pleasure be on him), which has been transmitted on his authority by Ibn Abí Shaibah and al-Dailami. [See *Kashf al-Khifā*, al-'Ajluni al-Jarrahi, vol. II, p. 290, *Hadith* No.

On the basis of this *hadith*, Imām Abû Hanifah (Allah's mercy be on him) argues that in the matter of adjudication the outer credit worthiness (*zāhiri 'adālat*) of a witness is to be kept in view.[93] But according to the *sāhibain*, there is no authority for outer credit worthiness. According to some jurists, this conflict of opinion (between Imām Abû Hanifah (Allah's mercy be on him) and *sāhibain*) is only with regard to the time and not with regard to an argument or a proof as Imām Abû Hanifah (Allah's mercy be on him) is giving this opinion (*fatwa*) in the 3rd century Hijrah.[94]

2301; *Al-Maqāsid al-Hasana,* al-Sakhawi, p. 385, *Hadith* No. 1022; *Nasb al-Rā'iyah fi Takhrij al-Hidāyah,* al-Zayla'i, vol. IV, p. 81].

93. It is well known among Ahnaf that a decision can be based on the evidence of a witness whose states are not known (*mastur*). [See *Al-Mabsūt,* al-Sarakhsi, vol. XVI, p. 63].

94. In all the manuscripts, this statement is available, but it dos not mean the third century *Hijrah* as Imām Abû Hanifah (Allah's mercy be on him) had died in 150 A.H. (i.e., in the second century *Hijrah*). It actually means the period of *tāb'a tābi'in* regarding the purity, righteousness, and goodness the Messenger of Allah (peace and blessings of Allah be on him) had given the testimony as the words of the *hadith* on the point are:

"*Khairul qurûni qarni thummallazina yalûnahum*

thummallazina yulûnahum."

(The best of all the ages is my period, then of those who come after me, and then of those who come after them).

The synonym of the word *qarns* is *jîl*, which means the people of an age and a people coming after a people. [See *Al-Qāmûs* under the root *q-r-n.*, vol. IV, p. 259]. Ibn Athír (Allah's mercy be on him) says in this *hadith* the reference is to the companions and then to those who were successors of the companions and the word *qarn* means the people of every age. [*Al-Nihāya fi Gharib al-Hadith wa 'l-Athr,* vol. IV, p. 51; *Jāmi' al-Usûl,* Ibn Athír, vol. X, p. 454]. Therefore, the companions are the people of *al-qarn al-awwal* (the first period) and the successors of companions are the people of *al-qarn al-thani* (the second period) and the successors of the successors of the companions are the people of *al-qarn al-thalith* (the third period)

Regarding the people of that age, the Messenger of Allah (peace and blessings of Allah be upon him) had given testimony of their purity and righteousness and had stated their attribute of goodness, while the *sāhibain* were g   age when there had occurred moral degradation and the falsity had become rampant.

86. Thereafter, he said:

"*illā mahdûdan fi haddin*"

(Except a person on whom the *hadd* punishment had been executed).

This *hadīth* is a proof in our (Ahnaf's) favour. In it such person has been excepted on whom *hadd* had been executed. There is no clarification of its being before his repentance or after his repentance.

87. Thereafter, he said:

"*au mujārraban 'alaihi shahādatu 'zûrin*"

(or a person who has been experimented as a false witness).

in which Imām Abû Hanifah (Allah's mercy be on him) also lived and is counted among them. Although, some later companions of the Holy Prophet (peace and blessings of Allah be upon him) were his contemporaries, [*Al-Jawāhir al-Mudi'ah*, al-Qarashi, vol. I, p. 28], but he is not counted among the successors of the companions. The *'ulamā'* have included their name in the category of the successors of the successors of companions (*tāb'u tābi'in*). The Messenger of Allah (peace and blessings of Allah be on him) had given the testimony of the truthfulness and righteousness of those people as has been stated by the *Sharih* (commentator). The word *qarn* is applied in many other shades of meaning. One of such meaning is *forty years*. According to some, it refers to *thirty years*. According to some others, it means *eighty years*. According to some still others, it means *hundred years*. Some say that it means *an age in general*. But the meaning we have stated is more proper and by adopting this meaning, all doubt is removed.

The reason is that a testimony is a *khabar* (news) which may be true or false. It will become a proof (*hujjat*) only when it is based on truthfulness (*sidq*). When a person is proved to be having given false evidence, the possibility of his giving false evidence is more. Hence the testimony of such a person is not admissible.

88. Thereafter, he said:

"Au zaninan fi wilā'in au qarābatin."

(or concerning whom there is doubt of being partial due to friendship or relationship).

"Zanin" is a person who is accused of some allegation or concerning whom there is some doubt. The Messenger of Allah (peace and blessings of Allah be on him) said:

"Lā shahādata li muttahammin"

(there is no testimony of a person against whom there has been proof of accusation).

Zanin fil-walā' refers to a person who is linked with the family of another person to such an extent that he considers their benefit as his benefit and their loss as his loss.

"Zanin fil-Qarābah" refers to a person whose evidence in favour of another person is in fact is an evidence in his own favour as the evidence of the parents in favour of their children.

89. Thereafter, he said:

"fā innallāha tawalla minkumus-sarā'ir

(Allah; the Almighty is the Guardian of all your secrets).

That is Allah, the Almighty alone knows the unseen. A judge is not made responsible to be acquainted with the internal affairs as it is not within the power of him.

90. Thereafter, he said:

"wa dara'a 'ankum bil-bayyināti wal-'amāni"

(and Allah, the Almighty has kept the punishment away from you on the basis of proof and oaths).

That is Allah Almighty has removed from you the disgrace of this world and the affliction of the next world on the basis of proof and oaths.

91. Thereafter, he said:

"iyyaka wal-ghadab wal-qalaq"

(avoid wrath and disturbance).

So far as the wrath is concerned, it is blameworthy as it is narrated that a man asked the Messenger of Allah (peace and blessings of Allah be on him), "Indicate me the thing that may be useful for me in this world and in the Hereafter." On that he said:

"Do not be angry."[95]

95. *Sahih* al-Bukhārī, Kitāb al-Adāb, on the authority of Abû Hurairah (Allah's pleasure be on him), vol. IV, p. 48; *Sunan* al-Tirmizī, Kitāb al-Barr wa al-Silah, on the authority of Abû Hurairah (Allah's pleasure be on him), vol. III, p. 250, *Hadith* No. 2089; *Al-Muwatta bi Sharh Tanwir al-Hawalik*, Imām Mālik, on the authority of Ibn Shahab, who on the authority of Hāmid bin Abdur-Rahmān bin 'Aûf, vol. II, p. 212 and *Sharh al-Muwatta*, al-Zurqani, vol. V, p. 254; *Musnad Ahmad bin Hanbal*, vol. II, pp. 175, 262, 466; vol. III, p. 484 and vol. V, pp. 34, 370, 372-373; *Majma 'al-Zawā'id*, al-'Irāqi wa ibn Hajar, vol. VIII, p. 70 transmitted by al-Tabarani, on the authority of Sufyān bin Abdullāh al-Thaqafi; *Mawarid al-Zam'ān ila Zawā'id Ibn Habbān*, al-Haithami, p. 484, *Hadith* No. 1971-72, transmitted by Ibn Habbān, on the authority of Jariyah bin Qudamah, on the authority of a man who had asked the Holy Prophet (peace and blessings of Allah be upon him), "Indicate me...."; *Al-Matālib al 'Aliyah bi Zawā'id al-Masanid al-Thamaniyah*, vol. II, pp. 403-404, *Hadith*

When leaving wrath is useful in this world and the Hereafter, then being angry is certainly harmful in both the worlds. Hence, when a judge will be in a state of anger, it will be impossible for him to do justice.

Likewise, the disturbance (of heart and mind) is blameworthy. The reason is that it causes petrubation of heart and mind and impatience (or rest!essness). These instructions are in the circumstance when the matter is of the nature of personal judgement (*ijtihād*). When there is a text (*nass*) then the decision must be immediately in accordance with the text (*nass*). The reason is that a text (*nass*) is clear and there remains no possibility of the matter remaining doubtful.

92. Thereafter, he said:

"wal-tā'zzi bin-nāsi"

(Do not feel agitated due to the people).

That is, a judge should not feel agitated by the overcrowding of the people at his door. The reason is that after accepting the responsibility of administration of justice, it is his responsibility to adjudicate upon the disputes of the people.

93. Thereafter, he said:

"wāt-tanakkur 'indal-khusûmi"

(and avoid simulation before the litigants).

That is, a judge should neither simulate nor speak loud upon the litigant public.

94. Thereafter, he said:

Nos. 2585-86, transmitted by Musaddad, on the authority of Abi Sa'id, on the authority of a man who asked the Holy Prophet (peace and blessings of Allah be upon him), "Indicate me...."

"fã innal qadã'a fi mawãtinil-haaqi yûjabullãhu bihil-ajra; wa yuhsamu bihiz-zukhrã"

(and verily, the administration of justice is the occasion of execution of the right (*haqq*) for which Allah will grant you a rich reward and give you a good compensation).

It is so because the administration of justice is an act of worship and it is superior than an act of supererogatory worship (*nafl al-'ibãdah*)

95. Thereafter, he said:

"wa man khallasat niyyatahu fil haqqi"

(one whose intention is clear on that which is the truth).

In another report, the words are as under:

"wa man khallasat niyyatahu wa lau 'ala nafsihi"

(and one whose intention is clear on that which is between him and Allah, though it affects himself).

It is so because the administration of justice is an act of worship and the purity of intention (*al-ikhlãs fi al-niyyah*) is a condition precedent in it. As Allah, the Almighty says:

"wa mã umirû illã li ya'budullãha mukhlisína lahud-dín"

> "And they have been commanded
> No more than this
> To worship Allah,
> Offering Him sincere devotion."   (98:5)

96. Thereafter, he said:

"wã abqa 'ala nafsihi, zãnahullãhu ta'ala"

(and one who maintains himself on this behaviour (of purity of intention), Allah, the Almighty ornaments him).

It is transmitted on the authority of the Messenger of Allah (peace and blessings of Allah be on him) who said:

"izã aslahal-'abdu sarïratahu aslahallãhu 'alã niyatahu"

(When a servant reforms his inner-self, Allah, the Almighty reforms his outer-self also).

It is so because he is working for the sake of Allah

97. Thereafter, he said:

"wa man tazayyana lin-nãsi bimã ya'lamullãhu ta'ala annahu laysa fi qalbihi shãnahullãhu."

(And the one who ornaments for the sake of [show to] the people, although Allah knows that his heart is not in accordance with his outward ornamentation, Allah disgraces him).

The reason is that such a person is a worthless, a hypocrite.

98. Thereafter, he said:

"fa mã zannuka bi thawãbillãhi ta'ala ma'a 'ãjili rizqihi wa khazã'ini rahmatihi. Wassalãm"

(So what do you think of the reward from Allah regarding what he accords Here as nourishment and of treasures of His mercy in the Hereafter? Salutation).

In other words, a judge who decides a case against law and justice to get worldly benefit and to be praised in the public but the reward from Allah is much more superior than the worldly gains.

The Principles of Exercising Personal Judgement (Ijtihād) and Administration of Justice (Qadā')

99. *It* is narrated that Abdullāh bin Mas'ûd (Allah's pleasure be on him) said, "There had been a period on us when neither we were the adjudicators nor we had as yet attained that position."[96]

In *kitāb Adāb al-Qādi* of Imām Muhamamd (Allah's mercy be on him) the words of Abdullāh bin Mas'ûd (Allah's pleasure be on him) are as under:

"Neither the solution of problems was asked from us nor we had attained that position."

Here the reference is to the period of the Messenger of Allah (peace and blessings of Allah be on him). People used to turn towards the Messenger of Allah (peace and blessings of Allah be on him), Hadrat Abû Bakr Siddíq (Allah's pleasure be on him) and Hadrat 'Umar Farûq (Allah's pleasure be on him) regarding the events with which they were confronted. At that time no one turned towards Abdullāh bin Mas'ûd (Allah's pleasure be on him). When Abdullāh bin Mas'ûd (Allah's pleasure be on him) acquired religious knowledge fully well and started exercising personal judgements (*ijtihād*), he became popular. When he came to Kûfah, four thousand people gathered around him. When Hadrat

---

96. *Al-Mabsût*, al-Sarakhsi, vol. XVI, p. 68.

'Alí (Allah's pleasure be on him) came to Kûfah and Hadrat Abdullãh bin Mas'ûd (Allah's pleasure be on him) along with other companion called upon him, Hadrat Alí (Allah's pleasure be on him) remarked, "Verily, you have fill d this city with knowledge and jurisprudence."[97]

100. Hadrat Abdullãh bin Mas'ûd (Allah's pleasure be on him) said: "After that the Divine decree made us reach this position where you are seeing us."

The object of saying so is to express thanks over the grace of Allah that they reached the position that they attain the ability to give *fatwa* and may be that the object of saying so is to mention the changing circumstances of time to such an extent that a man like him is being consulted for getting *fatwa*.

101. After that he said: "After today if any person is assigned a judicial post he should decide according to the book of Allah (*Kitãbullãh*) and if he does not find any thing in it he should decide according to the *sunnah* of the Messenger of Allah (peace and blessings of Allah be on him) and if he does not find any thing in *Kitãbullãh* and *sunnah Rasûl Allãh* then he should decide the matters according to the decisions of the righteous (*sulaha'*) and if the problem before him is such that no decision is available in *Kitãbullãh* or *sunna Rasûl Allãh* or in the decisions of *sulaha'* then he should exercise personal judgement (*ijtihãd*). None of you should say, 'It is my personal judgement (*ijtihãd*) and I fear.'"

In other words it is not proper for a judge to leave exercising personal judgment (*ijtihãd*) apprehending commission of a mistake by him. As the evil of leaving exercise of personal judgement (*ijtihãd*) is much greater than exercising it.

97. *Al-Mabsût*, al-Sarakhsi, vol. XVI, p. 68.

102. After that he said:

"The lawful is clear and the unlawful is also clear."[98]

In between these two are the doubtful affairs. An affair which puts you in doubt leave it and an affair which does not put you in doubt adopt it.

The statement, "the unlawful is clear" means that when a thing is proved on the basis of a text (*nass*) its *shari'ah* value (*hukm*) is clear.

The statement, "an affair which puts you in doubt" means a thing concerning which your heart is not satisfied, leave such thing; and a thing concerning which your heart is satisfied, adopt it. The Messenger of Allah (peace and blessings of Allah be on him) said: "There is satisfaction in the truth (*al-sidq*) and there is doubt in the falsity (*al-kizb*)."[99]

103. The same narration, which we have mentioned, has also been mentioned by Imām Khassāf (Allah's mercy be on him) on the authority of Qāsim bin 'Abdar-Rahmān, who, on the authority of his father, and who, on the authority of 'Abdullāh bin

---

98. Its basis is the *Hadith* mentioned by Imām Tabarani in his *Al-Jāmi' al-Saghir*, vol. i, p. 19 & p. 153; *al-Muntaqi*, Ibn Jarud, p. 194, *Hadith* No. 555; *Sahih* al-Bukhārī, Kitāb al-Buyu', vol.II, p. 3.

Regarding the statement of Hadrat Abdullāh bin Mas'ūd (Allah's pleasure be on him) that there had been a time on us..." See *Sunan* al-Darimi, vol. I, pp. 54-56, *Hadith* Nos. 167, 171-173; *Sunan* al-Nisā'ī, vol.VIII, pp. 230-231; *Jāmi' Bayān al-'Ilm*, Ibn 'Abd al-Barr, vol. II, p. 57; *Akhbār al-Qudāt*, al-Waki', vol. I, p. 76; vol. II, p. 188; *Sunan al-Kubra*, Al-Bayhaqi, vol. X, p. 115; *Al-Mabsūt*, al-Sarakhsi, vol. XVI, p. 68; *Musnad* Ahmad bin Hanbal, vol. VI, p. 153; *Takhrij ahadith Usūl al-Buzdawi*, Qāsim bin Qatlubagha, p. 251.

99. *Sunan* al-Tirmizi, Abwāb Sifah al-Qiyamah, vol. IV, p. 77, *Hadith* Nos. 2637-38; *Musnad* Ahmad bin Hanbal, vol.I, p. 200; *al-Maqāsid al-Hasanah*, al-Sakhawi, p. 214, *Hadith* No. 490; *Al-Mustadrak* al-Hākim, vol. IV, p. 99.

Mas'ûd (Allah's pleasure be on him), with the following additional words:

> "If a case comes before a judge regarding which he does not know the shari'ah value, he should admit [his lack of knowledge] and should not feel ashamed to ask it from someone else."

In some manuscripts, the words are:

> "He should escape himself from the Fire of Hell and should not feel ashamed asking the [the solution of such problem] from someone else."[100]

In other words, a judge should not use conjectures and surmises and thereby render himself liable to go to Hell.

<hr>

100. *Al-Mustadrak* al-Hākim, vol. IV, p. 94; *Al-Musannaf*, Abdul Rzzāq, vol. VIII, pp. 301-302, *Hadith* No. 15295; *Akhbār al-Qudāt*, al-Waki', vol. I, p. 76; *Jāmi' Bayān al-'Ilm*, Ibn 'Abd al-Barr, vol. II, p. 57.

104. *It* is narrated that whenever a problem was put to Hadrat 'Abdullāh bin 'Abbās[101] (Allah's pleasure be on him), he used to find it in the Holy *Qur'ān* and if its solution would have

101. He was called *hibr ummat*. He was a great scholar. He was the cousin of the Messenger of Allah (peace and blessings of Allah be on him). The *ahadith* transmitted on his authority find mention in *sahihain*. People used to come from far off places to get knowledge from him. He was counted one among the four companions each one of whom was named 'Abdullah (*'ibādallah arba'a*). He is one of those persons from whom many *ahadith* have been transmitted. A great number of *tābi'un* [successors of the companions of the Holy Prophet (peace and blessings of Allah be on him)] transmitted *ahadith* on his authority. He was born three years before *Hijrah*. He was only thirteen (or ten) years old at the time when the Holy Prophet (peace and blessings of Allah be on him) breathed his last. Hadrat 'Alí (Allah's pleasure be on him) had appointed him the governor of Kûfah. He had resigned from the office of the governor-ship before the martyrdom of Hadrat 'Alí (Allah's pleasure be on him). In the year 68 A.H. (or 69 A.H.), he died in Tā'if. His superiorities are detailed in the *sihah sitta* (the six authentic books of *ahadith*). For his biography, see *Tahzíb al-Asmā' wa al-Lughāt*, al-Nawawí, vol. I, part 1, pp. 274-276, biographical note no. 312; *Taqrib al-Tahzíb*, al-'Asqalani, vol. I, p. 425, biographical note no. 404; *Al-Isti'āb fi Asmā al-Ashāb*, Ibn 'Abd al-Bar, vol. III, pp. 342-49; *al-Isabāh fi Tamyiz al-Sahabah*, Ibn Hajar al-'Asqalani, vol. III, pp. 322-26, biographical note no. 4781.

been there, he used to tell it. If it was not found in the Holy *Qur 'ān* he used to find it in the *ahadith* of the Messenger of Allah (peace and blessings of Allah be on him), and if its solution would have been there, he used to tell it. If it was not found in the *ahadith* of the Messenger of Allah (peace and blessings of Allah be on him), he used to find it by returning towards the opinion of Hadrat Abū Bakr Siddíq (Allah's pleasure be on him) and the opinion of Hadrat 'Umar Fārûq (Allah's pleasure be on him). If it was not found in their opinions, he used to exercise his own personal judgement (*ijtihād*) and told the same.[102]

Hadrat Ibn 'Abbās (Allah's pleasure be on him) did so as he was young during the period of Hadrat Abû Bakr Siddíq (Allah's pleasure be on him) and Hadrat 'Umar Farûq (Allah's pleasure be on him) and a youth like him is bound to respect and honour an elder.

Exercise of Personal Judgement (Ijtihād) by the Messenger of Allah (peace and blessings of Allah be on him)

105. It is reported by Hadrat Umm Salmah (Allah's pleasure be on her) that the Messenger of Allah (peace and blessings of Allah be on him) said, "The matters concerning which revelation is not sent down to me, I adjudicate them by exercise of my personal judgement (*ijtihād*)."

This hadîth is the proof of adjudication by the Messenger of Allah (peace and blessings of Allah be on him) by exercise of his personal judgement (*ijtihād*). If the said *ijtihād* would have been

102. *Jāmi' Bayān al-'Ilm*, Ibn 'abd al-Barr, vol. II, pp. 57-58; *Sunan al-Darimi*, vol. I, p. 55, *hadíth* No. 168; *Sunan al-Kubra*, Al-Bayhaqi, vol. X, p. 112; *Al-Matālib al-'Aliyah bi Zawā'id al-Masanid al-Thamāniyah*, Ibn Hajar, vol. II, p. 248, *hadíth* No. 2129.

correct and valid then all the right; and if it would have been otherwise, then it was not maintained. Thus when he adjudicated a matter exercising his personal judgement (*ijtihād*) it became the *shari'ah*, but if later on, command was revealed in the Holy *Qur'ān*, it served as the repealing command for the said decision as the repeal of *sunnah* by the *Kitābullāh* is permissible.

106. Imām Sha'bi[103] (Allah's mercy be on him) said that whenever the Messenger of Allah (peace and blessings of Allah be on him) gave a decision and later on some command was revealed otherwise, the earlier decision was not set aside by the Messenger of Allah (peace and blessings of Allah be on him) and in fresh cases decision was made by him according to the new command. The reason is that the *Kitābullāh* became the repealing law of the *sunnah Rasûlullāh*. And the repeal was applicable on future decisions and not on the past decisions. [In modern terminology, the effect of the repealing law was prospective and not retrospective].

Administration of Justice by Qādi Shuraih (Allah's mercy be on him)

107. Hadrat 'Umar bin Khattāb (Allah's pleasure be on him) appointed Shuraih (Allah's mercy be on him) as a judge and

---

103. Amir bin Sharahbil al-Sha'bi was a *tābi'i* (successors of companions of the Messenger of Allah (peace and blessings of Allah be on him). He was one of the leading jurists of Kûfah. He was an eminent judge. He had seen 150 companions (Allah's pleasure be on all of them). A great number of *'ulamā* had transmitted *ahadith* on his authority and have mentioned his good traits of life. He died in 150 A.H. [See, *Tazkarah al-Huffāz*, al-Zahabi, vol. I, pp. 79-88, biographical note no. 76; Taqrîb al-Tahzîb al-Asqalāni vol. I, p. 387, biographical note no. 46. *Al-Hiliyah*, Abû Nu'aim, vol. IV, p. 310; *Al-Ma'arif*, Ibn Qutaibah al-Dinuri, p. 449; *Akhbār al-Qudāt*, al-Waki', vol. II, p. 413; *Hamish kitāb Adāb al-Shāfi'i wa manāqibuhu*, pp. 208, 334; *al-Mabsût*, al-Sarakhsi, vol. XVI, p. 85.]

in the meeting during *hajj* season asked him, "How do you adjudicate in the matter of properties of the people?"

He replied, "On the basis of proof and witnesses."

On that Hadrat 'Umar (Allah's pleasure be on him) remarked, "You secured your own person but destroyed the properties of the people."

❖ In securing own person indicates that whomsoever adopted the way of the Messenger of Allah (peace and blessings of Allah be on him) he will not be subjected to any punishment in this world nor in the world to come.

❖ In destroying the properties of the people, the indication is towards deterioration in the circumstances of the people as sometimes apparently an unjust person gives a just evidence and a just person gives an unjust evidence. Thus when there appears corruption in the states of the people, then whosoever under such circumstance relies upon the apparent evidence he destroys the properties of the people.

The Judicial Conduct (min adāb al-qudāt)

108. [Imãm Khassãf] Ahmad bin 'Umar (Allah's mercy be on him) said, "When the office of a judge is assigned to a person and he accepts it, then he should fear none but Allah, the Almighty, who has no partner."

The reason is that a man gets the desired things of both the worlds by means of piety (fear of Allah).

Allah, the Almighty says:

"And for those who fear Allah, He will make their path easy." (65:4)

109. He said, "He (the judge) should prefer obedience of Allah and should work for the sake of Hereafter."

It is so because the performance of a judge becomes the means of getting reward from Allah, the Almighty and the worldly benefits also come due to it. Hence, he should adopt the reward and compensation from Allah Almighty. For whatever is given by Allah, the Almighty is much better and lasting.

Hadrat 'Alí (Allah's pleasure be on him) said, "The world will perish even if it is made of gold and the Hereafter will remain eternally even if it is made of dust."

110. He further said, "He should make it his objective to reach the truth and justice by exerting his full effort in the matter of discharge of his liability."

The reason is that a judge is bound to decide according to the truth and justice. Therefore, he should fully exert to reach the truth.

Reader of a Judge

111. A judge should appoint a righteous Muslim as his reader. The reason is that a judge is to write and he cannot write each and every thing. The precondition of being righteous and Muslim for a reader is due to the fact that writing is of the genesis of administration of justice, hence, whatever are the conditions precedent for a judge, the same are for the reader of a judge.

Court-Staff

112. A judge may appoint a few persons as his staff to stand before him (in the court) for two reasons, viz.

Firstly, a court session is a dignified session and short of staff will lose its dignity and will lower its awe and prestige.

Secondly, parties are to be produced before the court and it is impossible for a judge to do so himself. The parties also do not appear themselves. Hence, the staff produces the parties in the court.

To prepare name slips of all the parties and to give preference in the matter of giving a call for hearing of the case

113. A judge may send his reader to the mosque to prepare slips of all the parties.

The Hanafi masters of law (*masha'ikh*) prior to Imām Khassaf (Allah's mercy be on him) had adopted the policy of "first come first served". A person who used to come first, his case was called, heard and decided first.

Imām Khassāf (Allah's mercy be on him) has depended upon the policy of making name slips of the parties as to depend on the policy of *first come first heard* resulted in dispute as every party claims to have come first and it will become a separate issue for a judge to decide. Hence, he adopted the policy of making name slips of the parties. This has also basis in the *shari'ah*. The Messenger of Allah (peace and blessings of Allah be on him) when intended to go on journey, he used to draw lots between his wives and the one whose name came in the draw was joined with him in the journey.[104]

The reason is that if a judge starts the hearing of the case of a party, he will be blamed as being partial. Hence, to save himself such blame, he should draw the lot. He should also do so as whatever is within his power he can withdraw the lot to avoid the

104. *Sahih* al-Bukhāri, Kitāb al-Hibah, vol. II, p. 61; kitāb al-Shahadat, vol. II, p. 69-73; kitāb al-Jihād, vol. II, p. 99; kitāb al-Maghazi, vol. III, p. 25; *Tafsir Sūrah al-Noor*, vol. III, p. 107; kitāb al-Nikah, vol. III, p. 172; *Sahih* Muslim, Fada'il al-Sahābah, vol. IV, p. 1894, *Hadith* No. 2445; kitāb al-Taubah, vol. IV, p. 2130, *Hadith* No. 2770; *Sunan* Ibn Mājah, Kitab al-Nikāh, vol. I, p. 634, *Hadith* No. 1970; kitāb al-Ahkām, vol. II, p. 246, *Hadith* No. 2347; *Jāmi' al-Usûl*, Ibn Athir, Vol. II, p. 330, *Hadith* No. 727; *Sunan* al-Darimi, kitāb al-Nikāh, vol. II, p. 68, *Hadith* No. 2214; kitāb al-Jihād, vol. II, p. 130, *Hadith* No. 2428; *Musnad* Ahmad bin Hanbal, vol. VI, pp. 114-117, 197 and 269.

blame of partiality. As when a judge distributes the inheritance, he draws lot although he can determine and fix the share of each heir without drawing a lot. But to avoid the blame of partiality, he withdraws the lot. The same is the situation here.

Mode of making name slips

114. The form of making slips is that the names of the plaintiff and the defendant should be written on each slip and they should be put in some drawer (*bunduqah*).[105] If 20 or 100 parties of litigants appear before a judge, he should make an assessment as to the number of the cases that can be decided by him on that day and he should draw lot between them. The parties whose names come in the first, their case be heard and decided first. Then again, the lot be drawn and so on and so forth the process be continued till all the cases for the day are disposed of.

If a judge feels that all the causes cannot be disposed of on one day, his reader should make slips of all the cases as we have already stated and thereafter, a bundle each of 20 slips or such number as a judge feels that he will be able to decide in a day, a

---

105. *Bunduqah* is a thing by means of which something is thrown. See Qāmûs, *madah bunduq*, vol. III, p. 222, where it is stated that *bunduqah* is a thing made of clay whereby something is thrown. Same is mentioned in *Al-Misbāh*, vol. I, pp. 63-64. (its plural is *banadiq*). The jurists in their books under the heading of drawal of lots for the purposes of disribution use the words *bunduqah*, *bunduq*, and *banadiq*. They have explained that it is made of clay and wax. See *Al-Mukhtasar al-Shāfi'i* on the margin of *Kitāb al-Umm*. Similarly, see *al-Mukhtasar*, al-Muzni min kalām alShāfi'i, on the margin of kitāb al-Umm, vol. V, p. 244; *Nihāya al-Muhtaj*, al-Ramali, vol. VIII, p. 272; *Adāb al-Qādi*, al-mawardi, vol. II, pp. 191-195; *Al-Fātawa al-Hindiyah*, vol. V, p. 206; *Hashiyah al-Tāhawi 'ala al-Durr al-Mukhtār*, vol. IV, p. 136; *al-Mughni*, Ibn Qudamah, vol. XI, p. 503; *Al-Sharh al-Kabir*, Ibn Qudamah al-Maqdasi, vol. XI, p. 505.

bundle of such number of slips be made fixing a slip marking some well-known mark on each such bundle. Now, in these bundles there will be many name slips and thereafter he should draw a lot about these bundles and whichever comes in the first draw, such cases be disposed of say on Saturday and the so on and so forth. Parties present should be informed of the bundle which contains their name so that they may remain well informed about their turn of hearing of their cases. In this manner, there will not be a crowd of parties in the court.

After drawing the lots, the judge should direct to notify on the court notice board that the cases of the parties of such and such bundle will be fixed for such and such date. In this manner all the parties will be informed of their dates of hearing and they will appear on that date in the court.

In this manner, lots will be drawn twice. Once for the bundles and second time for the names of the parties in the said bundles. The first will be collective and the second will individual lot. As is done in the matter of distribution of the war booty that once collective lot is drawn between the commanders of the army and secondly, the lot is drawn to distribute the war booty between the various flags.

115. Shams al-A'immah Imām Sarakhsi (Allah's pleasure be on him) said, "The thing on which Imām Khassāf (Allah's mercy be on him) depended is also good."[106] But the thing on which earlier leading jurists have depended is better than it. The reason

---

106. *Al-Mabsūt* al-Sarakhsi, vol. XVI, p. 80. Imām Sarakhsi (Allah's mercy be on him) has also added that Imām Muhammad (Allah's mercy be on him) has liked it that whosoever comes first in the court, his case will be heard firstly. The Messenger of Allah (peace and blessings of Allah be on him) has also said, "Ukashah has taken the precedence over you." In this *hadith* the indication is also towards it.

is that if a judge adopts the principle of drawing lots and every party knows the date of hearing of his case such as Saturday or Sunday or so on then it will be possible for him to decide all those cases when the proof and argument are clear or those are decided on oaths. But if the cases are of such a nature where a judge is to consult or deeply ponder upon and to exercise personal judgement (*ijtihād*) and cannot be decided the same day. it will be a sort of breach of promise. Hence, the policy of first come first heard should be adopted and the policy of drawing lots should be avoided.

116. Imām Khassāf (Allah's mercy be on him) said, "The first bundle of name slips be kept for Saturday, the second for Sunday, the third for day after Sunday and so on, if the judge be working during those days. And if for any day he is not to hold the court, he should inform the parties in advance and tell them that their cases will be heard next day."

The reason is that to take rest is also essential for a judge so that he may not feel tired and may be able to ponder in the mtatters to be heard by and may look after his own personal affairs also.

During the period of Imām Abû Hanifah (Allah's mercy be on him) Saturday was the holiday. On that day, no teaching work was done in the teaching institutions. During the period of Imām Khassāf (Allah's mercy be on him), the holiday was observed at times on Monday and at times on Tuesday. Some judges observed holiday on Saturday and some observed on Monday or Tuesday.

During the period of Imām Hisām (Allah's mercy be on him) the custom is to observe holiday on Tuesday as the duty of administration of justice is from the genesis of royal duties and the staff of the king does not perform their duty on Tuesday as they consider it as a condemned day as on that day Qābil had killed Hābil. Hence, the *fuqaha* used to tell to the litigant parties that Tuesday is the holiday.

Whether salary of a holiday will be deducted from the monthly salary of a judge

117. If a judge receives his salary from national exchequer (*bait al-māl*) whether he is entitled to receive the pay for a holiday or to that extent his pay will be deducted from his monthly salary?

The *fatwa* of Hanafi masters of law (*mashā'ikh*) of Balkh is that he is not entitled to receive the pay of a holiday and to that extent his pay will be deducted from his monthly salary.

The *fatwa* of Hanafi masters of law (*mashā'ikh*) of Bukhara is that a judge is entitled to receive pay for a holiday and there will be no deduction of any pay from his monthly salary. And this opinion is a valid opinion. Because a judge takes rest on such day and becomes fresh to decide cases the next day. This day of rest is also beneficial for the parties to the litigation. Hence, a judge is entitled to receive the pay of such day. It is like his receiving the pay for the night period in which he is not deciding the cases. The same is the situation here.

Its example is found in the matters of wills. If a person makes a will of the stems of date trees in favour of one man and a will of the date (fruit) in favour of another man while the date trees bear fruit one year and do not bear fruit the next year but the expenditure incurred in the matter of irrigation and other necessary affairs remains the liability of the man in whose favour the will of fruits has been made. The reason is that despite an interval of an year, the next year only, the said man gets benefit of the fruits in whose favours the will of fruits is made. Therefore, he shall be responsible for the expenditure of both the years. The same is situation here.

Whose case shall be heard first

118. If in the court of a judge the witnesses, the oath takers, the travellers, and the ladies are present and the judge deems fit to give precedence to make the name slips of the witnesses in all his court sitting he may do so. The reason is that to give respect and honour to the witnesses has been commanded. The Messenger of Allah (peace and blessings of Allah be on him) said, "Honour the witnesses as Allah, the Almighty revives the rights of the people through them."[107]

To leave the witnesses (without examination) who come to the court for giving evidence is not an honourable treatment to them.

119. And if a judge deems it proper to give precedence to the preparation of the draw slips (*riqā'*) of those who are to take oaths in all his court sittings, he may do so.

The reason is that to decide a case on the basis of oath is easy. While to decide a case on the basis of evidence it is necessary to prove the names of the witnesses, to ponder upon the words of evidence, the purging of the credit worthiness of the witnesses. In oath cases these things are not necessary for giving a decision.

120. If a judge deems it proper to give precedence to the preparation of name slips for draw purposes of the outstation witnesses (*al-ghurabā'*) in all court sittings, he may do so.

The reason is that the heart of an outstation person remains attached with his family and home. Over stay at court door and to attend the court again and again makes him disturbed.

---

107. *Al-Maqāsid al-hasanah*, al-Sakhawi, pp. 78-79, *Hadith* No. 154; Al-Jāmi' al-Saghir, al-Suyuti, vol. I, p. 55; *Al-Fawā'id al-Majmū'a fī al-Ahadīht al-Maudū'a*, al-Shawkani, p. 200, *Hadith* No. 4, under heading Kitāb al-Qadā'. [Imām San'ani has explained that thsi hadith is a forged one.] *Kashf al-Khifā*, al-'Ujluni al-Jarrāhi, vol. I, pp. 194-195, *Hadith* No. 509. At some places the additional words are, "through them the injustice is removed." See also *Talkhis al-Habir*, al-'Asqalani, vol. 4, p. 198, *Hadith* No. 2107.

Consequently he leaves his right and returns to his home. In this manner a judge wastes his right. This happens when the number of outstation attendants is not more. If their number is more the judge may adopt the principle of precedence of the policy of drawing the lots. If a judge fears the case of a party earlier than others on the ground of his being an outstation litigant, it will not be sufficient to allege that he is an outstation and he wants to go back to his place of residence. The judge should ask him to produce witnesses who may give testimony that he is really an outstation and intends to go back to his home. It is so transmitted on the authority of Imām Muhammad (Allah's mercy be on him).[108]

The reason is that in such a case the judge is giving precedence to an outstation applicant over the other outstation litigants. Hence, he is bound to give proof of his urgent return and of being an outstation person. However, in such evidence there is no condition precedent of a witness being *'adil* (creditworthy). The evidence of a *mastūr* (whose creditworthiness is not open).

One of our Imāms stated that the judge shall ask the outstation person, "With whom you intend to travel?" Then he should ask his co-travellers, "When are you going? Is such and such person also travelling with you? And at what time you are ready to depart?"

The same is the situation in the matter of an *ijārah* (lease). If a lessor shows some just excuse of his journey, the lease will be cancelled. However, the simple statement of the lessor that he wants to go on journey will neither prove his excuse nor the lease will be cancelled. The judge shall ask such lessor, "With whom you want to travel?" Then the judge will ask his colleagues, "When are you going to travel? Is such and such person travelling with you? Is he ready for travel?" If they reply in the affirmative, the

---

108. *Al-Mabsūt* al-Sarakhsi, vol. XVI, p. 81.

excuse will be proved and the lease will come to an end.

The same procedure will be adopted in the matter of taking a guarantee. Its details will be mentioned in chapter 29 of this book *Inshã Allãh.*

121. If the judge deems it proper to prepare the draw name slips of ladies first of all slips he may do so.

The reason is that they are *pardah nashin* and are bound to stay at home and can come out on some just excuse. If a judge decides their cases they will return home earlier and it will also maintain the observance of *pardah* by them.

If the judge deems it proper to fix a day for hearing of ladies cases he may do so. This is only when the matter is between the ladies. In case the matter is between the males and the females then he should not fix a separate day for the ladies.

122. If in a bundle twelve names are entered the judge should affix a label on the said bundle with a mark and thereafter he should draw the lot. After the lot the judge should direct the concerned official of the court to proclaim at the main gate of the court that such and such cases shall be heard on such and such day. But he should not proclaim the names of the female parties to avoid publicity of the ladies as their affairs are not to be made public. However he should send an honest old female court official to inform them that the turn of hearing of their cases shall be on such and such day. In this manner they shall attend the court on the date of hearing of their case and after the case hearing is over they would return to their homes.

Assistant Court Reader

123. If a judge deems it proper to appoint an assistant court reader to help him in the matter of preparation of the name slips of the parties he may do so and appoint a reliable person. In doing so there is an element of extra care and caution.

It is like the matter of purgation of witnesses (*tazkiah al-shuhûd*) where only a single person is sufficient for that purpose but there is an element of extra care and caution in getting the purgation done by two persons. The same is the situation here.

Court Diary

124. A judge should note in his court diary the turn and the date of hearing of each case. A judge needs to remember these matters as otherwise he will be disturbing the order list of cases. A human being is forgetful and the court diary will be helpful for a judge to proceed according to the turn of the cases.

Court Safe Box

125. After making necessary entries in the court diary the judge should keep it safe in the court box (*qumtar*).[109]

Court Seal

126. After making necessary entires the judge should affix his seal at the end otherwise it will not remain secure from any interpolation.

(Allah knows the best)

---

109. *Al-Qâmûs*, Maddah Q-M-R vol. II, p. 126 and Maddah, KH-R-T vol.II, p. 270; *Al-Misbâh al-Munir*, vol. I, p. 258.

CHAPTER 6

Taking Over Charge of Documents from the Office of the Dismissed Judge

Dismissal of a Judge on the Charge of Doubtful integrity or any Other Reason

127. **When** a successor judge takes charge of the office of the predecessor judge, the former shall send two reliable court officials to the later to get charge of the court documents and all other things.

The basis of this affair is that the head of the state can dismiss a judge on the basis of doubtful integrity or any other reason.

So far as the power of dismissal on the basis of doubtful integrity of a judge is concerned, there is no doubt about its being available to the head of the state.

So far as the power of dismissal on the basis of a reason other than doubtful integrity, the authority is a transmission from Imãm Abû Hanifah (Allah's mercy be on him) that a judge should not be kept on a judicial post for more than a year. The reason is that when a judge becomes busy in the disposal of judicial matters, his knowledge corrodes. Hence, he should be relieved of this office and in his place some other person should be appointed so that he may again continue his own further education. After lapse of one year, the head of the state should consider such cases. If he intends to relieve him from judicial function, he should say to him; "There is no fault in you but I apprehend that you have forgotten the knowledge, hence, you should leave this office and get fresh knowledge and then again come to us and we will again assign you the judicial duty."

Thus, whatever may be the basis of the removal of a judge from his office, the doubtful integrity or any other reason, the nominated judge shall send two reliable persons to him to get charge of all the things that were in his custody or control as a judge. For this purpose sending of one person is sufficient, but there is extra care in sending two persons.

Contents of Judicial Record

128. The office of a judge is the custodian of such files which include *al-sajillāt* (the register of judgements and orders of the judge), *al-sakûk* (the register containing proceedings relating to the contracts of sale, mortgage, etc.), *al-mahãdir* (the register containing the proceedings of the cases like the admission or denial of the defendant, the evidence or proof of the plaintiff, the judgement, the denial of the defendant to take oath, etc.), and *nasb al-awsiyā'* (appointment orders of trustees), and *nasb al-quyyam* (appointment orders of supervisors) regarding the *waqf* properties and the amount of expenditure.

Therefore, a judge prepares two copies each of such documents, one of which is given to the party and the other is kept as a record in the office to use whenever needed. The copy with the party may be interpolated, hence, it is not relied upon.

Separate inventory of judicial record and taking charge of them

129. At the time of receipt of the documents and files from the office of the outgoing judge, should collect the copies of court registers in a separate file, appointment orders of trustees of the properties of orphans in a separate file, orders fixing expenditure in a separate file, orders of appointment of supervisors of trusts where the trust property is under the supervision of the court, in a separate file (if the trust is not under the supervision of the court, then there is no need to prepare separate copies of such trust), the copies of documents concerning sales and mortgages in a separate file. In short, all kinds of copies should be collected in separate files.

As all these copies were in the custody of the outgoing judge and for him there was no matter in doubt, but it may be doubtful for the nominated judge. If two reliable persons do not collect all such copies and in some case need arises to the nominated judge, he will be compelled to find out the relevant persons and to have an access to them will be difficult for him.

130. Both the reliable persons should ask every matter from the outgoing judge as his reply concerning all such things will be a reliable proof (*hujjat*) although due to his removal, his status is that of an ordinary man. However, they (the two reliable persons deputed by the new judge) should ask the outgoing judge concerning all matters that may arise at that time in their mind so that if a problem arises later on, the solution could be made (in the light of the statement of the outgoing judge).

131. After receipt of the said documents from the outgoing judge, they should put their seal on them to avoid any interpolation (by way of an addition or omission).

132. The diary in which the outgoing judge had entered these copies will be either purchased by public money or by spending from his own pocket. If he voluntarily gives the said diary to the said reliable persons of the new judge, he may do so. If he refuses to give and it transpires that the same was purchased by public money, he shall be compelled to surrender it. The reason is that it was in his custody for the performance of public duty and not for his personal use. Hence, it will not be left in his custody.

If it was purchased by him from his own pocket or by the expenses of the litigant, then there is conflict of opinion between the Hanafi master of law (*mushā'ikh*). Some say he shall not be compelled to return it as it is his own property or it was a trust with him on behalf of the litigants who had born the expenditure. According to others, he shall be compelled to return it. And this is the valid opinion. The reason is that it was in his custody for administrative affairs and not for his personal use nor any litigant had given it to him for his personal use. It was given to him for the performance of the public job which has since been transferred to another judge.

Receipt of the Trust Money and the Property of the Orphans

133. The two representatives should take charge in the presence of the outgoing judge. In case he is not present himself, he cannot be compelled. The reason is that when presence of the nominated judge is not essential for this purpose, the presence of the outgoing judge is also not essential, but the outgoing judge should send his two representatives to hand over the charge of the articles to the two representatives of the nominated judge. The representatives of the nominated judge should ask about all the things from representatives of the outgoing judge so that their replies may be used if any problem arises later on.

134. The said representative shall receive the properties of the orphans and the trust amount as all these were in the custody of the outgoing judge.

Prisoners Affairs

135. The said representatives should note down the names of the prisoners. It is so because when a judge sends a person to prison, it is necessary for him to record the name, father's name, grand father's name, cause and date of confinement of the prisoner. As sometimes testimony is to be recorded to know as to whether the prisoner is a pauper. Hence, there should be complete particulars with the judge.

The nominated judge should receive a copy of it from the outgoing judge and should also note it down in his diary and keep it in the court box after affixing his seal. He should enter the same date in his diary that has been entered by the outgoing judge. He should not enter in it the date when he starts his work as the basis of confinement of the prisoner can only be the said copy and no other thing can become a proof thereof.

136. The said representatives shall ask the outgoing judge about the prisoners and the cause of their confinement. After that the judge should ask the prisoners about the cause of their confinement.

The nominated judge shall call the prisoners and their opposite parties. If the statement of the outgoing judge, the statement of the prisoner and the statement of the party at whose instance the prisoner is kept in confinement are in conformity with each other, the prisoner shall be sent back to the prison. If there is any difference of the parties upon the decision of the outgoing judge on the basis of some proof and argument, then the nominated judge should not pay heed to the statement of the outgoing judge.

If the nominated judge calls the prisoners and their opponents and the prisoner confesses the claim of the complainant and the complainant also demands that the prisoner should be kept in confinement, the nominated judge should send back the prisoner to jail.

At this point, this is the statement of Imām Khassāf (Allah's mercy be on him). However, in chapter 11 of this book, he has stated that if a person admits the liability of a right of any other person on himself, he will not be confined to jail on his first admission. But here the Imam has stated that such a person shall be confined to jail.

The reason is that confinement is a punishment which is necessary only when the defendant is either harsh in his behaviour or is making lame excuses to postpone the paying back of the right of another. By his admission, as aforesaid, that he is liable to pay the right of the claimant. no lame excuse is expressed. But in case the defendant does not pay back the liability and the plaintiff is to sue him again, the judge should send him to jail. So far as the situation mentioned above is concerned, it was that the nominated judge found the prisoner in the jail and the outgoing judge had put him behind the bars due to his harsh behaviour. In such circumstances, it is permissible for the nominated judge to send him back to the prison.

This is the difference between the two statements of Imām Khassāf (Allah's mercy be on him). The point indicated by Imām Muhammad (Allah's mercy be on him) in his book is that there is no difference between the first or the second admission of the defendant. The reason is that once the defendant makes an admission of the right of the plaintiff. the judge should send him behind the bar and compel him to make payment of the debt due on him.

This is when a prisoner makes an admission of the liability on him but if he denies and states that the plaintiff has brought a suit against him without having a cause of action against him and he has been wrongfully confined to jail, his statement will not be considered and the plaintiff (complainant) shall be asked to produce his evidence. Thereafter, if the plaintiff produces witnesses and the judge knows that they are creditworthy (*'adil*), he shall maintain the confinement of the prisoner (defendant). The reason is that the creditworthiness of the witnesses is to be got known when the judge does not know of it himself. If he knows it and the witnesses are *'adil* then there is no need to make further probe. Its example is that if goods are destroyed and their price is not known, then their price is got ascertained through the expert of price assessement. But when the price is known, there is no need to turn to any one else.

If the *'adālat* (credibility) of the witnesses is not known to the judge, the statement of the outgoing judge in this behalf is not an authoritative proof (*hujjat*). The nominated judge should get information about the credibility of the witnesses and should release the prisoner (defendant) on furnishing bail bond [to the satisfaction of the court].

The defendant is not to be kept in prison as at that time the credibility of the witnesses is not clear. Merely on the basis of witnesses the right is not proved against the defendant. Hence, he cannot be kept in prison. Without furnishing bail bond, he cannot be released. Therefore, a judge should remain careful for the benefit of the litigant public. The care lies in it that the judge should get bail bond from the defendant till the credibility of the plaintiff's witnesses becomes clear. If later on the credibility becomes clear, the judge should send the defendant to prison and if it is not clear, the defendant should not be kept in prison.

137. If there are such persons amongst the prisoners whose opposite party does not appear before the court and the prisoners claim that they have been kept in prison without any cause of action against them that there is no opponent of them, the judge should investigate the excuse of such a person, i.e., the judge should make an inquiry into it.

The method of inquiry is that when the judge sits in his court he should direct the court official to proclaim every day, "Whoever has got a right against such and such prisoner should attend the court." If any person in response to that proclamation appears in the court, well and good, otherwise if the judge deems it proper to release the prisoner, he should make such proclaimation for sufficient number of days. It is like the asking of the judge to a defendant to take oath and says him each time. "I offer you to take oath and if you deny to take it the matter will be decided against you on account of such denial." If the defendant denies to take oath even third time, the judge decides the case against him. The same is the situation here.

If the opposite party of a prisoner appears in the court, the judge should also summon the prisoner [to dispose of the matter]. If the opposite party of a prisoner does not appear in the court, the judge may, within his discretion, wait for a few days and should not make haste in releasing the prisoner and then after taking personal bond release the prisoner.

According to some jurists, the taking of bail bond in both the circumstances is the statement of Imam Abu Yusuf and Imam Muhammad (Allah's mercy be on both of them) while Imam Abu Hanifah (Allah's mercy be on him) is not in favour of taking the bail. The basis of it is the two following examples.

❖ When a judge divides inheritance between the heirs of a deceased person, he takes surety (*daman*) from them as an extra care.

❖   When a judge decides to pay debts out of the inheritance of the deceased, he takes surety (*daman*) from the creditor.

According to Imām Abû Hanifah (Allah's mercy be on him) in both these circumstances, a judge should not demand surety while according to *sāhibain*, a judge should demand surety as an extra care. The same is the situation in the aforesaid problem.

Shams al-'Aimmah Imām Sarakhsi (Allah's mercy be on him) states that the correct thing is this it is the statement of three Imāms. According to Imām Abû Hanifah (Allah's mercy be on him) the difference between the said two forms is that the matter of division of inheritance and the matter of payment of debt. the right of the heir and the creditor is clear while the proof right of any other person is doubtful and for the sake of an ambiguous right to delay or postpone the payment of right till the limitation period of surety is not permissible.

So far as the form of problem mentioned in the book is concerned, there the right is certainly proved one as the act of the outgoing judge shall be considered as just and useful, but there is no information about the plaintiff. Hence, for an ambiguous right surety shall not be demanded.

138. If a prisoner states, "I have been confined in the jail for an amount of one thousand dirhams payable by me to such and such person of which I have made an admission before the outgoing judge," the nominated judge shall summon the opposite party. If the opposite party appears and the nominated judge knows him personally or the witnesses give evidence of his lineage and thereafter the prisoner states, "Here is the amount of this person which I want to give him. You kindly direct him to receive and I may be released from the prison." The nominated judge shall direct the payment of that amount to be given to that person as the prisoner has made admission that it belongs to him.

If the nominated judge does not know the opponent party personally, he should release the prisoner. Here Imām Khaṣṣāf (Allah's mercy be on him) has not been mentioned as to whether the surety will be taken from the prisoner. This is according to the meanings which we have already stated above.

Likewise, if the prisoner does not give the amount to the said person but the claimant submits before the nominated judge, "I want to deal with this prisoner softly. You kindly grant him some time and release him." In such circumstance, the nominated judge should release him. Thus, this form and the first form are the same.

If it is difficult for the nominated judge to determine as to whether the plaintiff is actually such and such person and son of such and such person, in that circumstance also the nominated judge shall order the prisoner to make payment of amount payable to him.

By all means, the nominated judge should release the prisoner in both these circumstances, but the proper thing is not to make haste in passing the release order and it should be delayed for a while and thereafter, the prisoner should be released after taking personal bond from him. It is so because it may be that the prisoner and the other person might be playing some fraud on the court and the actual opponent of the prisoner may be some other person. Hence, the judge should take surety as an extra care in the matter and then pass the release order.

139. Similarly, if the prisoner states, "I was imprisoned for non-payment of an amount of one thousand dirhams of this person which I want to give him back. Kindly direct him to receive the said amount from me and get me released from the prison." If the judge does not know the plaintiff nor the plaintiff produces witnesses, he will direct the said person to receive the amount on the basis of the admission of the prisoner.

So far as the release is concerned, the judge should not make haste in the matter of his release and should get the proclamation issued. If in response of the proclamation someone attends the court, well and good; otherwise the judge may, in his discretion, wait for a few days and thereafter order the release of the prisoner after taking surety from him.

If the prisoner states, "I have no surety," or he states, "There is no need for me to give surety as I have no opposite party, therefore. I am not going to give a surety." the judge should consider a statement and should not make haste in releasing him till a proclamation is issued. The waiting period may be one month or such time as the judge considers properly. If the opposite party comes, well and good, otherwise the judge should release him.

140. Here Imām Khassāf (Allah's mercy be on him) has himself posed a question:

If any one says that the nominated judge should release every prisoner except a prisoner who admits the right of another person and he wants to keep him in the prison or a person produces credible witnesses against the prisoner.

A person whose opposite party does not appear in the court, the judge should not keep such person in prison. The reason is that such a person has been kept in prison by the judge for the sake of the right of another person and when there is no opposite party to him, the judge is bound to release him. Imām Khassāf (Allah's mercy be on him) has replied that we look to the order to imprisonment passed by a judge as being passed in a matter in which the imprisonment of the said person was necessary. It is so because according to us a judge is himself a credible person and is competent to proceed in the matter even otherwise.

141. Imãm Khassãf (Allah's mercy be on him) then posed another question.

If any one says that when the judge does not release the said prisoners, it is also not proper for him to deal in any manner with the affairs of the prisoners. Neither he should order their imprisonment nor restrain others from doing so. The reason is that the proceedings in the court are based on some proof. He has no proof to imprison or release the prisoners.

Imãm Khassãf (Allah's mercy be on him) then replies to this question and says, "When the judge states that neither I pass any order in this matter nor I stop them from it." Thereafter, if the Superintendent Jail or any other person releases such prisoners, then whether the judge shall release them? No, he should not release them. As to release them is not in his power, he should not release anyone. However, he should investigate the correct circumstance in their matter and proceed according to that which he considers valid.

142. The causes to confine a person in jail may be as under:

- *al-dayn* (non-payment of debt); or
  due to punishments that are related to the rights of men, i.e.,
- *al-qisãs fi al-nafs* (*qisas* of life), or
  al-qisãs fi al-tarf (*qisas* of limb); or
  due to punishments that are related to the rights of God, i.e.,
- *al-zina* (adultery);
- *al-sariqah* (Theft);
- *shurb al-khamr* (Intoxication); or
  due to punishment that is related to a right both of men and God, i.e.,
- *qazf* (false accusation of adultery).

143. So far as imprisonment due to liability of debt is concerned, we have already stated above about it.

144. If the prisoner has been confined due to such punishments that are related to the rights of men (*huqûq al-'ibãd*), e.g., when the prisoner states, "I have been confined in prison as I had made a confession of *qisãs* in favour of such and such person", the judge shall summon the prisoner as well as his opposite party. If the opposite party makes such claim, the judge will see if the *qisãs* is concerning the life, he can enforce the punishment due to his confession as in such circumstance the allegation of partiality cannot be levelled against him. Similarly, if the *qisãs* is concerning any limb ('*udw*), even in that circumstance he can enforce the punishment on him.

However, the judge should not make haste in releasing him as in that circumstance allegation of partiality can be levelled against him as it may be that some other person's right of life or property may be against the prisoner and he wants to get him released and thereby the said right may be lost. Therefore, a judge should postpone the matter for a time and issue a proclamation and thereafter release him on furnishing personal (bail) bond.

145. If the prisoner is kept in confinement for the punishment that are related to the rights of Allah, the Almighty, e.g., the prisoner states, "I had made four confessions before the outgoing judge and for that he had kept me in the prison to execute *hadd*, the nominated judge will not execute the *hadd* on this prisoner. It is so because the confession of the prisoner before the outgoing judge is not an authoritative proof for the nominated judge. The nominated judge should conduct *de novo* trial. If the prisoner confesses in four sittings of the judge, then his confession is valid (for nominated judge). If the prisoner is married one, the judge shall stone him to death; and if he is unmarried, he will be given the punishment of stripes. After that the judge should wait for some time and again issue a proclamation concerning him. If any party comes, he will summon both the parties and the prisoner to appear before him, otherwise release him on furnishing personal bail bond.

If the prisoner resiles from the confession, his resile is valid. The reason is that if he had resiled from his confession before the outgoing judge, such resile would have been valid. Likewise. his resiling from his confession before the nominated judge is also valid. Hence, the judge shall not execute *hadd* on him, but he should also not release him because there is possibility of some trick from his side. Hence, he should issue a proclamation and thereafter think over the matter for sometime and then release him after getting personal bond.

146. If a prisoner states. "As the charge of *zina* was proved against him, hence the outgoing judge had kept him in jail," the nominated judge should not execute *hadd* on the basis of evidence of the witnesses. The reason is that the evidence before the outgoing judge is not reliable for the nominated judge.

Likewise, if after the lapse of the fixed period the witnesses give evidence before the nominated judge, such evidence is also not reliable because evidence after the lapse of fixed time is not an authoritative proof (*hujjat*). However, if the accused prisoner makes the confession, his confession is an authoritative proof (*hujjat*). In such circumstance, the nominated judge should start *de novo* trial.

When it is proved that the nominated judge is not to execute the *hadd* on the accused prisoner on the basis of the evidences of witnesses, he should not release him immediately as the possibility of any trick is there and he should direct the issuance of a proclamation concerning him and should ponder upon his matter and thereafter release him after taking personal bond from him.

147. If a prisoner states: "I was kept in confirmment as I had confessed having committed theft [of the property] of such and such person," the nominated judge will execute the sentence of amputation of hand irrespective of the time limit (*taqādum al-'ahd*) had elapsed. The reason is that the confession of commission of a theft is an authoritative proof in both the circumstances as his confession of commission of *zina* is an authoritative proof in both the circumstances. Thereafter, the nominated judge should not make haste in releasing the prisoner as there may be a possibility of some fraudulent excuse concerning which a probe should be made and thereafter he should be released on furnishing bail bond as we have already stated.

148. If a prisoner makes statement: "I have been confined by the outgoing judge in his court on a charge of theft against me, the witnesses have given testimony," the nominated judge should not execute the *hadd* on the basis of the said evidence of the witnesses as we have already stated.

Likewise, if the witnesses give testimony before the nominated judge after the lapse of the time limit (*taqādum al-'ahd*), the *hadd* shall not be executed. The reason is that after the time limit (*taqādum al-'ahd*) is lapsed, the testimony in theft is inadmissible. Therefore, the hand shall not be amputated. However, the nominated judge shall not make haste in release of the prisoner and should proceed as we have already stated.

149. If a prisoner states, "I was confined as I have confessed the drinking of wine or being intoxicated having taken wine or the proof had came in the court against me and to execute the *hadd* for that offence, the outgoing judge had confined me to execute the *hadd*." The nominated judge should not execute the *hadd*.

According to Imām Abū Hanifah (Allah's mercy be on him) and Imām Abū Yūsuf (Allah's mercy be on him) even in the new circumstance the nominated judge should not execute the *hadd*. The reason is that according to them the *hadd* of drinking wine on the basis of confession or proof becomes necessary only when the wine is present in the abdomen of the drunkard irrespective of the smell of wine is present or not in his mouth. Hence, to execute *hadd* on him is not necessary. However, the nominated judge should not make haste in his release and proceed as we have already stated.

150. If a prisoner states, "I have been confined as I had levelled allegation of *zina* on such and such person and the outgoing judge had kept me to execute *hadd* on me." Thereafter, the said person also verifies the said statement of the prisoner, the nominated judge should execute the *hadd* on him. The retraction from confession by the prisoner will not be valid. However, the matter of *zina* is different from it (as in the matter of *zina* an offender can retract from his confession).

The Matters regarding the Properties and Trusts *(umûr al-amwãl wa'l-wada'i')*

151. So far as the properties and the trusts are concerned, if the outgoing judge states such and such property belonging to such and such person is in the possession of such and such person, the nominated judge will enquire from the possessor concerning it. After that there may be four situations, viz.

- ❖ The person in possession of the property states, "The outgoing judge had given me the possession of the property in question and had informed me that it belongs to such and such person;" or
- ❖ The person in possession of the property states, "The outgoing judge had given me the possession of the property in question but I do not know who is the owner of this property; or

❖ The person in possession of the property in question denies the whole statement of the outgoing judge; or

❖ The person in possession of the property states, "The outgoing judge had given me the possession of the property in question but it is of such other person (i.e., it is not the property of the person named by the outgoing judge.

In the first and the second case, the nominated judge should accept the statement of the outgoing judge and the property shall belong to the person in whose favour the statement has been made. The reason is that the possession of the property has come in possession of such person through the outgoing judge and thus, it is to be considered as in the possession of the outgoing judge, who, due to his dismissal from the office became like an ordinary person. It is like the admission of the ownership of another person by a person which is accepted in the matter of the possession of the properties. The same is the situation here.

The precedent case is that which is mentioned in the books of jurisprudence as under:

"Where a certain property is in the possession of a certain person and he makes an admission that the said property has been given to him by such and such person and that such and such person states that the owner of the said property is certain other person. The person in whose possession of the property is shall be ordered to deliver the property to that owner in whose favour the admission has been made. It is so because the person in possession of the property has admitted that the possession of the property is on behalf of the person who had given it to him and the giver of the property has admitted that actually the said property is owned by another person. In such circumstance, his such admission is valid and he will be directed to deliver the property in whose favour the admission has been made."

In the third case, the statement of the person in possession shall be accepted and nothing will be his liability due to the statement of the outgoing judge.

In the fourth case, there can be two situations.

Firstly, while returning the property to the nominated judge the person in possession of the property in question makes the statement: "The outgoing judge had given me this property while it actually belongs to such and such other person."

Secondly, the person in possession of the property makes the statement before the nominated judge: "This property belongs to such and such person and the person in whose favour the outgoing judge has made admission is not that person." And thereafter, he further says, "The outgoing judge had given this property to me."

In the first case, the statement of the outgoing judge shall be reliable. The property shall be ordered to be handed over to the person in whose favour the outgoing judge had made admission. The reason is that he stated that the property was given to him by the outgoing judge. In other words, he admitted that the property was in the possession of outgoing judge. After this admission, he makes the admission that the property in question belongs to such and such other person. His second admission shall not be valid.

In the second case, the nominated judge shall direct him to hand over the property in question to the person in whose favour he made the admission. If the property is of the goods which are similar (*mithli*), he shall give the consideration of the value of the similar property to the person in whose favour the outgoing judge had made admission. The reason is that his first admission is valid as the property was in his custody. Therefore, it is necessary to deliver the property to that person in whose favour he had made admission. Later on, when he made statement that the property in question was given to him by the outgoing judge and the outgoing judge says that the said property belongs to some other person, he admitted as well that the property in question was in the custody of the outgoing judge and the outgoing judge admits the ownership of another person. And this man in possession of property by making an admission in favour of a different person is destroying the right of the said person in whose favour the outgoing judge had made admission. Therefore, he is bound to give compensation of that property provided that the property is of the goods which are similar (*mithli*).

152. If the outgoing judge states the amount of ten dirhams in possession of such and such person is the property of such and such orphan, which he had got from the inheritance of his father and the person in possession of the said amount also verifies such statement of the outgoing judge, the nominated judge shall accept the statement of the outgoing judge. It is so because in a way the possession on that amount was of the outgoing judge. Thereafter, it will be seen that there is no claim from any other heir regarding the said amount. If there is no such claim, the property shall belong to the orphan in whose favour the said admission was made. If, on the other hand, the heirs bring a suit that they have not as yet received their rights, in that case their statement will be accepted and the said amount will be treated as common between the or ophan and the other heirs.

The reason is that in a way there was possession of the outgoing judge on the said amount and he had made admission that the said amount belongs to the said orphan. Thus, by way of the said possession, his admission is valid that the owner of this amount was their father, but by way of that possession his admission is not valid to the extent that the other heirs had also received their rights. When it is not proved that they had received their rights, the amount became common between the orphan and the other heirs.

However, the nominated judge should take extra care and caution in the matter of an orphan minor and should take oath from the other heirs regarding non receipt of their rights. It is so because a minor is not capable to understand his own affairs and the judge should keep his affair before him. The precedent of it is the case where a judge decides a debt of a deceased person. In that case, he takes oath from the creditor in the following words. "By the token of Allah, I have not received back the debt nor I have relieved him of the responsibility."

The reason of such procedure is that the deceased person is not in a position to look after his own affairs and it is the judge who looks his affairs.

The affair relating to movable and immovable properties and general goods (umûr al-'iqâr wa'l-diyâ' wa'l-'urûd)

153. If there are movable or immovable properties or general goods instead of the dirhmas, the same is the situation as we have already described.

154. If there is liability on a person in the form of written document and the outgoing judge explains the cause (*sabab*) of such property and in that document he witnesses that the said property belongs to such an orphan, which he got from his father' and the other heirs have already received their rights, the said property will belong to the said orphan and the other heirs will have no share in it.

The reason is that the testimony of the outgoing judge that the said heirs had received their shares from the said inherited property is a sort of decision of the outgoing judge. It is like the case where the outgoing judge informs of some of his decisions and he has also witnesses concerning it and the said witnesses, if later on, give testimony against that decision, the statement of the outgoing judge shall be accepted. The same is the situation here. If they give evidence against the contents of the document and the outgoing judge gives his own evidence, the statement of the outgoing judge shall be accepted. However, merely in the presence of the document the statement of the outgoing judge shall not be accepted.

If the outgoing judge gives the evidence that this property belongs to such and such orphan but does not mention the inheritance of his father, the property shall belong to the said orphan.

If the other heirs bring a claim of their rights in the said property, they will have no share in it as the outgoing judge has made this admission that the said property belonged to the orphan and he has also possession on it as such his admission is valid. For the ownership of an orphan of a property, it is not necessary that it should be the inheritance of his father.

If the other heirs claim that the said property is the inheritance of their father. Their such claim shall not be valid without proof.

When the orphan becomes major, he will be asked about the said property. If he denies it being the inheritance of his father and also does not accept the rights of the other heirs, the statement of the orphan shall be accepted.

And if the orphan admits the rights of the other heirs. His admission shall be a proof against him (orphan). Hence, his statement will be accepted. This is the detail that has been described in the matter of the properties and the deposits.

Matters relating to (Trusts) Waqf Properties and their Trustees

155. So far as the trust properties which are in the custody of the trustees are concerned, if regarding them the outgoing judge states: "Regarding such and such property the witnesses had given evidence before me that such and such person son of such and such person has made it a trust for such purpose and I had delivered my decision on that basis. I gave this property in the custody of such son of such person and directed him to spend the income of that property on the items fixed by the founder of the trust." The trustee in whose custody this property is also verifies the same then there can be three types of statements from the heirs of the founder of the trust, viz.:

1. The heirs of the founder of the trust admit it and verify the statement made by the outgoing judge [in that behalf];

2. The heirs of the founder of the trust deny it but there exists some proof against them, e.g., the decision of the outgoing judge against them or the admission of the founder himself;

3. The heirs of the founder of the trust deny it and there is also no proof available against them.

In the first case, the nominated judge shall enforce the decision of the property being a trust property on the basis of the admission of the heirs. It is so because by fiction of law the said property was in the control of the outgoing judge and he admitted that it belonged to the deceased and he disclosed that it was made a trust by the deceased. The heirs who have stepped into the shoes of the deceased have also verified it. Thus, their verification will be deemed as if it is the verification made by the founder of the trust himself had he been alive and made it.

In the second case, the effect is also the same because the availability of any proof against the heirs is like the availability of the proof against the founder of the trust himself.

In the third case, the said property shall be an inheritance between the heirs. As had the founder of the trust been alive, his own statement would have been reliable and the admission of the outgoing judge in his favour that the said property belongs to him and a suit for declaration against him that he had made this property a trust would not have been valid. The same is the situation here. The nominated judge should ask the heirs to take oath and if they take oath he should return this property as inheritance.

If the outgoing judge makes a statement: "This property has been made a trust for such and such purposes." But he does not state. "The said property has been made a trust by such and such deceased person and it is in the possession of such and such person." If the person in possession of the said property also verifies it, then the nominated judge should enforce his own decision. He should not ask clarification as to who had made it a trust. The reason is that if he makes any question, the answer of it, sometimes, demands details, e.g., if he replies that such and such deceased person had made it a *waqf* and the heirs deny it, it will become impossible for the judge to enforce his order. The judge should put a question only when it could be useful and should not question unnecessarily otherwise it will become difficult for him to enforce the order.

Accountability of Trustees

156. The judge should conduct accountability of the trustees in whose custody are the properties of the Muslims and the incomes derived from them.

It is so because it is narrated that Hadrat 'Umar Fãrûq (Allah's pleasure be on him) used to put his governors to accountability at the end of every year.

The reason is that a judge is himself responsible for the control of the properties which belong to the orphans and the properties which have been made a trust.

Sometimes he is unable to exercise the control himself and in some affairs he seeks the help of the other persons. Therefore, it is necessary for him to conduct accountability so that he may remain informed of the correct situation.

If he feels any dishonesty on the part of any person made responsible for the exercise of control of any property, he should dismiss him and appoint some other person. And if he finds that a person who has been entrusted with the responsibility is honest, he should maintain him in that office.

Matters relating to Al-Awsiyā' and Al-Quwwām and their Accountability

157. Imām Khassāf (Allah's mercy be on him) has pointed out the difference between *al-wasiyy* and *al-qayyim*.

A person whom the judge appoints as an acting *wasiyy* his statement will be admissible in all such matters in which the statement of the *wasiyy* is admissible.

A person whom the judge appoints as a *qayyim* of the properties and *qābid* (who's function is to sell the produce and to cultivate the lands), his statement will be admissible in the matters for which he is made responsible.

The reason is that a *qayyim* (or *mutawalli*) is a person who is responsible to take care of the property, to supervise it and to collect its incomes. He does not have the power to appropriate them and if he exercises any control he violates the law (*shari'at*) as if a person with whom a deposit of any amount is made and he appropriates it, he commits a breach of law.

A *wasiyy* is a person whose responsibility is to appropriate the property and also to take care of it. He is like an agent (*wakil*) who can appropriate the property and take care of it. But this difference was in the past, while now in our period there is no difference between a *qayyim* (*mutawalli*) and a *wasiyy*.

158. The judge should accept the statement of *wasiyy* and *mutawalli* in such matters in which the claim is brought for spending on property or the person of an orphan or during this period some claim is brought in respect of such other matters.

The reason is that a *wasiyy* and a *mutawalli* are acting on behalf of the judge. As the statement of the judge is admissible in such affairs in which there may be some doubt so the statement of a *wasiyy* and a *mutawalli* will be admissible in such affairs.

If a *wasiyy* or *mutawalli* claims that he has incurred an expenditure from his own pocket with the intention to get it refunded from the property of an orphan or trust he cannot bring such a claim. The reason is that he is bringing the claim of such a debt for his own person which was liability of the orphan or the trust property. Hence merely on the basis of making a claim it cannot be valid.

If he brings a claim of having incurred expenditure from the property of the orphan or the trust and such property is in his possession then he claimed the expenditure from a thing which was in his possession as a deposit (*wadi'at*) and he has the authority to spend out of it then in such circumstance the judge should accept his statement.

If a *wasiyy* or *mutawalli* is accused of any blame in any matter, the judge should take oath from him concerning such blame (being false).

Imām Khassāf (Allah's mercy be on him) has stated in this manner but the latter jurists have difference of opinion.

According to some jurists the oath will be taken from a *wasiyy* only in the circumstance when a claim of some known thing is made against him. If the claim against him is not of a known thing he shall not be put to take oath.

According to most of the 'ulama he shall be put to oath as an extra care and caution in the matter of an orphan and the trust property.

If the judge feels any kind of dishonesty on the part of *wasiyy* then he should take extra care and caution in the matter of an orphan and trust property and take oath from the *wasiyy*.

159. If the *wasiyy* of the property of an orphan or a *mutawalli* of the property of a *waqf* claims that the outgoing judge had fixed his monthly or annual salary to such and such extent the nominated judge should not pass an order merely on the basis of such claim.

Like wise if the outgoing judge gives the statement that he had fixed salary, his statement will not be admissible as in the present circumstance his statement is not a proof (*hujjat*).

If regarding the proceedings of the outgoing judge some proof is available, in such circumstance the nominated judge shall enforce the order. It is so because the statement of outgoing judge stood proved in the circumstance when he was holding the office of a judge (competently). The statement of a judge of the period when he is competent to hold office of a judge, is a proof. However, the present judge should see in this matter that if the wages are equal or less than the actual work, then he should enforce it and if the wages are more then he should enforce to the extent of that which is equal to the work done and set aside the extra amount of wages. And return the said extra amount to the orphan if the wages had been received from the orphan.

The reason is that a judge is bound to take care and supervise the orphan and the above said over payment of wages by a judge from the property of the orphan is an act violative of his duty as a supervisor.

When it is not permissible for the former judge to give more wages than the wages equal to the work done, how can it be permissible to do so for the later judge?

160. If a *wasiyy* or a *mutawalli* of a *waqf* property makes the statement: "I collected the incomes and sold them under the orders of the outgoing judge and spent them on such and such property and now such and such amount is in balance with me, the nominated judge will accept this statement concerning the property that was in his possession as he was the custodian (*amin*) of that property and the statement of a custodian is admissible.. The portion of his statement should not be accepted that he had spent it under the order of the outgoing judge and then spent it on such and such property.

The property of an orphan or *waqf* that goes out of his possession is still his liability. The reason is that by doing so he claims to have the authority vested in himself, while by mere claim the authority (*sabab walāyat*) is not proved.

Likewise, if an outgoing judge makes a statement of this nature, the nominated judge should not accept his statement as in the present circumstance, his statement cannot become a proof (*hujjat*).

If the proof becomes available that the outgoing judge, when he was holding the office of a judge competently, had given him the permission, the nominated judge should get its ratification and enforce his own order. If no proof is available, then he should not enforce the order.

The jurist Abû Ja'far[110] (Allah's mercy be on him), in the

110. His name was Muhammad, his father's name Abdullāh, his grandfather was Muhammad, and his great-grand father was 'Umar. He was a jurist of Balkh, and known as Hindawani. The author of *Hidāyah* has mentioned him in the chapter of Sifah al-Salāh. He was a great juristic leader of Balkh. According to Imām Sam'ani, he was popular with the title of Abû Hanifah Khurd in the *fiqh Hanafi*. He

commentary of this book, has stated that if the said person is well-known and popular in his good conduct (*al-salāh*), the judge shall not make such person liable to pay compensation (*daman*) applying the principle of juristic equity (*istihsān*). It is so because he has done the same which the judge would have done. Had this matter been before the judge, he would also have exercised such appropriation. Hence. such person shall not be made liable to pay compensation (*daman*) applying the principle of juristic equity.

There are (many) other forms of this nature some of which are as under:

❖ When a person makes arrangement of coffin and burial of a deceased person from the property of such deceased person without prior permission of the judge;

got expertise in *fiqh* from his teacher Abû Bakr Muhammad bin Abî Sa'id, who was popular with the title al-A'mash. The later was a pupil of Abû Bakr al-Askaf, who was a pupil of Muhammad bin Salmah, who was a pupil of Abû Salmān Jûzjani, who was a pupil of Imām Muhammad bin Hasan, who was a pupil of Imām Abû Hanifah (Allah's mercy be on all of them). He introduced the 'Ilm of *hadith* in Balkh and Mawaraun-Nahr. He had issued his *fatawas* in difficult matters. He had presented the solution of complicated and mysterious problems. He died in Bukhāra in 362 A.H. when he was 62 years old. Nasr bin Muhammad Abû al-Laith al-Faqih had learnt *fiqh* from him. Yûsuf bin Mansûr bin Ibrāhim al-Sawi and transmitted on his authority *Kitāb al-Mukhtalif* of Abû al-Qāsim al-Sighar. He had also written a commenary of *Kitāb Adāb al-Qādi* of Imām Khassāf (Allah's mercy be on him). [*Al-Jawāhir al-Mudi'ah*, al-Qarashi, vol. II, p. 68, biographical note no. 211; *Tāj al-Tarājum fi Tabaqāt al-Hanafiyyah*, Ibn Qatlubagha, p. 63, biographical note no. 190; *Tabaqāt Ashāb al-Hanafiyyah*, Ibn Hanā'i, manuscript nos. 19-a-b; *Tabaqāt al-Fuqahā*, Tash Kubrazādah, pp. 65-66; *Al-Lubāb fi Tahzib al-Ansāb*, vol. III, p. 394; For his commentary of *Kitāb Adāb al-Qādi* of Imām Khassāf (Allah's mercy be on him), see *Kashf al-Zunun*, Haji Khalifah, vol. I, p. 46].

❖ When a pious person of the area takes the *waqf* property of the mosque and spends it on the mosque according to the need.

In both these cases, applying the principle of juristic equity (*istihsān*), such a person shall not be made liable to pay compensation (*daman*).

The valid view is the same which Imām Khassāf (Allah's mercy be on him) has expressed, i.e., the liability of payment of compensation (*daman*) shall be imposed. Similarly, in the above said cases the liability of payment of compensation (*daman*) shall be imposed. However, if the judge, in the above said cases or the earlier mentioned cases, does not impose the liability of payment of compensation (*daman*) applying the principle of juristic equity (*istihsān*), then the matter shall still remain between the said persons and Allah, the Almighty. So far as the general command is concerned, the liability of making payment of compensation (*daman*) shall be imposed on such persons.

Shams al-'A'immah Imām Hulwāni[111] (Allah's mercy be on him) has stated the same in the book *Sharh Nafaqāt* (Imām

111. His name was Abdul-'Azíz. His father's name was Ahmad. His grandfather's name was Nasr and his great-grandfather's name was Sālih. His title was Shams al-'A'immah. He belonged to Bukhāra. He was called al-Hulwāni as he used to sell sweets. He was the leading Hanafi jurist of his time. He learnt *hadíth* from Abū Abdullāh Ghanjar Bukhārí. He got the science of *fiqh* from Qādi Abū Alí al-Husain bin-al-Khidr al-Nasafí. Many persons have transmitted on his authority including Shams al-'A'immah Imām Abū Bakr Muhammad bin Ahmad bin Abí Sahl al-Sarakhsi (Allah's mercy be on him) who had learnt *fiqh* from him and got the highest degree of knowledge from him and also got his blessings. Besides these, Abū Bakr Muhamamd bin al-Hasan bin Mansūr al-Nasafi and Abū al-Fadl Bakr bin Muhammad bin Alí al-Zaranjari have also transmitted on his authority. Al-Mabsoot is included among his writings. He died in 448 A.H. (or 449 or 456). He wrote a commentary of Imām Khassāf's

Khassāf).

Likewise, the same will be the treatment in the matter of fruits and incomes which are obtained without any settled agreement. However, if they are obtained under some settled agreement like the incomes of the shops, then in such a case liability for payment of compensation shall not be imposed.

The reason is that when the permission of the outgoing judge is not proved in this behalf, he became a usurper and when a usurper gives a usurped thing on payment and receives such payment (*ujrat*), then such a payment becomes his property. Hence, the imposition of liability on him of making payment of compensation (*daman*) cannot be thought of irrespective of his being popular in good conduct or not.

161. If the nominated judge says to the *mutawallis*, "I shall not receive from you the whole amount in lumpsum and will receive from you the whole amount by monthly or yearly installments, then there can be two situations, viz.:

❖ If the *wasiyy* or *mutawalli* is popular in his good conduct and honesty and he says, "I possess this much amount," the nominated judge shall not compel him to give separate accounts and will accept his statement along with his oath.

❖ If the *wasiyy* or *mutawalli* is not popular in his good conduct and honesty, the judge should take extra care and caution and check his accounts minutely.

(Allah's mercy be on him) book *Adāb al-Qādi*. [See *Al-Jawāhir al-Mudi'ah*, al-Qarashi, vol. I, p. 318, biographical note no. 318; *Taj al-Tarajum fi Tabaqāt al-Hanafiyyah*, Ibn Qatlubagha, p. 35, biographical note no. 104; *Tabaqāt Ashāb al-Hanafiyyah*, Ibn Hana'i, manuscript no. 20b; *Tabaqāt al-Fuqaha*, Tash Kubrazadah, p. 70; *Miftāh al-Sa'adah*, Tash Kubrazadah, vol. II, pp. 272-273; *Al-Lubāb fi Tahzib al-Ansāb*, Ibn al-Athir, vol. I, p. 380].

❖ If any person insists and says that such and such amount is in balance and in my possession, the judge should not compel him to make clarification. The reason is to compel him amounts to cause harm to him. If he admits of any thing, then in the matter of expenses his statement shall not be accepted. The judge has no power to cause harm to anyone, hence. he has no power to compel him or to make him liable to pay *daman*. It is so because if such a person is accused of dishonesty then mere levelling accusation of dishonisty cannot become the cause to impose liability of payment of *daman* on him. When the power to compel or impose liability to make payment of *daman* is not available to a judge, then he should take oath from the said person and should avoid causing him any harm.

All the above situations are available when the outgoing judge has been dismissed from his office.

If the outgoing judge dies then there is no difference in his death and dismissal. The answer we have given in the matter of the *Mutawallis* and prisoners in the circumstance of dismissal of a judge, is also here in the circumstance of death of a judge.

Knowledge of the People of the Area where a Judge is Posted

162. When a person is appointed as a judge in a city, it is befitting for him that before entering into the city, he should get himself introduced with the jurists, pious, honest, and just people of that city so that he may deal with them according to their status. It is due to the following two reasons.

1. A judge has to turn towards the jurists for decision in the matters coming before him and to purge the creditworthiness

of the witnesses he had to turn towards the pious, honest, and just people so that when the witnesses appear before him to give evidence, it may be possible for him to decide the cases according to the correct situation. It is so because when the proof comes about the creditworthiness of witnesses, they are considered to be so unless there occurs some change in their states.

2. When a judge will enter the city, the people will come to see him including the jurists. Hence, it is necessary for him to get introduction with the residents of that city so that he may give proper treatment to them according to their situation and status.

When a judge is in need of introduction with the residents of the city, it is better for him to send someone in advance as his vice (*nã'ib*), who may obtain the necessary information and will inform the judge when he comes there

When a judge comes in the city, he should ask an honest person of the city as to who are honest persons in the city. He should also enquire this fact from other persons of the city as it may be that his vice (*nã'ib*) might have kept secret the names of some persons. After the creditworthiness and honesty of a person is clear, then he should ask about the creditworthiness of others. In his court room, the judge should give due place to every person.

If the nominated judge belongs to the same city, even then he should also do like this. The reason is that after joining the office of a judge even those people will come to see him who had never met him earlier. He has to get introduction and information about them. Therefore, sending of an envoy on his behalf prior to his own arrival in that city is for the purpose of knowing about the people of that city.

In both the cases, the judge should note the names of those persons so that, at the time of their need, they could be approached.

(Allah knows the best)

CHAPTER 7

To Hold Court in Mosque

Conflict of Opinion of 'Ulamā in respect of holding Court in the Mosque premises

163. *Hasan Basri* (Allah's mercy be on him) stated: "One day at noon time I came in the Masjid al-Madínah (*Masjidun-Nabwí*) and found Ibn 'Affān (Hadrat 'Uthmān Ghaní) (Allah's pleasure be on him) sitting there and made a pillow by collecting pebbles into a heap and putting his cloth sheet on it. His continence was handsome and beard beautiful. The marks of healed measles were apparent on his cheeks and the wrist were hairy. Meanwhile, a water carrier came with a water skin. He was disputing with another person and he started considering their matter."[112]

This *hadíth* throws light on many points some of which are as under:

---

112. *Adãb al-Qãdi*, ImāmKhassāf with marginal notes by al-Jassas, p. 18a; *Fath al-Qadir*, vol. V, p. 4566; Sunan al-Kubra, Al-Bayhaqi, vol. II, p. 447; *Adãb al-Qãdi min al-Hãwi al-Kabir*, al-Mawardi, vol. I, p. 207, note no. 266; *Sirãj al-Mulûk*, al-Tartûshi, p. 53; *Rawdah al-Qudãt*, Ibn al-Samnani, vol. I, p. 99, no. 210.

❖ Hadrat 'Uthmān Ghaní (Allah's pleasure be on him) was of handsome continence and beautiful beard.

There is no harm in sitting in the mosque for administration of justice Hadrat 'Uthmān Ghaní (Allah's pleasure be on him) generally held court sittings in the mosque and prior to him Hadrat 'Umar Fārûq (Allah's pleasure be on him) also held court sitting in the mosque. Likewise, it is befitting for a ruler and a judge to hold court sittings in the mosque so that people may come to them easily.

164. The *'ulamā* have conflict of opinion regarding the matter of holding court sitting in the mosque. According to Ahnaf, there is no harm in it.[113]

Imām Shāfi'i (Allah's mercy be on him) considers it abominable (*makruh*).[114]

Imām Mālik (Allah's mercy be on him) has explained it like this that if the judge is sitting in the mosque at the parties come to him, there is no harm to decide their case in the mosque, but if the judge goes in the mosque with the intention to hold court in it, then it is abominable (*makruh*).[115]

The argument advanced by Imām Shāfi'i (Allah's mercy be on him) that in the court of a judge a polytheist (*mushrik*) will also appear who is impure (*najas*) as per Holy *Qur'ān*. Likewise, a .

---

113. *Fath al-Qadir*, vol. V, p. 465; *al-Hidāyah*, al-marghinani, vol. III, p. 103; *Al-Fatawa al-Hindiyyah*, vol. III, p. 330; *Al-Mabsut* al-Sarakhsi, vol. XVI, p. 81; *Bada'i' al-Sana'i*, al-Kasani, vol. IX, p. 4100; *Rawdah alQudāt*, Ibn al-Samnani, vol. I, p. 98, note no. 207.

114. *Kitāb al-Umm,* vol. VIII, p. 241; *Adāb al-Qādi*, al-Mawardi, vol. I, p. 205 (264)

115. This opinion of Imām Mālik (Allah's mercy be on him) has been quoted by Ibn Farhûn from *al-Mudawwinah* of Imām Mālik. [*Tabsara al-Hukkam*, Ibn Farhûn, vol. I, p. 24].

woman who is going through menses will also appear whose admission in the mosque is prohibited (*mamnû'*). Therefore, the holding of court sitting by a judge in the mosque is abominable (*makruh*).

The proof in support of our (Ahnaf's) argument is the following *hadith* of the Messenger of Allah (peace and blessings of Allah be on him):

"innamã buniyati 'l-masãjida li zikr illahi wa 'l-hukmi"

(The mosques are built for remembrance of Allah and for administration of justice).[116]

The Messenger of Allah (peace and blessings of Allah be on him) has declared both the acts of worshipping Allah (*'ibadat*) and the deciding of cases (*fasl al-khusûmãt*) as equal.

The following *hadith* is a proof of this declaration.

"innã rasûlallãhi (sallallahu 'alayh wasallam) kãnã yafsulû bayna 'l-khusumi fî mu'takafihi"

(Verily, the Messenger of Allah (peace and blessings of Allah

---

116. This *hadith* has been transmitted on the authority of Abû Hurairah (Allah's pleasure be on him), and in it the incident of a bedouin (*a'rabi*) who had urinated in the mosque. The words of *hadith* are: *"innã hazã'l-masjid la yabalu fîhi wa innamã buniya li zikrillãhi wa lissalati"* (Verily, this is a mosque in which urination is not to be passed and it is constructed for remembrance of Allah and to offer prayers in it. [See *Sunan* Ibn Mãjah, Kitãb al-Tahãrah, vol. I, p. 176, *hadith* No. 529; *Sahíh* Muslim, Kitãb al-Nahi 'an-Nashd al-Dallah, vol. I, pp. 397-98, *hadith* Nos. 79, 81; *Jãm' al-Fawã'id min Jãmi' al-usûl wa Majma' al-Fawã'id*, edited by al-Yamani, Vol. I, p. 175, *hadith* Nos. 1219-20; *Sunan al-Kubra*, Al-Bayhaqi, vol. X, pp. 102-103. In all these narrations, the word *"al-hukm"* is not present. See also *Nasb al-Ra'iyah fî Takhrij Ahadith al-Hidãyah*, al-Zayla'i, vol. IV, pp. 70-71; *Al-Dirayah fî Takhrij Ahadith al-Hidãyah*, Ibn Hajar al-'Asqalani, vol. II, p. 168].

be on him) used to decide cases between the parties while he was observing *i 'tikāf).*[117.]

"wa 'l-khulafa 'ur-rāshidūna kānū yajlisuna fi 'l-masajidi li fasli 'l-khusumat"

(The Righteous *Caliphs* (Allah's mercy be on all of them) also used to sit in the mosque to decide disputes).[118]

To the argument of Imām Shāfi'i (Allah's mercy be on him) that a polytheist (*mushrik*) also appears in the court of a judge while he is impure (*najas*), our (Ahnaf's) answer is that here the impurity referred to is not the impurity of body, but the reference is to the impurity of belief. By coming of a polytheist in the mosque, the land of the mosque does not become impure. However, a woman passing through her menses period is after all a Muslim and she will avoid entering in the mosque during such period and will inform the judge of her state of menses. On receipt of such information, the judge shall not put her to the inconvenience of coming to the mosque, but would himself go to her to hear her case or will come uptil the main gate of the mosque as is the court

117. *Nasb al-Ra'iyah fi Takhrij Ahadith al-Hidāyah,* al-Zayla'i, vol. IV, p. 71; *Al-Dirayah fi Takhrij Ahadith al-Hidayah,* Ibn Hajar al-'Asqalani, Vol. II, p. 168, *hadith* No. 820; *Sahih* al-Bukhārī, Bab al-Taqadi wa'l-Mulazamah fi'l-Masjid min Kitāb al-Salāt, vol. I, pp. 62-63; Bāb Raf al-Sawt fi'l-Masajid, vol. I, p. 64; Bāb al-Mulazamah min Kitāb al-Istiqrād, vol. II, p. 41; Bāb al-Sulh bi al-Dayn wa'l 'Ayn min Kitāb al-Sulh, vol. II, p. 77; *Sahih* Muslim, Bāb Istihbāb al-Wad' min al-Dayn min Kitāb al-Musāqāt, vol. III, p. 1192, *hadith* No. 1558; *Sunan* al-Nisā'i, Bāb Ishārah al-Hākim 'alal-Khasmi bi al-Sulhi min Kitāb Adāb al-Qudāt, vol. VIII, p. 244; *Sunan* Abû Dā'ûd, Bāb al-SUlh min Kitāb al-Aqdiyah, vol. III, p. 304, *hadith* No. 3595.

118. *Al-Dirāyah fi Takhrij Ahadith al-Hidayah,* Ibn Hajar al-'Asqalani, vol. II, p. 168, *hadith* No. 820, *Nasb al-Ra'iyah fi Takhrij Ahadith al-Hidayah,* al-Zayla'i, vol. IV, p. 72.

practice in the matter of animals like goats, cows etc., as these animals are not brought into the mosque and the judge hears the case outside the mosque premises and hears the evidence. The same is the situation here.

165. It is narrated that Hadrat 'Umar bin Abdul-'Azíz (Allah's mercy be on him) had issued a circular letter to all the judges in which he had directed as under:

No judge shall court sitting in a mosque as by doing so the polytheist will also enter into it, who are impure.[119] As Allah, the Almighty has said:

"innamã 'l-mushrikûna najasun"

(Verily, the polytheists are impure).   (9:28)

166. Another report says that Hadrat 'Umar bin 'Abdul-'Azíz (Allah's mercy be on him) had written a circular letter that no judge should hold court in the mosque to decide cases.[120]

167. Imãm Khassãf (Allah's mercy be on him) has mentioned the *ahadith* in support of both sides with a view to showing that there was difference of opinion among the past jurists in this matter. Some of them have declared it abominable while some others have not declared it so.

To Hold court sitting on the Way

168. 'Abdul-Rahmãn bin Qays reported, "I saw Yahyã bin Ya'mar[121] deciding cases sitting on the way."[122]

---

119. *Sunan al-Kubra*, Al-Bayhaqi, vol. X, p. 103.

120. *Sunan al-Kubra*, Al-Bayhaqi, vol. X, p. 103.

121. The title of Yahyã bin Ya'mar was Abu Sulaymãn. He was also called Abû 'Adí al-'Udwain al-Basarí. He was a great jurist and judge. He was posted in Marû. He has transmitted Ion the authorities of Hadrat Abû Zarr, Hadrat 'Ammar, Hadrat 'Ã'ishah, Hadrat Abû Hurairah, Hadrat Ibn 'Abbãs, and Hadrat 'Umar (Allah's pleasure be on all of

The reason is that when a judge accepts the responsibility of the office of a judge, it becomes necessary for him to decide the cases. The moment the parties bring their case before him, he should dispose it off without delay. But, while sitting on a way, he should sit in a manner whereby the passer-byes do not feel any inconvenience in traffic. If, by sitting there, the road traffic suffers then he should sit for that purpose on a side of the road.

A judge can stand on the road to decide a case provided that by his standing at that place the passer-byes do not feel any hindrance in the traffic. If any inconvenience occurs in the traffic, he should not stand there for that purpose and should leave that place but should not decide a case while he is walking as in that state he will not be able to have a firm opinion. Hence, he should stop at some proper place and then decide the case.

Deciding Cases by a Judge at His Residence

169. Ibn Mubārak has narrated on the authority of a person

them). And on the authority of him, 'Abdullāh bin Buraidah, Qitādah, Yahyā bin 'Aqil, 'Atā Khurasāni, Sulaymān Taimi, Ishāq bin Suwid al-'Udwi (Allah's mercy be on all of them) transmitted *ahadith*. According to some historians, it is he who, for the fist time, dotted the *Mushaf 'Uthmāni*. He was an eloquent jurist. He had learnt Arabic language from Abû al-Aswad. When Hujjaj banned his entry in the province, he was welcomed by Qutaibah bin Muslim and was appointed the judge of Khurasān. He had many deputies. All agree on the *ahadith* transmitted on his authority. He is reliable in *hadith*. He died before 100 A.H. or after 100 A.H. [See *Tazkarah al-Huffāz*, al-Zahabi, vol. I, pp. 75-76, note no. 73; *Taqrib al-Tahzib*, al-'Asqalani, vol. II, p. 361, note no. 209; *Tārikh*, Khalifah bin Khayyāt, vol. I, p. 306, wherein his date of death is mentioned as 90 A.H.; *Tabaqāt*, Ibn Khayyāt, pp. 203, 322; *Tārikh al-Islām*, al-Zahabi, vol. IV, p. 68; *Akhbār al-Qudāt*, al-Waki', vol. V, pp. 305-306].

122. *Sahih* al-Bukhāri, Kitāb al-Ahkām, vol. IV, p. 159; *Akhbār al-Qudāt*, al-Waki', vol. III, pp. 305-306.

who had said, "I had gone to the house of Yahyā bin Ya'mar and he said to me, 'No one should come to the house of a judge.'"[123]

The *'ulamā* have interpreted these words of Yahyā bin Ya'mar in two ways.

❖ One interpretation is that when a judge feels tired hearing the cases and goes to his own house for taking rest, it is not proper for the litigants to follow him to his residence.

❖ The second interpretation is that none of the parties should visit the house of a judge as it will bring an allegation of partiality against the judge. Therefore, to keep such allegation away from the judge, no party should come to the judge at his residence.

170. It is narrated about Shuraih (Allah's mercy be on him) that he used to decide the cases at his residence on a day when there was rainfall.[124]

It may be for the following reasons.

❖ One reason may be that he had done so for his own convenience because to go to mosque on a rainy day would have been inconvenient for him. As such the rainfall became a just excuse for him. The precedent lies in the *hadíth* of the Messenger of Allah (peace and blessings of Allah be on him) wherein the rainfall has been declared a just excuse. The words of the *hadíth* are: "*izābtalatin-ni ālfa's-salātu*

123. *al-Mabsût* al-Sarakhsi, vol. XVI, p. 82; *Al-Fatawa al-Hindiyyah*, vol. III, p. 320.

124. *Akhbār al-Qudāt*, al-Waki', vol. II, p. 225; *Sahíh* al-Bukhārí, Kitāb al-Ahkām, vol. IV, p. 159; *Al-Mabsût*, al-Sarakhsi, vol. XVI, p. 82; *Fatawa Tatār Khāniyah*, on the margin of *Al-Fatawa al-Hindiyyah*, vol. III, p. 320; *Al-Hidāyah*, al-Marghinani, vol. III, p. 103; *Fath al-Qadir*, vol. V, p. 366.

fi'r-rihāl" (When your shoes become wet, you may offer your prayer at your residences).[125]

When on account of disability caused by rain, the abandonment of congregational prayer is permissible, then the abandonment of visiting the mosque for the purposes of administration of justice is much more permissible.

The second reason may be that he might have liked to sit in his house with a view to keeping the mosque secure from mud as the feet of the people become polluted with mud due to rainfall and he thought it proper to pollute his own residence with the mud than to pollute the mosque with it.

Form and Style of Judge's Dress

171. It is narrated that Hasan bin Ibrāhīm said, "I saw Mahārib bin Daththar[126] deciding cases in the mosque while he had coloured his hair with a black dye.

125. *Talkhis al-Habir*, al-'Asqalani, vol. II, pp. 31-32, *hadith* No. 565; *Sahih* al-Bukhārī, Kitāb al-Azān, vol. I, pp. 80-81, 84; *Sahih* Muslim, Kitāb Salāt al-Musāfirīn, vol. I, p. 484, *hadith* Nos. 697-699; *Sunan* al-Nisā'i, Kitāb al-Azān, vol. II, pp. 14-15; *Sunan* Abū Dá'ūd, Kitāb Iqāmah al-Salāt, vol. I, p. 278, *hadith* Nos. 1057-1065; *Sunan* Ibn Mājah, Kitāb Iqāmah al-Salāt, vol. I, p. 302, *hadith* Nos. 936-939; *Sunan* al-Darimi, Kitāb al-Salāt, vol. I, p. 235, *hadith* No. 1278; *Múwattā'* Imām Mālik, Kitāb al-Nidā' fi al-Safar, vol. I, p. 71 (from *Tanwir al-Hawālik*); *Musnad* Ahmad bin Hanbal, vol. I, p. 277; vol. II, pp. 4, 10, 53, 63, 103; vol. III, p. 316; vol. IV, pp. 167, 220, 346, vol. V, pp. 8, 13, 15, 19, 22, 24, 74, 75, 370, 377.

126. Mahārib bin Daththār al-Sadusi al-Kūfī was a leading and reliable jurist. He was an abstemious (*zāhid*) and pious person . He transmitted *hadith* on the authority of Hadrat 'Ibn 'Umar, Hadrat Abdullāh, Hadrat Jābir bin Abdullāh (Allah's pleasure be on all of them) and from a great number of *Tābi'un*. All agree on his being a

There is conflict of opinion on this subject. According to some jurists to colour the hair with dye is abominable (*makruh*).[127] The reason is that the old age is a light of Allah and to make a change in the light of Allah is not a commendable behaviour.

The generality of *'ulamā* do not consider it abominable. They quote the following report in support of their argument.

It is transmitted that Hadrat Abû Bakr Siddíq (Allah's pleasure be on him) used to dye his hair with *hinā* and *katam*.[128]

Hadrat Abdullāh bin 'Abbās (Allah's pleasure be on him) said, "As I like that my spouse should decorate her for me. Similarly, she likes that I should decorate myself for her."[129]

On this subject there are two transmissions on the authority of Imām Abû Yûsuf (Allah's mercy be on him).

creditworthy (*thiqah*) transmitter of hadíth. He died during the period of governorship of Khālid bin Abdullāh. [See *Tahzib al-Asmā' wa al-Lughāt*, al-Nawāwí, vol. I, p. 2, no. 84; *Akhbār al-Qudāt*, al-Waki', vol. III, p. 25; *Al-Ma'ārif*, Ibn Qutaibah al-Dinuri, p. 490; *Tabaqāt*, Ibn Khayyāt, p. 161; Taqríb *al-Tahzíb*, al-'Asqalani, vol. II, p. 230, note no. 932, where it is mentioned that he died in the year 116 A.H; *Akhbār al-Qudāt*, al-Waki', vol. III, p. 31].

127. Imām Mawardi al-Shāfi'i has gone to the extent that he said, "To colour hair with a dye is an absurdity and due to it the testimony will be rejected." [See *Kitāb al-Shahādat min al-Hāwi al-Kabír*, p. 4521].

128. It is a red colour used as a dye. See *al-Lisān*, maddah h-m-r, vol. IV, p. 210; *Sahíh* Muslim, Kitāb al-Fadā'il, vol. IV, p. 1821, *hadíth* No. 2341, *Sunan* Abû Dā'ûd, Kitāb al-Tarajjul, vol. IV, p. 86, *hadíth* No. 4209; *Musnad* Ahmad bin Hanbal, vol. III, pp. 100-108, 178, 192, 198, 206 and 251; *Al-'Iqd al-Farid*, Ibn 'Abd Rabbihi, vol. II, p. 354; *Majma' al-Zawā'id*, al-'Irāqi wa ibn Hajar, vol. V, pp. 59-60; *Mawārid al-Zam'ān ila Zawā'id IbnHabbān*, al-Haithami, p. 356, *hadíth* No. 1476.

129. *Al-Durr al-Manthûr fi al-Tafsir bi'l-Ma'thûr*, vol. I, p. 276; *Tafsir*,, al-Qurtubí, vol. III, pp. 123-124.

❖ According to one narration, if anyone colours his hair with dye during the state of war, there is no harm in it. They have analogically deduced this value from the permission of growing nails and moustaches abnormally. As there is no harm in their growing during the state of war.

The growing of moustaches untrimmed is with a view to make oneself awful in the eyes of the enemy and the non-paring of nails is to use them as a weapon of war. To do so is not permissible when the state of war is over. The same is the command here.

❖ The second narration is that if a person colours his hair with a dye for the sake of his spouse or maid to look beautiful in her eyes, there is no harm in it.

172. It is narrated on the authority of Abû Tālût that he said, "I saw Qādi Shuraih deciding cases in the mosque while he was wearing a silk shawl."[130]

The object of Imām Khassāf (Allah's mercy be on him) by the mention of this report is that a judge should wear a dignified dress while holding court so that he may appear respectful in the sight of litigant public.

The proof in support of it is the report that the Messenger of Allah (peace and blessings of Allah be on him) used to wear a gown of sable-skin on the occasion of *'idayn, jumu'ah*, and when the foreign deputation called upon him.[131]

---

130. *Akhbār al-Qudāt*, al-Waki', vol. II, pp. 215-217; *al-Mabsût*, al-Sarakhsi, vol. XVI, p. 80.

131. *Nasb al-Ra'iyāh fi Takhrij Ahadith al-Hidayāh*, al-Zayla'i, vol. II, p. 209; *al-Dirayah fi Takhrij Ahadith al-Hidāyah*, Ibn Hajar al-'Asqalani, vol. I, p. 218, *hadith* No. 281; *Kitāb al-Umm*, Imām al-Shāfi'i, vol. I, p. 206; *Mukhtasar al-Muzani min Kalām al-Shafi'i*, vol. I, p. 151; *Musnad Imām Shāfi'i*, vol. VI, p. 107; *Al-Matālib al-'Aliyah bi Zawā'id al-masanid al-Thamaniyah*, Ibn Hajar, vol. I, p.

173. Abû Tâlib said, "Qãdi Shuraih continued deciding the cases of litigants till late in the night and when the people came early in the next morning, he said to them loudly, 'Have you been a victim of oppression during the night just passed.'"[132]

Cases of Jews and Christians and Women

174. Jãbir narrated: "Amir Sha'bi used to hear and decide the cases of the Jews, the Christians and the menstruating women at the outer gate of the mosque."[133]

According to us there is no harm of coming of *zimmis* (non-Muslims) into the mosque. However the women who are menstruating or post pregnancy period, there cases should be heard and decided at the outer gate of the mosque.

Proper Place of Sitting for Holding Court

175. Imãm Abû Hanifah (Allah's mercy be on him) said, "A judge should sit in the *jami'a Masjid* as it is the most popular public place."

The reason is that the parties consist of the local residents and also outstation persons. Hence, a judge should hold court sittings at a place which is a well known public place.

176. There is no harm in it if a judge holds court sittings in the muhalla mosque. It is so because it is not necessary for a judge to go to the parties himself. If a judge fixes a place for holding court, he should intimate the parties about it.

171, *hadith* No. 621; *Sunan al-Kubra*, Al-Bayhaqi, vol. III, p. 280; *Majma' al-Zawã'id*, al-'Irãqi wa ibn Hajar, vol. II, p. 198.

132. *Akhbãr al-Qudãt*, al-Waki', vol. II, p. 336; *al-Mabsût*, al-Sarakhsi, vol. XVI, p. 80.

133. *Akhbãr al-Qudãt*, al-Waki', vol. II, pp. 415-416.

177. Likewise, if a judge holds court sittings at his own residence there is no harm in it. He should permit the people and should not restrain anyone to enter his residence. In such circumstance, he may make such a person to sit with him who used to sit with him when he was holding court sitting in the mosque.

The reason is that if he sits all alone, he may be accused of partiality.

Opening Session of a Court

178. When a judge enters in the mosque, it is better for him to offer two or four *rak'āts* of *nafl* prayer as it is transmitted on the authority of Abû Sa'íd al-Khudari (Allah's pleasure be on him) that the Messenger of Allah (peace and blessings of Allah be on him) said:

"man dakhal'l-masjida fa'l-yuhayyihu bi rak'atayni"

Whosoever enters a mosque, he should offer two *rak'ats* of prayer of *tahiyyatul-masjid.*)[134]

He may offer four *rak'āts* of *nawāfil* as it is also reported that the Messenger of Allah (peace and blessings of Allah be on him) said:

"al-salātu khayrun dā'imun, faman sha'ā istaqall wa man sha'ā istakthar"

(The best act of worship is that which is constant. So whosoever may desire to make increase in it and whosoever may

---

134. *Mawārid al-Zam'ān ila zawā'id Ibn Habbān*, al-Haithami, p. 102, *hadith* No. 325; see also p. 52 of this book; *Sahih* al-Bukhārí, kitāb al-salāt, vol. I, p. 61; kitāb al-tahajjud, vol. I, p. 139; *Sahih* Muslim, kitāb salāt al-musafirin, vol. I, p. 495, *hadith* No. 714; *Sunan* al-Tirmizi, kitāb al-salāt, vol. I, p. 198; *Talkhis al-Habir*, al-'Asqalani, vol. II, p. 20, *hadith* No. 536.

desire to make a decrease in it).[135]

But to offer four *rak'āts* in *nawafil* is superior as this is a *nafl* worship of daytime and it is better to offer four *rak'āts* prayer in daytime.

179. There is conflict of opinion among the *'ulamā* in the matter of offering the prayer of *tahiyyatul-masjid* immediately on entrance in the mosque and then hold court siting or first sit and then to stand up for the said prayer. According to some of the *'ulama* the judge should after his entry into the mosque sit down and then stand up for offering of the said prayers. According to the generality of the *'ulama* the judge should after his entry in to the mosque offer the prayer *tahiyyatul-masjid*.

180. A judge should pray Allah, the Almighty that He may grant him courage and fortitude (*tawfiq*) and guide him towards the truth and secure him from sins. After this he should begin his court work.

Best Court Sitting is that which Faces Qiblah

181. A judge should sit facing Qiblah in all his court sittings.

The authority in this behalf is the following *hadith* of Messenger of Allah (peace and blessings of Allah be on him):

"khayrul-majālisi mā istaqbala bihi'l-qiblata."

(The best session is that which is facing the Qiblah).[136]

---

135. *Al-Jāmi' al-Saghir*, al-Suyûti, vol. II, p. 51; *Kashf al-Khifa'* al-'Ujluni al-Jurrahi, vol. II, p. 38, *hadith* No. 1616; *Musnad* Ahmad bin Hanbal, vol. V, p. 265; *Mawārid al-Zam'ān ila zawā'id Ibn Habbān*, al-Haithami, p. 52, *hadith* No. 94.

136. Al-Maqāsid al-Hasanah, al-Sakhawi, pp. 76-77, *hadith* No. 153; *Kashf al-Khifa'* al-'Ujluni al-Jurrahi, vol. I, p. 192, *hadith* No. 505; *Al-Jāmi' al-Saghir*, al-Suyûti, vol. I, pp. 42, 55; *Bahjah al-Majālis*, Ibn Abd al-Barr, vol. I, p. 41; *Adāb al-Qādi*, al-Mawardi, vol. I, p. 219.

During that period this was the custom but now a days a judge sits taking the support of arch (*mihrāb*) which is also in accordance with the following practice of the Messenger of Allah (peace and blessings of Allah be on him) that after completing the prayer he (peace and blessings of Allah be upon him) used to sit taking support of the arch and thereafter as' ed the Companions (Allah's pleasure be on them):

"hal ra'a minkum ru'yan"

(Has any one of you seen any dream?)[137]

Similarly when a sermon deliverer (*khatib*) delivers a sermon from the pulpit (*mimbar*) his back is towards the *qiblah*. The reason is that when a judge will sit in a court while his back is towards *qiblah* the parties appearing before him in the cases will be facing the *qiblah* and thereby the chances of their inclination to tell a lie will reduce.

Place of standing of court Guard

182. The court guard shall stand in front of the judge at a place from where they may not hear the proceedings.

The reason is that the session of a judge is a dignified and awe inspiring session. Therefore his guard should stand before him so that he may look dignified (respectful) in the eyes of the litigant public.

---

137. *Sahih* al-Bukhārí, kitāb alta'bír, vol. VI, p. 148; *Sahih* Muslim, kitāb al-ru'ya, vol. IV, pp. 1778-79, *hadíth* No. 2629; p. 1781, *hadíth* No. 2275; *Sunan* al-Darimi, kitāb al-ru'ya, vol. II, pp. 53-54, *hadíth* No. 2162; *Sunan* al-Tirmizi, kitāb al-ru'ya, vol. III, pp. 368-369, *hadíth* No. 2389; p. 372, *hadíth* No. 2396; *Sunan* Abû Dā'ûd, kitāb al-sunnah, vol. IV, p. 208, *hadíth* No. 4634; *Muwatta* Imām Mālik, (Tanwír al-Hawālik), vol. II, p. 237; *Musnad*, Ahmad bin Hanbal, vol. II, p. 146; vol. IV, p. 244; vol. V, pp. 14, 44, 50.

Place of keeping Court Box

183 A judge should keep his court box in front of him on his right side.

The reason of keeping it in front of the judge is that the court box is a tool of the judge as it contains the registers of his orders, the registers containing the proceedings of the cases. the copies of all sorts of contracts. The tool or the weapon of a ruler (or a judge) must be in front of him.

The reason of keeping it on the right side of the judge is that there is a report:

"kanā yakhtārul-tayammun fī kulli shay'in"

(He, i.e., the Messenger of Allah (peace and blessings of Allah be on him) liked the right side in everything).[138]

184. The reader should bring this box from the residence of the judge to the mosque and keep it before the judge as it is the tool of the judge and he should put it in front of him. The precedent on this point is that such sort of things were kept by the Messenger of Allah (peace and blessings of Allah be on him) in front of him.

Even today the court practice is that the judges keep the files before them.

138. *Sahih* al-Bukhāri, kitāb al-wudū, vol. I, p. 30; *Sunan* Ibn Mājah, kitāb al-taharah, vol. I, p. 141, *hadith* No. 3, 301-302; kitāb al-janā'iz, vol. I, p. 469, *hadith* No. 1459, *Sunan* Abū Dā'ūd, kitāb al-janā'iz vol. III, p. 197, *hadith* No. 3145; *Sunan* al-Tirmizi, kitāb al-Janā'iz, vol. II, pp. 229-230, *hadith* No. 995; *Sunan* al-Nisā'i kitāb al-janā'iz, vol. IV, p. 30; *Musnad* Ahmad bin Hanbal, vol. VI, p. 408; *Al-Kashshāf,* al-Zamakhshari, vol. III, p. 299; *Kitāb al-Kāfi al-Shāf fi Takhrij ahadith al-Kashshaf,* p. 141, *hadith* No. 289.

Seat of Court Reader

185. Court reader should sit at a place away from the judge from where the judge could see him so that he may not indulge in any illegal activity, such as taking of bribe or committing any fraud by addition or omission in the evidence (or court proceedings).

Seat of Jurisconsults

186. Jurisconsults (*ahl al-fiqh*) and creditworthy persons (*ahl al-amānah*) shall be seated near the judge. The reason of seating arrangement of jurisconsults near the judge is that they have to give advice. This object can be achieved only when they are seated at a near distance. However, the matter of the court guard is altogether different from them. They are to stand at a distance away from the judge because they are standing to maintain the decorum of the court. Such objective can be achieved only when they stand at a distance away from the judge.

Likewise, the creditworthy persons (*ahl al-amānah*) are to be seated near to the judge. The reason is that the creditworthy persons come in the court to give evidence or to note the conversation of the judge. In the first case, a judge should give them proper respect and in the second case, the object can only be achieved when they sit near the judge.

Draw of Name Slips

187. After that the judge should open his court box or his Court Reader should open it but the later should not put his hand into it so that he may not put any thing into it which was not already in it. The judge should himself bring out the name slips of the litigants cases of that day. The method of making such slips has already been stated earlier.

Conflict of Opinion among 'Ulamã regarding questioning the Plaintiff about His Suit

188. When both the parties to a suit appear before the judge, he should ask the plaintiff: What is your claim?

There is conflict of opinion in this matter. According to some 'ulamã the judge should remain silent and the plaintiff should himself state his case and the judge should not put any question about it.

The stand of Imãm Khassãf (Allah's mercy be on him) is that a judge shall ask such question to the plaintiff. The reason is that the session of a judge is an awful session and a person who has not seen such session he will be perplexed and will not be in a position to submit his claim. Therefore, a judge should make him intimate by his conversation so that he may be able to plead his case before him.

Accordinig to Imãm Muhammad (Allah's mercy be on him), it is a discretion of the judge to put or not to put a question [as suggested by Imãm Khassãf (Allah's mercy be on him)]. To proceed either way is valid.

Pleading in Writing

189. When a suit is brought before a judge, he should record it at verbatim without any addition or omission and thereafter to look into it if the claim is correct or not.

If the claim is not correct, the judge shall not put it to the defendant nor ask him to answer the facts alleged. He should tell to the plaintiff that his suit is not correct and he should correct it and re-institute it (in a valid manner).

At that time such a direction by the judge is only of the nature of an advice (*fatwa*) and a judge should advise only of a matter of which he has knowledge.

If the claim is correct, then according to the Hanafi masters of law (*masha'ikh*) the judge should not ask any question from the defendant but should become attentive to the defendant who has heard the claim of the plaintiff and will himself give the reply. Therefore, a judge should listen to him attentively.

According to Imām Khassāf (Allah's mercy be on him), the judge should become attentive towards the defendant and should ask him: "Such and such is the claim against you, what do you want to say about it?" If the defendant admits the claim, the judge should record it on a sheet of paper along with date and direct the defendant to produce the object regarding which he has made an admission. The judge should record the admission at verbatim without any addition or omission. The judge should also record the identification of both the parties if he knows them personally. The language of recorded proceeding should be in the following form:

"A the son, of B has made admission of the right of C the son of D."

If the judge does not know both the parties to the suit personally, then the form of recording of admission shall be as under:

"A person who has given statement that he is A, son of B, has made an admission of the right regarding the person whom he says is C, son of D."

If the judge knows one of the parties to the suit, but does not know the other, he should record the identity of the person whom he knows. And the person whom he does not know he should record his identity as stated by that person in his own words. This is to be done only when the defendant makes an admission of the claim of the plaintiff as alleged in the suit. In case the defenedant denis the claim, the judge should record the denial on the same sheet of the paper on which he had recorded the claim of the plaintiff.

The reason is that the need to be acquainted with the denial arises only after a claim is made and a suit is instituted because sometimes it so happens that the plaintiff makes a claim of his deposit and the defendant totally denies it. Thereafter, the defendant states that he had returned the deposit in question or the same had been destroyed. In such circumstance, his such claim will not be admissible. This proves that the need to be acquainted with the denial arises only after the suit is instituted. Therefore, the judge should record such denial on the same sheet of paper on which he had recorded the plaint of the plaintiff.

The judge should record the denial statement of the defendant at verbatim and should not translate it in Arabic. He should translate it into Arabic when there is no possibility of any addition or omission in it. He should also not write any ambiguous or common word that may create any doubt. If this is not possible, then he should record it in the language of the defendant and should also enter date on it.

Imām Khassāf (Allah's mercy be on him) has mentioned this procedure of recording proceedings. However, now a days a different procedure is in vogue in the courts, which is better than this. The new procedure is that when a plaintiff comes to the court, he consults some counsel (*wakil*) and the later advices him to get the plaint written by a petition writer (*kātib*) and scribed on a sheet of a paper. He should also write the title of the parties and when the other party also comes, both should appear before the judge along with the said plaint. In this manner, it will be convenient for judges and also for the parties and they will not have to visit repeatedly the court and the petition writer (*kātib*).

Demand of Proof from the Plaintiff in Case of Denial of the Claim by the Defendant

190. If the defendant denies the claim, then according to the Hanafi masters of law (*mashā'ikh*) the judge should not ask any question from the plaintiff while according to Imãm Khassãf (Allah's mercy be on him), the judge should ask the plaintiff. "Have you any proof as the defendant has denied your claim.?"

Whether Proof can be Demanded from the Plaintiff where a Plaintiff demands oath from the Defendant?

191. Where a plaintiff applies to the court to take oath from the defendant regarding his claim, then according to the Hanafi masters of law (*mashā'ikh*), the judge should not demand witnesses from the plaintiff. According to Imãm Khassãf (Allah's mercy be on him), the judge should ask the plaintiff, "Have you witnesses?" As it is narrated that when the case of a Hadrami and a Kindi came for decision before the Messenger of Allah (peace and blessings of Allah be on him), he asked the plaintiff:

"*a laka bayyinatun? Qãla: lã.*"

(Have you got proof?" 'No,' said he.)

"*qãla: laka yaminuhu*"

He (peace and blessings of Allah be on him) said to the Hadrami: "Then there is his oath for you."[139]

139. *Sahih* Muslim, kitāb al-aymãn, vol. I, pp. 123-124, *hadith* Nos. 223-224; *Sahih Muslim bi Sharh al-nawãwi*, vol. II, p. 159, 162; *Talkhis al-Habir*, al-'Asqalani, vol. IV, p. 208, *hadith* No. 2137; *Sunan* Abû Dã'ûd, kitãb al-aymãn, vol. III, p. 221, *hadith* No. 3245; kitãb al-'aqdiyah, vol. III, p. 312, *hadith* No. 3623; *Sunan*, al-Tirmizi, kitãb al-ahkam, vol. II, pp. 398-399, *hadith* No. 1355; *Tuhfah*, al-Ahwazi, p. 1355; *Musnad* Ahmad bin Hanbal, vol. III, pp. 379, 423, 426; vol. IV, pp. 192, 317; vol. V, pp. 25, 79, 211-212; *Jãmi' al-Usûl*, Ibn Athir, Vol. XII, p. 296, *hadith* No. 9249; *Sunan* Darãqutni, vol. IV, p. 211, *hadith* No. 26; *Sunan al-Kubra*, Al-Bayhaqi, vol. X, p. 254; *Nasb al-Ra'iyah fi Takhrij Ahadith al-Hidãyah*, al-Zayla'i, vol. IV, p. 94; *al-Dirayah fi Takhrij Ahadith al-Hidãyah*, Ibn Hajar al-'Asqalani, vol. II, p. 175,

192. If the plaintiff states: "I have no proof." Then the judge should take oath from him.

The reason is that the oath is the right of the plaintiff as the proof is the right of the defendant. The basis of it is the following hadith of the Messenger of Allah (peace and blessings of Allah be on him):

"innamā laka shahidāni au yaminahu."

(Either you plaintiff) produce two witnesses or the defendant is to give his oath).[140]

This proves that to take oath from the defendant is the right of the plaintiff.

193. If the plaintiff states, "Yes, my witnesses are present," or he states, "Yes, they are present in the court," the judge shall not accept the demand of the plaintiff to take oath from the defendant and should not take oath from the defendont. All the leading jurists (*a'immah*) are agreed upon this point.

Imām Qudûri[141] in his commentary of Imām Khassāf's book *Adāb al-Qādi* stated that if the plaintiff replying in the affirmative

hadith No. 839; *Sunan* Ibn Mājah, kitāb al-ahkām, vol. II, p. 778, hadith No. 2322; *Adāb al-Qādi*, al-Mawardi, vol. II, pp. 97, 98, 263, 349, 372; vol. III, sec. 4104.

140. *Talkhis al-Habir*, al-'Asqalani, vol. IV, p. 198, hadith No. 2107; *Sahih* al-Bukhārī, kitāb al-rahn, vol. II, p. 52; kitāb al-shahādat, vol. II, p. 71-72; kitāb al-diyat, vol. IV, p. 129; *Sahih* Muslim, kitāb al-aymān, vol. I, p. 123, *hadith* No. 221; *Musnad* Ahmad bin Hanbal, vol. V, p. 211.

141. His name was Ahmad. His father's name was Muhammad. His grand-father's name was Ahmad. His great-grand father's name was Ja'far, and his great-great-grand-father's name was Hamdān. He was famous with the title Abū al-Hasan bin Abī Bakr al-Baghdādi al-Qudûri. He was a well-known jurist and Imam. He was the author of *Al-Mukhtasar (Al-Qudûri)*. He was born in 362 A.H. He learnt *fiqh* from Imām Abū Abdullāh Muhammad bin Yahyā al-

said, "I have the witnesses," then, according to the view of Imām Abū Hanifah (Allah's mercy be on him), the judge should not accept the demand of the plaintiff (to take oath from the defendant), but according to Imām Abū Yūsuf (Allah's mercy be on him), the judge should accept the demand of the plaintiff and shall take oath from the defendant.

The view of Imām Muhammad (Allah's mercy be on him) on this issue is not confirmed one (*mudtarab*). Imām Qudūri has mentioned his opinion being in conformity with the opinion of Imām Abū Hanifah (Allah's mercy be on him), while Imām Khassāf (Allah's mercy be on him) has written that his opinion is in conformity with the opinion of Imām Abū Yūsuf (Allah's mercy be on him).

Jurjani. Abū Nasr Ahmad bin Muhammad bin Muhammad learnt *fiqh* from him and also wrote a commentary of his book *Al-Mukhtasar*. He transmitted *hadith* on the authority of Muhammad bin Ali bin Suwayd al-Mu'addab and Ubaydullāh bin Muhammad al-Jaushani and from him the chief justice Abū Abdullāh al-Damighani and Khatib transmitted the *hadith* onward. Khatib stated, "I copied *hadith* from him." From him very few *ahadith* have been transmitted. He is of those personalities who became expert in *fiqh* on account of their high intellectual acumen. The leadership of Hanafi *'ulamā* ended at him. He was greatly respected among them. He was daring in his speech. He often recited the Holy *Qur'ān*. Ibn Hanna'i has counted him amongst the category of *ashāb tarjih*. He died in the year 428 A.H. See *Tārikh Baghdād*, al-Khatib, vol. IV, p. 377; *Wafiyyāt al-A'yān*, Ibn Khalqan, vol.I, p. 26; *Al-Nujūm al-Zāhira*, Ibn Taghri Burdi, vol. V, pp. 24-25; *Al-Lubāb fi Tahzib al-Ansab*, Ibn al-Athir, vol. III, pp. 17-18; *Al-Bidāyah wa'l-Nihāyah*, Ibn Kathir, vol. XII, p. 4; *Shazarāt al-Zahab*, Ibn al-'Imad al-Hanbali, vol. III, p. 233; *Mir'at al-Janān*, al-Yafi'i, vol. III, p. 47; *Al-Jawāhir al-Mudi'ah*, al-Qarashi, vol. I, pp. 93-94, note no. 180; *Tāj al-Tarājum fi Tabaqāt al-Hanafiyyah*, Ibn Qatlubagha, p. 7, note no. 13; *Tabaqāt al-Hunafa*, Tāsh Kubrazada, p. 79; *Rauda al-Jannāt*, al-Khawansari, pp. 66-67; *Tabaqāt*, Ibn Hanā'i, pp. 22b, 23a; *Miftāh al-Sa'ādah*, Tash Kubrazadah, vol. II, p. 280; *Mu'jam al-Musannifin*, Taunki, vol. I, pp. 155-157, *Kashf al-Zunūn*, Haji Khalifah, vol. I, p. 46.

The argument of *sahibain* (Imãm Abû Yûsuf and Imãm Muhammad) is that the oath is the right of the plaintiff which is proved by the text (*nass*). When the plaintiff makes a demand of his right to be fulfilled by the defendant, the judge should accept such demand.

The argument of Imãm Abû Hanifah (Allah's mercy be on him) is that the *shari'ah* has declared the taking of oath essential in the absence of the witnesses as the Messenger of Allah (peace and blessings of Allah be on him) had asked the plaintiff, "Have you the witnesses (proof)?" And when the plaintiff had replied in the negative, the Messenger of Allah (peace and blessings of Allah be on him) had said, "For you is the oath of the defendant."

Besides this, oath is a substitute (*al-khalf*) of proof and a substitute is taken into consideration in the absence of the original (*al-'asl*).

Anyhow, there is conflict of opinion regarding this issue.

A judge who does not adopt the stand of taking of oath may not take the oath and a judge who adopts the stand of taking oath may take the oath.

194. Where a plaintiff states before the judge, "My witnesses are present, please hear their evidence," the judge shall call the witnesses. As the judge has already recorded the claim of the plaintiff and now he should hear his witnesses and if he finds that the evidence is in accordance with the claim, he should collect the whole evidence and send it to the reader to prepare a file.

195. When the plaint and written statement are recorded in black and white, the judge shall read it out to the plaintiff that he has used for such subject matter and should also read out the written statement to the defendant. If both the parties reply in the affirmative, the judge should keep the pleadings in his custody as a court record.

Whether a Witness Should Himself Begin to Give Testimony

196. *When* the witness appears in the court before the judge he shall not begin the evidence himself till the judge asks him: "Of what you want to give evidence?"

After that the judge should put before him questions about each and every relevant fact with details and get information from him.

Imām Tahāwí[142] (Allah's mercy be on him) said; "If a witness starts giving his evidence himself there is no harm in it."

142. His name was Ahmad. His father's name was Muhammad. His grandfather's name was Salamah. His great-grandfather's name was Muslim. His great-great grandfather's name was Abdul Mãlik. His great-great-great-grandfather's name was Salamah. His great-great-great-great-grandfather's name was Sãlim. His great-great-great-great-great-gandfather's name was Hubãb. He was famous as al-Uzadi, al-Hijri, al-Misrí, al-Tahāwí. His surname was Abû Ja'far. He was an eminent Imãm of Hanafiyyah. He was born in 227 A.H. He learnt *fiqh* form his maternal uncle Abû Ibrāhím Isma'il bin Yahyā al-Muzani (who was a pupil of Imãm Shāfí'i). And transmitted *al-Musnad* of Imãm Shāfí'i on his authority. Abû BakrAhmad bin Muhammad bin Mansûr al-Damighani learnt *fiqh* from him. He has left behind a great juristic heritage of ten books including *Ma'ani al-Athãr* and *Bayãn Mushkil al-Athãr*. His *al-Mukhtasar* is very popular. He compiled all those books when he separated from his maternal uncle and adopted the Hanafi school of thought. He has a high rank among the Hanafi *fuqaha*. He died in 321 A.H. See *Al-Jawāhir al-Mudi'ah*, al-Qarashi, vol. I, pp. 102-105, biographical

The reason behind the statement of Imām Khassāf (Allah's mercy be on him) is that to give evidence before its demand is a sign of falsehood as the Messenger of Allah (peace and blessings of Allah be on him) said:

"thumma yafshû'l kizba fa yashhadur-rajulu qabla'an yastashhada wa yahlafu qabla 'an yastahlafa."

(Thereafter, the falsehood will spread to such an extent that before the seeking of an evidence from a person he will give it and before the seeking of an oath from a person he will take it).[143]

note no. 205; *Tāj al-Tarājum fi Tabaqāt al-Hanafiyyah*, Ibn Qatulbagha, pp. 8-9, biographical note no. 15; *Tabaqāt al-Fuqahā*, Tāsh Kubrazādah, p. 45; *Tabaqāt*, Ibn al-Hāna'i, pp. 17 a-b; *Al-Hāwi fi Sirah al-Imām Abi Ja'far al-Tahāwi*, Muhammad Zāhid al-Kauthari,. *Miftātah al-Sa'adah*, Tāsh Kubrazādah, vol. II, pp. 275-276; *Mu'jam al-Musannifin*, Taunki, vol. I, p. 155; *Muqaddamah Kitāb al-Shurūt al-Saghir wa'l-Kabir*, Rūmi Uzjah and *Muqaddamah Kitāb Mukhtasar al-Tahāwi*, Abul Wafā al-Afghāni, pp. 1-14.

143. *Sunan* al-Tirmizi, kitāb al-fitan, vol. III, p. 315, *hadith* No. 2254; kitāb al-shahādat, vol. III, p. 376, *hadith* No. 2404; *Sunan* Ibn Mājah, Kitāb al-ahkām, vol. II, p. 791, *hadith* No. 2363; *Mawarid al-Zam'ān ila zawā'id Ibn Habbān*, al-Haithami, p. 568, hadith Nos. 2282-83; *Musnad* Ahmad bin Hanbal, vol. I, p. 18; *Talkhis al-Habir*, al-'Asqalani, vol. IV, p. 204, *hadith* No. 2130; *Sahih* al-Bukhāri, kitāb al-shahādat, vol. II, p. 68; kitāb al-fada'il, vol. II, p. 186; kitāb al-riqāq, vol. IV, p. 81; kitāb al-aymān wa'l-nuzur, vol. IV, pp. 104-108; *Sahih* Muslim, kitāb al-fada'il, vol. IV, p. 1962, *hadith* Nos. 210-212; p. 1964, *hadith* No. 214; *Sahih Muslim Sharh* al-Nawāwi, vol. XVI, pp. 84, 86, 87, 89; *Sunan*, Ibn Mājah, kitāb al-ahkām, vol. II, p. 791, *hadith* Nos. 2362-63; *Sunan*, Abū Dā'ūd, kitāb al-sunnah, vol. IV, p. 214, *hadith* No. 4657; *Musnad*, Ahmad bin Hanbal, vol. I, pp. 378, 417, 434, 438, 442; vol. II, pp. 228, 410, 479; vol. IV, pp. 267, 276, 277, 426, 427, 436, 440; vol. V, p. 350; *Adāb al-Qādi*, al-Mawardi, vol. I, p. 270, *hadith* No. 439; p. 465, *hadith* No. 1028; kitāb al-shahadat min al-hawi al-kabir, p. 4030; *Kashf al-Khifā* al-'Ujluni al-Jurrahi, vol. I,

When it is counted amongst the science of falsehood and it is necessary to avoid falsehood, hence, the witness should remain silent till the judge asks him, "Of what have you come to give evidence?" The reason behind what has been stated by Imãm Tahãwí (Allah's mercy be on him) is that a witness who gives evidence without its demand is the best witness as the Messenger of Allah (peace and blessings of Allah be on him) said:

"'a lã 'unabbi'ukum bi khayrish-shuhada'i? qãlû 'na'am, yã rasûlallãh.'" Qãla, "an yash-hada qabla an yatluba minhu."

(Should I not inform you of the best of the witnesses? They (the Companions) submitted, "Yes, O Messenger of Allah (peace and blessings of Allah be on him)!" He (peace and blessings of Allah be upon him) said, "A person who gives evidence before it is demanded from him.")[144]

When such a witness is the best witness, why his evidence be treated as a sign of falsehood?

The interpretation of the prophetic words *"qabla an yastash-hada"* is *"qabla an yatahammala"* (i.e., before bearing the testimony he gives the testimony). The example of it is in the

pp. 475-76, *hadith* No. 1265; *Mishkãt al-Masãbih,* al-Khatíb al-Tabrizi, vol. III, p. 218, *hadith* Nos. 6001-2; *Sunan al-Kubra,* Al-Bayhaqi, vol. X, p. 160; *Sunan* al-Nisã'i, vol. VII, pp. 17-18.

144. *Sahih* Muslim, kitãb al-aqdi'ah, vol. III, p. 344, *hadith* No. 19; *Sharh* al-Nawãwí, vol. XII, pp. 16-17; *Tanwir al-Hawãlik,* vol. II, p. 107; *Sharh al-Mu'awattã,* al-Zurqani, vol. IV, p. 473; *Sunan* Ibn Mãjah, kitãb al-ahkãm, vol. II, p. 792, *hadith* No. 2364; *Sunan* Abû Dã'ûd, kitãb al-aqdi'ah, vol. III, pp. 373-74, *hadith* Nos. 2397-99; *Tuhfah,* al-Ahwazi, pp. 2397-99; *Jãmi' al-Usûl,* Ibn Athir, vol. X, p. 561, *hadith* No. 7678; *Musnad* Ahmad bin Hanbal, vol. I, p. 18; vol. IV, pp. 115-117; vol. V, p. 193; *Sunan al-Kubra,* Al-Bayhaqi, vol. X, p. 159; *Talkhis al-Habir,* al-'Asqalani, vol. IV, p. 204, *hadith* No. 2131.

following verse of the Holy *Qur 'ān*:

"*wastash-hadû shahidayni min rijālikum.*"

"....And make two persons from among you as witnesses...."

(2:282)

Here the word *istishhād* means to bear evidence.[145]

In What Words a Judge should put Questions to a Witness

197. When a judge puts a question to a witness, he should say, "Of what fact you want to give evidence?" A judge should not say to the witness, "How will you give evidence?"

The reason is that such an utterance on the part of a judge would amount to put a leading question to a witness.

Summary Evidence and its Details

198. Where a witness gives evidence and fully explains it and thereafter, the second witness gives the evidence by saying, "I give the testimony like the testimony of my co-witness." The judge shall not accept it till each witness gives his own independent statement in evidence.

The reason is that it will be an ambiguous form and there is possibility that he may be referring by such statement to the earlier part or the middle part of the final part of the statement of the first witness. Likewise, there is possibility that he may be concealing certain facts and is intending to avoid some harm and thus makes the matter complicated for the judge. The evidence is an authoritative proof (*hujjat*) in deciding the cases. Therefore, it is not necessary for a judge to base his decision on an evidence which carries such possibilities.

145. *Sharh Sahih Muslim*, al-Nawāwi, vol. XII, p. 17.

Shams al-A'immah Imām Hulwāni (Abû Muhammad Abd al-Aziz Ahmad) has said that Imām Khassāf (Allah's mercy be on him) has taken care and caution by stating that the summary evidence of witnesses should not be accepted. Otherwise, according to us, if the first witness gives evidence and fully explains all the facts and thereafter, the second witness states, "I give the same testimony which the first witness had given," it will be taken as sufficient. The reason is that the second witness has based his own testimony on the testimony of the first witness and (it is a rule that) a building is like its basis.

Shams al-A'immah Imām Hulwāni (Allah's mercy be on him) has further stated that this issue demands further details. If a witness is eloquent and can state the evidence with full details, the summary will not be accepted from him as is the stand of Imām Khassāf (Allah's mercy be on him). If he is a non-Arab ('*ajami*) and non-eloquent, his summary (*brief*) evidence will be accepted provided that the awe of the court room does not become a hindrance and he is able to express the evidence with his own tongue. If the awe of the court room becomes a hindrance and he is unable to utter a single word of evidence from his tongue, then his evidence will not be accepted.

Shams al-A'immah Imām Sarakhsi (Allah's mercy be on him) said that this issue demands such detail as that if a judge feels that a witness is dishonestly making a false evidence, he should ask details of the evidence from each witness as is the stand of Imām Khassāf (Allah's mercy be on him). But if the judge does not feel any dishonesty on the part of any witness, then he should not ask explanation of evidence from each witness and should give decision according to his opinion. The proof of this is available on a narration transmitted on the authority of Imām Muhammad in which he said, "If the judge accuses the witnesses being false witnesses, he should separate them, i.e., he should put them questions separately, but if there is no such accusation against the witnesses then he should not separate them.

Imām Khassāf (Allah's mercy be on him) said that all such interpretations are needed at the time when the second witness states, "I give the evidence of the fact of which the first witness has given evidence." But if he states, "I give the evidence on the evidence of the first witness," then such evidence shall not be accepted as is agreed upon by all the jurists.

The reason is that it is an evidence of the evidence and not an evidence of the truth.

Likewise, if the witness says: *"alā mithli mā shahida'l-awwalu."* (As the first witness has given evidence, I give the similar evidence).

The reason is that the word *"mithl"* is sometimes used as a preposition (*silah*). For example, the Qur'ānic verse is:

"....laysa ka mithlihi shay'un...."   (42:11)

i.e., *laysa kahuwa shay'un"*

Therefore, his aforesaid statement and this statement, "I give evidence on the evidence of the first witness" are similar. Hence, evidence of such nature shall not be accepted.

Likewise, when the second witness states:

"ash-hadu 'alā mithli mā shahida'l-awwalu"

In this form his evidence shall not be accepted. The reason is that the word *"mithl"* is sometimes used as a preposition and sometimes it is used in the sense of the word *"min"*. In other words, the witness stated, *"ash-hadu 'alā man shahid'l-awwalu"*. Hence, this evidence shall not be accepted.

199. If any person gives written testimony in respect of the right of any person or he writes down his evidence on a paper and the other person reads it or makes it to be listened and the witness states, "Whatever has been stated in this writing in favour of the plaintiff and against the defendant, I gave testimony of it" or he states, "The thing whose qualification has been mentioned in this writing belongs to the plaintiff and the possession of the defendant on it is illegal and it is necessary for the defendant to hand it over to the plaintiff." Such a statement is a valid evidence. The reason is that sometimes the evidence is long and it is impossible for a witness to keep it preserved in his memory. If the witness does not give evidence in writing, the right of the plaintiff will become void. Therefore, to give evidence in writing is permissible.

Evidence regarding an Object Present in the Court

200. If evidence is required regarding an object present in the court (in view of the judge), the witness has to point out towards the plaintiff, the defendant, the object concerning which he is giving evidence.

Evidence concerning a Deceased or Absent Person

201. If the evidence relates a deceased person whose was is present in the court or an absentee whose agent (*nā'ib*) is present in the court and the witness states his name and his father's name, the judge should not accept his evidence till he also discloses his grandfather's name. The reason is that by telling only the parentage the identity is not made. It neither makes distinction nor removes the doubt.

If the witness gives the name of both the father and the grandfather of the person in question distinct and the doubt is also removed. The reason is that two individuals are included in the pluaral (*jamā'at*). Thus the mention of two persons is like the mention of ten and a hundred persons.

202. Imãm Khassãf (Allah's mercy be on him) has declared it a condition precedent for identification of a person to disclose his father's name and his grandfather's name. He has stated the same in his book *al-Shurut*.

Our Hanafi masters of law (*mashã'ikh*) have conflict of opinion in this matter.

According to some the above statement is of Imãm Abû Hanifah and Imãm Muhammad (Allah's mercy be on them) while the statement of Imãm Abû Yûsuf (Allah's mercy be on him) is that in the matter of identification of a person the mention of his father's name is sufficient. Imãm Muhamamd (Allah's mercy be on him) has taken a broad view in his writrings and he abandoned the mention of the name of grandfather.

Shams al-A'immah Imãm Hulwãni (Allah's mercy be on him) has stated that the aforesaid view is only of Imãm Abû Hanifah (Allah's mercy be on him). In this matter the view of *sahibayn* is that the mention of father's name is sufficient.

203. Imãm Abû Zaid al-Kabír[146] (Allah's mercy be on him) has described this conflict of opinion of the leading jurists (*a'immah*) in the same way in his book al-Shûrut. According to him if a witness mentions the name of the deceased or absent person and the name of his father and the profession in which he

---

146. His name was Ahmad. He was son of Zayd. His surname was Abû Zayd al-Shurûti. He was one of the *Hanafi fuqahã* of Irãq. He has many writings including *Kitãb al-Shurût al-Kabir, Kitãb al-Shurût al-Saghír*, and *Kitãb al-Watha'iq*. See *Al-Fihrist,* Ibn al-Nadim, p. 307; *Al-Jawãhir al-Mudi'ah*, al-Qarashi, vol. I, p. 68, biographical note no. 109; *Al-Tabaqãt al-Saniyyah*, al-Tamimi, vol. I, p. 407, biographical note no. 195; *Kashf al-Zunûn*, Hãji Khalífah, vol. II, p. 1046.

is engaged, it will not be a sufficient identity of such deceased or absent person.

The object of Imãm Khassãf (Allah's mercy be on him) is that a judge should not accept his evidence till the witness also gives the name of deceased or absent person's grandfather's name, his tribe's name, his profession's name or the circle in which the deceased or the absent person was well known.

The reason is that the identification is a condition precedent. The thing with which identification is complete fulfils the condition. Hence it is sufficient.

204. If the witness gives the name, the father's name, and the grandfather's name or the name of father, tribe, or profession as is stated by Imãm Khasãf (Allah's mercy be on him) and there are two persons in the same locality (*muhallah*) or in the same tribe or in the same profession, the judge shall not accept the evidence of the witness till he states another thing besides the above things which makes the distinctions apparent and removes the doubt.

The aforesaid form is to be followed in case the deceased or the absent person concerning whom the witness is giving evidence is not a popular and well-known person.

In case such a person is a popular and well-known person as were Imãm Abû Hanifah (Allah's mercy be on him) and Ibn Abí Layla (Allah's mercy be on him), then it is not a condition precedent to mention the name of anything. The reason is that the object of mentioning the name is to get (true and beyond any doubt) identification, which is already there.

Suit of Ownership of a House

205. If a plaintiff institutes a suit (for declaration) that the house in possession of the defendant belongs to him, the judge should examine the plaintiff and record his statement regarding the following particulars.

- ❖ In which city the house in dispute is situated?
- ❖ In which *muhallah* of that city it is situated?
- ❖ In which street of that *muhallah* it is situated?
- ❖ What are its boundaries?

The reason is that a plaintiff is entitled to get written statement of the defendant only after his suit is correct and a suit is correct when the subject matter is known and the subject matter is known when all the aforesaid particulars are mentioned in the plaint. Therefore, where the plaintiff describes only two boundaries of the house in dispute, his suit will not be entertained.

If the plaintiff describes three boundaries then according to us, his suit will be entertained, but according to Imãm Zufur (Allah's mercy be on him) it will not be entertained.

206. If the plaintiff describes any of the boundaries of the house in dispute incorrectly, then there is agreement of opinion that his suit shall not be entertained. Some of the Hanafi masters of law (*mashã'ikh*) have taken a different view but the valid view is that his suit shall not be entertained.

Imãm Zufur (Allah's mercy be on him) has taken the non-mention of one boundary of house in dispute as mentioning incorrect boundary, but the three leading jurists (*a'immah thalathah*) differentiate between the two situations.

207. If the house in dispute is a well-known house, then according to Imãm Abû Hanifah (Allah's mercy be on him) to describe its boundaries is still essential but according to the *sahibayn*, it is not essential.

It is so because the *sahibayn* take the popularity of the house on the analogy of the popularity of the plaintiff and the defendant, while Imãm Abû Hanifah (Allah's mercy be on him) differentiates between the two situations.

The correct place of discussion of such matters is *Kitãb al-Shahãdat*. In chapter 52 of this book, further details will be given on this subject. [*Insha Allah*]

Likewise, if the subject matters of the suit is any property or agricultural land instead of a house, the same procedure will be adopted for its disposal as aforesaid.

Suit for Existing Goods

208. If a plaintiff institutes a suit concerning the goods in possession of the defendant, the defendant shall be directed by the court to produce the same in the court and when such thing is produced in the court to point towards it is a condition and there is no need to state its kind, age, price, description, and qualities. It is so because by pointing out towards it, such thing becomes known.

Suit for Destroyed Goods

209. If the suit property had been destroyed, the form of suit will be proper when its sex, age, description, quality, and price are stated.

It is so because such a thing will only become known when the aforesaid facts are disclosed.

Likewise, in the suits for all movable properties, assets, and clothes, etc., the aforesaid facts are to be described essentially.

Further details on this subject are coming in chapter 21.

210. A judge should not decide cases while he is in a state of anger.

It is so because the Messenger of Allah (peace and blessings of Allah be on him) forbade a judge to decide cases while he is in anger.[147]

211. A judge should not decide cases while he is in a state of hunger.

It is so because hunger badly-affects the power to adjudge.

212. A judge should not decide cases while he is in a state of agony and grief.

It is so because agony and grief adversely affect the power to adjudge as the anger does.

213. A judge should not decide cases while he is in a state of surfeit (*kaziz*).

---

147. *Sahih* al-Bukhārí, kitāb al-ahkām, vol. IV, p. 159; *Sahih* Muslim, kitāb al-aqdi'ah, vol. III, pp. 1342-43, *hadith* No. 16; *Sharh Sahíh Muslim*, al-Nawāwí, vol. XII, p. 15; *Sunan* Abû Dā'ûd, kitāb al-aqdi'ah, vol. III, p. 302, *hadith* No. 3589; *Sunan* al-Tirmizí, kitāb al-ahkām, vol. II, p. 396, *hadith* No. 1349; *Sunan* al-Nisā'i, kitāb adab al-qudāt, vol. VIII, pp. 237-38; *Musnad* Ahmad bin Hanbal, vol. V, pp. 36, 38, 46, 52; *Kitāb al-Umm*, Imām Shāfi'i, vol. VI, pp. 86-87, 201; *Al-Mukhtasar*, vol. V, p. 241; *Musnad* Imām Shāfi'i, vol. VI, pp. 274-75; *Musnad* Abí 'Awana, vol. IV, p. 16; *Sunan al-Kubra*, Al-Bayhaqi, vol. X, pp. 104-105; *Sunan*, Darāqutni, vol. IV, pp. 205-206, hadith No. 13; *Al-Muhalla*, Ibn Hazm, vol. IX, p. 365; *Majma' al-Zawā'id*, al-'Irāqi wa ibn Hajar, vol. IV, p. 194; *Al-Matālib al-'Aliyah bin Zawā'id al-Masanid al-Thamaniyah*, Ibn hajar, vol. II, pp. 247-248, *hadith* No. 2125; *Akhbār al-Qudāt*, al-Waki', vol. I, p. 81; *Jāmi' al-Usûl*, Ibn Athir, vol. X, pp. 549-550; *Talkhis al-Habir*, al-'Asqalani, vol. IV, p. 189, *hadith* No. 2091; *Jāmi' Masanid al-Imām al-A'zam*, vol. II, pp. 260, 279.

It is so because over eating causes inconvenience affecting adversely the power to adjudge rightly.

From the above said affairs a judge has been forbidden apprehending injustice to any party as his responsibility is to do justice to all.

214. According to our (Hanafi) masters of law (*masha'ikh*) if a judge is in his full youth, he should go to his wife before sitting for deciding cases. It is so to avoid his inclination towards a young lady appearing before him as such an inclination would be against justice.

215. A judge should remain attentive towards the parties with his ears, heart, and mind.

It is transmitted that Hadrat 'Umar Fãrûq (Allah's pleasure be on him) said:

"*al-fahm; al-fahm.*"

(Deeply ponder upon, deeply ponder upon).

216. A judge should maintain equality in the matter of paying attention and looking towards the parties.

Hadrat 'Umar Fãrûq (Allah's pleasure be on him) had in his letter to Hadrat Abû Mûsã al-Ash'arí (Allah's pleasure be on him) instructed, among other things, "To maintain equality between the parties."

217. A judge should not play joke with any of the parties as to play joke with others is forbidden for all persons, it is forbidden for a judge even with more stress.

218. A judge should not laugh turning his face to anyone party as it will make such a party varying against his opponent and hoping an inclination of the judge towards him.

219. A judge should not whisper with any one of the parties nor make any indication of anything towards him leaving the other party.

It is so because such behaviour on the part of a judge will bring a blame of partiality to him. The other party will think that either the judge is helping his opponent or is telling something to him or is leading him to adopt a certain direction.

220. A judge should maintain equality in the matter of his sitting.

Hadrat 'Umar Farûq (Allah's pleasure be on him) said, "A judge should take account of all the necessary affairs and to do so is necessary for him."

Recording of Identity of plaintiff, Defendant, and Witnesses in the Proceedings Register

221. When the reader writes the proceedings of a case, he should record the name of the plaintiff, his father's name, his grandfather's name, his surname (*kunyah*), his profession, his tribe, and such things in which he is popular in the proceedings register.

It is so because all these particulars are necessary for the identification of the plaintiff fully.

222. If the judge does not know the plaintiff personally, the reader (of the court) should state his identity. It is not necessary for him to do so, however, if the reader states his identity, it would be more proper for the identification of the plaintiff. It is so because there is no harm in making such an identification by the reader.

223. When the reader states the identification of the plaintiff, he should not mention any defects of him. He should mention his good features. For example, if the plaintiff is one eyed, the reader should not describe him with it.

224. The same procedure should be adopted in the matter

of identification of the defendant and the witnesses. The identification of the defendant is necessary as unless the parties (plaintiff and defendant) are not fully identified, the truth will not be enforced. The identification of the witnesses is necessary as they can only be examined when they are fully identified to be the witnesses.

225. The reader should record the place of residence, the name of locality (*muhallah*), and the mosque in which they offer congregational prayers. It is so because if their creditworthiness is not already known to the judge, he shall have to know it and such information will be obtained from the people of his locality.

226. The reader should record the names of the witnesses, their description, their home addresses, and the places where they offer congregational prayers on a separate paper and then paste it on the proceeding register.

This proceeding will be taken only when a judge has no information about the witnesses, otherwise no such proceedings are needed.

The Attesting witness of a written contract or document or will or a Power of Attorney

227. If the witnesses give evidence upon a written contract or a document or a will, the reader shall copy it in the proceedings register.

It is so because the judge has to send these proceedings to the 'ulamā to get their *fatwa*. Therefore, it is necessary to write it down to present it to the 'ulamā.

Description of Women

228. When the reader prepares the file of a woman and intends to state in it her description, he should leave the space blank to be filled by the judge himself.

It is so because if the reader states her description, then thereafter the judge will also have to see her face and in this manner two persons will be seeing her face. Therefore, if only the judge records her description, it is better and in this manner only one person will be seeing her. There is more *pardah* in seeing by one person as compared to seeing her by two persons. Therefore, only such procedure is better whereby there is much *pardah* (*astar*).

If a judge sees a woman and states her description, it is permissible. If he dictates such description to the reader, it is also permissible. The reason is that in both the cases the seeing is, only, by one person.

A woman, whether she is a plaintiff or defendant, the statement of her description is necessary as in all circumstances her identification is necessary. Hence in all circumstances, statement of her description is necessary.

229. If the judge deems it proper to entrust this function to his reader, he may do so and in that case the reader shall record her description. It is so because at times the judge is not free to perform this function and as such he may delegate it to his reader provided that the reader is a pious and creditworthy person.

When the reader reads such file before the judge, the later should see towards the face and the description of the woman given in the file and compare it. The judge should take extra care and caution and also avoid publicity of her description.

Preference in the Matter of Hearing of Cases

230. If some outstation litigants appear before a judge and bring a suit against a resident litigant or they file suit against each other or a resident litigant files such against an outstation litigant, the judge should hear the cases of the outstation litigants first. If their number is so excessive that the turn of each people is going to be affected (to their inconvenience), then the judge should fix some time for their cases.

Details on this subject have already been given in chapter 6, above.

231. The judge should not detain them from performing their journey. However, if some right is proved against them or the hearing of their case prolongs, then he should consider them equal to the resident litigants.

In other words, the judge should give preference to the outstation litigants as to delay their matter is to hinder their journey. Therefore, he should not become a hindrance in their journey except that a right of someone is established against them. If there is no such right established against them then he should give them preference. If their case prolongs, then they shall be taken equal with the resident litigants.

Joining of Funeral and Visiting Sick by the Judge

232. If a judge joins funeral (*janāzah*) of deceased person and visits a sick person, there is no harm in it. It is so because these affairs relate to the rights of a Muslim upon another Muslim.

The Messenger of Allah (peace and blessings of Allah be on him) said:

"*sittum-min huqûqil muslim 'alal-muslimi. ..*"

(There are six rights of a Muslim upon another Muslim...).

Out of these, Imām Khassāf (Allah's mercy be on him) has described only two rights, viz., he should join the funeral of a deceased Muslim and visit a sick Muslim to ask his health.[148]

By appointment to an office of a judge the rights of other Muslims on a judge do not extinguish. However, a judge should not stay for a longer period of time at such occasions. He should also not give anyone a chance to have a conversation with him regarding any proceedings pending before him in his court. It is so because any party may ᴜᴄᴄᴜme the judge of being partial.

Acceptance of Invitation

233. If there is a general invitation, a judge may accept it as it is reported:

"kāna yaqdi baynannāsi wa yujibud-da'wah"

(The Messenger of Allah (peace and blessings of Allah be on him) used to decide the cases between the people and also accept the invitation).[149]

---

148. *Sahih* Muslim, kitāb al-salām, vol. IV, p. 1704, *hadith* No. 4; p. 1705, *hadith* No. 5; *Sunan* Ibn Mājah, kitāb al-jana'iz, vol. I, p. 461, *hadith* No. 1433; *Musnad* Ahmad bin Hanbal, vol. II, p. 68; *Sahih* al-Bukhārī, kitāb al-janā'uiz, vol. I, p. 148; *Sunan* Abū Dā'ūd, kitāb al-adāb, vol. IV, p. 307; *Al-Mustadrak* al-Hākim, vol. I, p. 349; *Sunan* al-Nisā'i, vol. IV, p. 54; *Al-Jāmi' al-Saghir*, al-Suyûtí, vol. I, pp. 148-149; *Al-Targhib wa'l-Tarhib*, al-Munzari, vol. II, p. 100; *Mishkāt al-Masābih*, al-Khatīb al-Baghdādi, vol. I, p. 485; *hadith* Nos. 1524-25; *Sahih*, al-Bayhaqi, vol. III, p. 379; *Al-Matalib al-'Aliyah bi Zawā'id al-Masanid al-Thamaniyah*, Ibn Hajar, vol. II, p. 368, *hadith* No. 2489; *Mawarid al-Zam'ān ila zawā'id Ibn Habbān*, al-Haithami, p. 504, *hadith* No. 2064; *Majma' al-Zawā'id*, al-Irāqi wa ibn Hajar, vol. VIII, pp. 184-86.

149. *Sunan* Ibn Mājah, kitāb al-tijārat, vol. II, p. 770, *hadith* No. 2296; kitāb al-zuhd, vol. II, p. 1398, *hadith* No. 4178; *Sunan* al-Tirmizí, kitāb al-janā'iz, vol. II, p. 241, *hadith* No. 1022; kitāb al-ahkām, vol. II, p. 397, *hadith* No. 1353; *Sahih* al-Bukhārī, kitāb al-Hibah, vol. II, p. 58; kitāb al-nikāh, vol. III, p. 167; *Talkhis al-Habir*, al-'Asqalāni,

The Messenger of Allah (peace and blessings of Allah be on him) said:

"man lā yajibud-da'wata faqad 'asa Abā'l-Qāsim."

(One who does not accept the invitation, he disobeys Abû al-Qāsim (peace and blessings of Allah be upon him).[150]

The reason is that when there is general invitation, it is not particularly for the judge.

234. If the invitation is particular then the judge should not accept it as the object of such an invitation is to invite the judge alone and by its acceptance he is taking the meals in the capacity of a judge.

235. What is a general invitation and what is a particular invitation? There is difference of opinion in this behalf.

According to some an invitation to a marriage party (*da'wah 'urs*) or a circumstance party (*da'wah khitān*) or any other party like it is a general party.

According to some others, an invitation where more than ten persons are invited is a general party and where less than ten persons are invited is a particular party.

Shams al-A'immah Imām Sarakhsi (Allah's mercy be on him) said, "Where the host knows that the judge will not participate in his invitation and even then he holds the party, it will be termed as a general party. Hence the judge should accept such an invitation.

vol. III, p. 70, *hadith* No. 1316; *Al-Matālib al-'Aliyah bi Zawā'id al-masanid al-Thamaniyah*, Ibn Hajar, vol. II, p. 43, *hadith* No. 1606.

150. *Talkhis al-Habir*, al-'Asqalani, vol. III, p. 195, *hadith* No. 1558; *Sahih* al-Bukhārí, kitāb al-nikāh, vol. III, p. 168; *Sahih* Muslim, kitāb al-nikāh, vol. II, p. 1055, *hadith* No. 110; *Sunan* Ibn Mājah, kitāb al-nikāh, vol. I, p. 616, *hadith* No. 1913; *Sunan* Abû Dā'ûd, kitāb al-at'amah, vol. III, p. 341, *hadith* No. 3742; *Tanwir al-Hawālik*, kitāb al-nikāh, vol. II, p. 14.

Where the host knows that the judge will not participate in his invitation and he does not hold the party, it will be termed as a particular party. Hence the judge should not accept such invitation."[151]

236. The above situation is only at the time when there is no relationship between the host and the judge. In case there is relationship between the host and the judge, then the judge should accept the invitation even if it is a particular party. The reason is that to accept the invitation of a party hosted by a relative is to join relationship (*silah al-rahm*) and to join relationship is compulsory (*fard*) for the judge.

Imām Khassāf (Allah's mercy be on him) has stated in the same way and he has not mentioned any difference of opinion on this issue among the *'ulamā*.

Imām Tahāwi (Allah's mercy be on him), in his *al-Mukhtasr*,[152] has mentioned the following difference of opinion on this issue among the *'ulamā*:

---

151. *Al-Mabsūt*, al-Sarakhsi, vol. XVI, p. 81.

152. *Mukhtasar al-Tahāwi* is the first *Mukhtasar* on the *Hanafi* school of thought. It is the best book in the matter of arrangement of subjects. Its narrations are the most authentic narrations. It is strong in the matter of *darāyat*. It is most preferable from the point of view of *fatwa*. Imām Tahāwi has mentioned the problems in this book in a well-known and popular way and has strengthened it by attributing its transmission on the authority of leading Hanafi jurists as has been mentioned at page 4 of the *muqaddimah of Mukhtasar*, al-Tahāwi by Abū al-Wafā' al-Afghāni. This book was published from Cairo in 1370 A.H. and many eminent leading jurists wrote commentaries on it including the commentary of Jassas and the commentary of Isbijabi. See *Miftāh al-Sa'adah*, vol. II, pp. 182, 276; *Kashf al-Zunūn*, vol. II, p. 1627; *Al-Hāwi fi Sirah al-Imām Abi Ja'far*, al-Tahāwi, p. 35.

❖ According to Imām Abû Hanifah and Imām Abû Yûsuf (Allah's mercy be on them), the judge should not accept the particular invitation of his relative.

❖ According to Imām Muhammad (Allah's mercy be on him), the judge should accept the particular invitation of his relative.[153]

237. The judge should accept the particular invitation of his relative only when such a relative is not a party to any case pending before the judge for adjudication. If he is a party in any such case then the judge should not accept his invitation.

238. A judge should not accept the particular invitation of a non-relative who had never invited the judge on any invitation before his appointment as a judge. A judge should accept the invitation of a non-relative who had been inviting the judge even before his becoming a judge.

Acceptance of Presents

239. The same is the rule concerning the acceptance of presents. A judge should not accept any present from anyone except when the giver of the present is related to the judge.

Imām Tahāwi has stated the same in his *al-Mukhstasar* and has not mentioned any disagreement of the *'ulama* on this subject.[154]

240. The judge should not accept the present of a non-relative who had not been sending him presents before his becoming a judge.

153. *Mukhtasar al-Tahāwi*, Abu al-Wafā' al-Afghāni, p. 326.

154. *Mukhtasar al-Tahāwi*, Abu al-Wafā' al-Afghāni, p. 326.

If a person used to send him presents prior to his becoming a judge and there is a case of such person pending before him, he should not accept the present of such a person. Imām Khassāf (Allah's mercy be on him) has stated the same in the end of chapter 14 of the book. If there is no case pending with the judge and the gift presented is equal to or less in value of the gift he used to send to the judge. the judge should accept the gift as such a gift is not being received by him on account of his judgeship. If the value of the gift presented is more than the gifts he used to send, the excess value be returned to that person by the judge as it is being given on account of his judgeship.

(Allah knows the best)

CHAPTER 8

Joint Sitting with a Judge (as amicus curiae)

241. *It* is transmitted by Abdul-Rahmān bin Sa'īd (Allah's pleasure be on him): "I saw Hadrat 'Uthmān bin 'Affān (Allah's pleasure be on him) sitting in the mosque when two persons brought a dispute before him and he directed one of them to call Hadrat 'Alī (Allah's pleasure be on him) and directed the other to call Hadrat Talha (Allah's pleasure be on him), Hadrat Zubair (Allah's pleasure be on him), and a group of Companions of the Messenger of Allah (peace and blessings of Allah be on him). When all of them came, he asked both the litigants to state their respective stands and they stated. After that he turned towards the said invitees and asked their opinion. They expressed their opinion which was in conformity with the opinion of Hadrat 'Uthmān Ghanī (Allah's pleasure be on him) and he decided the dispute accordingly and did not delay in execution of the decision. After that both the litigant parties stood up to depart and accepted the decision.[155]

The following guidance is available from this *hadith*:

❖ The relations between Hadrat 'Uthmān and Hadrat 'Alī (Allah's pleasure be on both of them) were cordial and the

155. *Sunan al-Kubra*, Al-Bayhaqi, vol. X, p. 112.

opposite *propaganda* of the innvators (*ahl al-bid'ah*) is not correct.

❖ To administer justice in the premises of a mosque is permissible.

❖ To ask *fatwa* from others by a judge and to decide accordingly is permissible.

❖ To consult mutually is commendable act.

❖ If any aspect of a matter under adjudication is not clear, a judge should consult and if it is clear, then there is no need to consult in that behalf.

❖ This *hadith* of Hadrat 'Uthmān Ghani (Allah's pleasure be on him) shows that the *shari'ah* value (*hukm*) regarding the matter in dispute was not clear.

❖ The words, "As the opinion of all the invitees was in conformity with the opinion of Hadrat 'Uthmān (Allah's pleasure be on him). Hence he decided between the two litigants accordingly" shows that there was consensus of opinion of the Companions (*ijmā' sahābah*).

❖ The words, "Hadrat 'Uthmān Ghani (Allah's pleasure be on him) did not delay in execution of the decision" shows that the right had become clear and, therefore, there was no scope for them to delay, as he did not consider permissible to delay the performance of a compulsory act.

242. It is transmitted on the authority of Isma'il bin Abi Khālid (Allah's mercy be on him): "I saw Justice Shuraih sitting as a court in the mosque wearing a turban on his head whose side was hanging on his shoulders and he had worn a silken shawl and a group of *'ulamā* was sitting with him in that session including Abû 'Amr al-Shaybāni[156] and al-Sha'bi[157] (Allah's mercy be on

156. His name was Sa'd. His father's name was Abas. He was of Kûfah

all of them).

The following guidance is available from the contents of this report:

- ❖ To decide cases in the mosque is permissible for a judge.

- ❖ A judge should wear a turban.

- ❖ In some countries the judge wear caps according to the custom of those countries. Thus there is no harm in wearing a cap by a judge. However, to wear a turban is better.

243. A'mash[158] (Allah's mercy be on him) reported: "Qāsim

and his surname was Abû 'Amr al-Shaybāni. He had got the period of the Messenger of Allah (peace and blessings of Allah be on him) but had not seen him. He went to Madínah Tayyibah after the death of the Messenger of Allah (peace and blessings of Allah be on him). Thereafter, he went to Kûfah. All agree in his being a creditworthy (*thiqah*). He died in 95 or 96 A.H., while he was of the age of 120 years. See *Al-Isabāh fi Tamyiz al-Sahābah*, al-'Asqalani, vol. II, p. 110, biographical note no. 3670; *Al-Isti'āb fi Asmā'il Ashāb*, Ibn Abd al-Barr, vol. II, p. 53; *Tazkarah al-Huffāz*, al-Zahabi, vol. I, p. 68, biographical note no. 62; *Taqrib at-Tahzîb*, al-'Asqalani, vol. I, p. 286, biographical note no. 79, *Tahzib at-Tahzîb*, al-'Asqalani, vol. III, p. 468; *Khulâsa Tahzib al- Kamāl*, al-Khazraji, p. 114, *Shazarāt uz-Zahab*, Ibn al- 'Imad al-Hanbali, vol. I, p. 113; *Tabaqāt al-Qurā*; Ibn al-Jazari, Vol. I, p. 303; *Al-'Ibr wa Diwān al-Mubtada wa'l-Khabār al-Musamma bi Tārikh*, Ibn Khaldûn, vol. I, p. 116; *Tabaqāt*, al-Suyûtí, vol. XXVI, p. 60.

157. *Akhbār al-Qudāt*, al-Waki', vol. II, p. 226.

158. His name was Sulaymān. His father's name was Mihrān. He was known as al-A'mash. His surname was Abû Muhammad al-Kûfî. He was a slave of Bani Kahíl. His family belonged to Tabristan. He heard the *hadith* from a number of tabi'in. He was born in Kûfah in the year when Hadrat Imām Husayn (Allah's pleasure be on him) was martyred. Ibn 'Uyainah stated that he excelled in three attributes from his companions:

- ❖ He was the best of all the reciters of the Holy Qur'ān of his time.

- ❖ He was the *hāfiz* of *ahadith* more than anyone else.

bin Abdur-Rahmān[159] (Allah's mercy be on him) asked me to come if it be possible and to sit with him in his session of administration of justice. I went to him and sat with him in the said session. Two litigant persons brought their case before him. I criticised him on a certain point and remarked that he has said this thing in such and such manner although Hadrat Abdullāh bin Mas'ūd (Allah's pleasure be on him) has said: 'Of you a person should decide only in accordance with the knowledge he has, otherwise, he should confess his ignorance and should not feel ashamed in asking others.'[160]

❖ He was ahead of all the experts in *'ilm al-farā'id*.
He died in 148 A.H. See *Tabaqāt*, Ibn Sa'd, vol. VI, p. 338; *Mizān al-I'tidāl*, al-Zahabi, p. 3517; *Tahzib al-Tahzib*, al-'Asqalani, vol. IV, p. 223; *Al-Jam Bayna Kitābai*, al-Kalābāzi, vol. I, p. 179; *Tazkarah al-Huffā*, al-Zahabi, vol. I, p. 154, biographical note. No 149; *Hāmish Adāb al-Shāfi'i*, Shaikh Abd al-Ghani Abd al-Khaliq, p. 315; *Tabaqāt al-Huffāz*, al-Suyūti, p. 67, biographical note no. 144.

159. His name was Qāsim. His father's name was Abdur-Rahmān. His grand father was Abdullah bin Mas'ud. His surname was Abū Abd al-Rahmān. He was al-Hazli al-Kūfi. He was a judge of Kūfah during the period of Hadrat 'Umar bin Abdul-'Azíz. He has transmitted *hadith* on the authority of his father, Hadrat Abū Zarr Ghifāri, Hadrat Abdullāh bin 'Umar, Hadrat Jābir bin Samurah (Allah's pleasure be on all of them). From him the *hadith* has been transmitted by A'mash, Mas'ūdi, and Mis'ar, etc. (Allah's mercy be on them). Ibn Sa'd said that he was creditworthy (*thiqah*) and excessive narrator of *hadith* (*kathir al-hadith*). Yahyā bin Sa'íd has also declared him *thiqah*. He did not take salary for administration of justice or legal opinion. He died when Khālid bin Abdullāh al-Qasri was the governor of Kūfah. See *Akhbār al-Qudāt*, al-Waki', vol. III, pp. 6-9; Tahzib al-Asmā' wa al-Lughāt, al-Nawāwi, part I, vol. II, p. 54, biographical note no. 60; *Taqrib al-Tahzib*, al-'Asqalani, vol. II, p. 118, biographical note no. 27.

160. *Akhbār al-Qudāt*, al-Waki', vol. III, p. 8.

The following guidance is available from the above report:

- ❖ If a judge deems it proper to ask a *faqih* to sit with him in his judicial session, he should make a request to him to sit with him for that purpose, but he should not compel him to do so.

- ❖ If there is any slip on the part of a judge, it is essential for the person sitting with him to stop and correct him as the jurisconsult A'mash (Allah's mercy be on him) had stopped Justice Qãsim bin Abdur-Rahmãn during the proceedings (and corrected him). The reason was that he knew that Justice Qãsim will consider it advantageous and will not feel ashamed asking him (the solution of the difficult point of law). However, in our period the judges are not stopped during the proceedings. The words of the report: "You have said this thing like this while Abdullãn bin Mas'ûd (Allah's pleasure be on him) had said it like that."

- ❖ May be these were the words of A'mash (Allahs' mercy be on him) as he apprehended that Justice Qãsim will feel embrarrassment in asking from him and on that he said that Abdullah bin Mas'ûd (Allah's pleasure be on him) has said, "A person should decide according to the extent of his knowledge, otherwise, he should confess his ignoance and should not feel ashamed in asking from someone else." Or it may be the words of Justice Qãsim that Abdullãh bin Mas'ûd (Allah's pleasure be on him) has said: "A person should decide according to the extent of his knowledge, otherwise, he should confess his ignorance and should not feel ashamed in asking from someone else." And Ibn Abdur-Rahmãn confesses his inability in the matter in issue and does not feel ashamed.

244. Idris has transmitted on the authority of his father who said, "I saw Mahārib bin Daththar deciding cases while Hammad and Hākam were sitting on his sides. Mahārib at a time looked towards Hammād and at a time looked towards Hākam while both the parties were sitting before him."[161]

The same guidance is available from this transmission which was available from the earlier quoted reports.

245. Ma'mar, on the authority of Ayyûb and he on the authority of Imām Muhammad (Allahs' mercy be on all of them), transmitted: "It was the opinion of *fuqaha* that the authority vested in a ruler is not vested in the judge. That is, a ruler can make another person to sit near or away from him but a judge cannot do so..."

The reason is that people visit a ruler to meet with him. Therefore, he should give a person place of sitting according to his status and rank. However, they visit a judge for decision of their disputes. Therefore, he should maintain equality between them in every respect.

This *Sharī'* value (*hukm*) is not particular due to being a ruler or a judge. Rather it relates to the aforesaid status (circumstance) which we have described. When a ruler is deciding cases between the parties, he should maintain equality between the parties and when a judge is sitting to meet the visitors, he should give them place of sitting according to their rank and status, i.e., make them sit near or away from him.

---

161. *Akhbār al-Qudāt*, al-Waki', vol. III, p. 30; *Al-Mughni*, Ibn Qudamah, vol. XI, p. 396; *Al-Sharh al-Kabir*, Ibn Qudamah, vol. XI, p. 400; *Matālib ulin-Naha fi Sharh Ghāya al-Muntahā fi'l-Jam' bayn al-Iqnā' wa'l-Muntaha*, vol. VI, p. 478; *Kitāb al-Shûra bayn al-Nazariyyah wa'l-Tatbiq*, Qahtān Abdur-Rahmān al-Dûri, p. 162.

246. It is transmitted on the authority of Hadrat 'Alí (Allah's pleasure be on him) that a guest was staying with him who asked about something. On that Hadrat 'Alí (Allah's pleasure be on him) put him the question as to whether he has the opponent party in the case and he replied in the affirmative. On it Hadrat 'Alí (Allah's pleasure be on him) said to him, 'Please leave my place as I have heard the Messenger of Allah (peace and blessings of Allah be on him) saying; 'Do not be a host to a party to a dispute unless the other party is also with him.'[162]

The reason is that if a judge hosts one of the litigant party, the other may blame him with partiality.

247. Imãm Abû Hanifah (Allah's mercy be on him) said, "There is no harm if a judge makes a person sit near him who is considered reliable due to his piety (*al-diyanah*), honesty (*al-amãnah*), and legal acumen (*al-fiqahah*). He should make him seated at a place from where he could hear the conversation taking place between the judge and the parties to the litigation. The condition precedent is that such a person must possess the qualities of piety, honesty, and legal acumen."

The reason of imposing the condition of piety and honesty is that young ladies have also to appear in a court of law before the judge and if the person so allowed to be seated is impious and dishonest, there is apprehension of indecency (*fasãd*).

162. *Al-Musannaf*, Abd al-Razzãq, vol. VIII, p. 300, *hadith* No. 15291; *Sunan alKubra*, Al-Bayhaqi, vol. X, pp. 137-38, *Kanz al-Ummãl*, al-Burhãnpuri, vol. III, *hadith* No. 2621; *Al-Matãlib al-'Aliyah bi Zawã'id al-Masanid al-Thamaniyah*, Ibn Hajar, vol. II, p. 150, *hadith* No. 2136; *Majma' al-Zawã'id*, al-'Irãqi wa ibn Hajar, vol. IV, p. 197; *Talkhis al-Habir*, al-'Asqalani, vol. IV, p. 193, *hadith* No. 2106; *Nasb al-Ra'iyah fi Takhrij Ahadith al-Hidãyah*, al-Zayla'i, vol. IV, p. 73; *Al-Dirayah fi Takhrij Ahadith al-Hidãyah*, Ibn Hajar, al-'Asqalani, vol. II, p. 169, *hadith* No. 822, *Al-Mabsût*, al-Sarakhsi, vol. XVI, pp. 75-76; *Adãb al-Qãdi*, al-Mawardi, vol. II, p. 264, *hadith* No. 3035.

The reason of imposing the condition of possessing legal acumen is that the object of counselling is to have access to the truth and to deduce the *sharī'* value (*hukm*) and this object can be achieved only after consultation with a *faqih*.

248. It is not befitting a judge to consult the jurisconsults sitting with him acbout any matter in the presence of the parties in whicn proceedings had advanced.

The reason is that the parties may not know about the conversatin that takes place between the judge and the counsellors and the opinion of the judge may not become known (to them) before time.

Earlier it was mentioned in the hadíth of Hadrat 'Uthmān bin 'Affãn (Allah's pleasure be on him) that he had consulted Hadrat Talhah and Hadrat Zubair (Allah's pleasure be on both of them). The reason is that in that period piety and honesty were dominant upon the people and the Messenger of Allah (peace and blessings of Allah be on him) has himself given the testimony about the people of that age being truthful and virtuous.

During that period if there was any dispute concerning any matter there had been the doubt of its being true or false and to get a decision people used to go to the judge so that the truth and false may become manifest. But now there has been degradation in the moral standard of the people and they concoct fraudulent excuses.

Hence if a person will give an advice to the judge in presence of the parties, they will become aware of it and will exercise fraud and excuses [with *mala fide* intention].

249. If the judge does not consider it proper to make any other person sit with him as his counsel or otherwise he may act as he deems proper provided he is well acquainted with the knowledge of administration of justice. If he is not so acquainted, then it is better for him to consult with the *fuqaha* concerning the problems coming before him and to make the *fuqaha* sit with him is the best course for him.

(Allah knows the best)

CHAPTER 9

Consultation by a Judge

250. *It* is transmitted on the authority of Abû Hurairah (Allah's pleasure be on him) that he said about Hadrat 'Umar (Allah's pleasure be on him)":

"ma ra'aytu ahadan ba'da rasûlillâhi sallallâhu 'alayhi wasallam akthara mushâwaratin li ashâbihi minhu"

I did not see any one consulting with his companions more than him [Hadrat 'Umar (Allah's pleasure be on him) after the Messenger of Allah (peace and blessings of Allah be on him).][163]

The reason is that the Messenger of Allah (peace and blessings of Allah be on him) used to consult his companions in every matter even in the matter of the food and dishes of his own family.[164]

The Messenger of Allah (peace and blessings of Allah be on him) did so to be benefited by the blessings of consultation. Besides this, in doing so was the following of the Divine Command, which is as follows:

---

163. *Sunan* al-Tirmizi, kitâb al-jihâd, vol. III, p. 129, *hadith* No. 1767' *Sunan al-Kubra*, Al-Bayhaqi, vol. X, p. 109; *Al-Kâfi al-Shâfi fi Takhrij Ahadith al-Kashshâf*, Ibn Hajar, p. 33, hadith No. 269.

164. *Tafsir* Ibn Kathir, p. 420.

"wa shāwir hum fi 'l - 'amr"

"....And consult them in all the affairs...." (3:159)

There are may *ahadith* on this subject that have been referred to by Imām Khassāf (Allah's mercy be on him) here and other places.

251. While explaining the Qur'ānic verse.

"wa amruhum shura baynahum"

"....And their affairs are settled by them by mutual consultation...." (42:38)

Hasan Basrī (Allah's mercy be on him) has said:

"innahu wallāhu mā tashawāru qaumun qattun illā waffaqahumullāhu ta'ālā li afdala mā bi hadratihim"

(By God, as and when a people mutually consulted about the problem faced by them, Allah, the Almighty granted them courage and fortitude of finding out a better solution).[165]

It is so because the better from is correct and valid form and the same is the objective. Thus, when they mutually consult, Allah, the Almighty blesses them with a better form and thus they find out the better, i.e., the correct form of the issue before them.

252. Imām Khassāf (Allah's mercy be on him) has referred to another *hadith* on the authority of Hasan Basrī (Allah's mercy be on him) which has the same meaning as that of the earlier hadith.

253. It is transmitted on the authority of Ziyād[166] that he

165. *Al-Kāfi al-Shāi fi Tajhrij Ahadith al-Kashshāf*, Ibn Hajar, p. 146, *hadith* No. 360; *Tafsir*, al-Kashshāf, vol. III, p. 407; *Tafsir*, al-Qurtubi, vol. IV, p. 251.

166. He was popular by the name Ziyād bin Abī Sufyān or Ziyād bin

said, "Men are of three kinds: a complete man, a half complete man, and nothing." A perfect man is he who possesses his own personal judgement and he is not dependant on any other person. A half man is he who has no independent opinion of him but when any problem comes he consults another person competent to exercise personal judgement. Nothing is he who is neither able to exercise his own judgement nor consult anyone else.[167]

The above statement of Ziyâd is a word of wisdom. Ziyâd was of such persons whose talk was full of wisdom. Ziyâd had stated so to excite upon consultation.

Ubayyah or Ziyâd bin Sumayyah. His surname was Abû al-Mughirah. According to some, he was born in the year of *Hijrah* of the Holy Prophet (peace be upon him) and according to some others, he was born in the year of battle of Badr. The *'ulamâ* have stated that he had not seen the Messenger of Allah (peace and blessings of Allah be on him) nor narrated any *hadith* from him. He was a sagacious, eloquent, Arab leader, and speaker. Hadrat 'Umar bin al-Khattâb (Allah's pleasure be on him) had appointed him governor of some areas of Basrah. According to some, Hadrat Abû Mûsâ al-Ash'arî (Allah's pleasure be on him) had assigned him this office. Ziyâd was his Secretary (*kâtib*). Later on, Hadrat 'Alî (Allah's pleasure be on him) appointed him the governor of Fâris. When Hadrat 'Alî (Allah's pleasure be on him) appointed him the governor of Fâris. When Hadrat 'Alî (Allah's pleasure be on him) was martyred and Hadrat Hasan (Allah's pleasure be on him) handed over the affair of the State in favour of Hadrat Mu'âwiyah (Allah's pleasure be on him), the later joined him in his lineage and later on appointed him the governor of Kûfah and Basrah. He died in 53 A.H., while he was holding that office. See *Al-Isâbah fi Tamyiz al-Sahâbah*, al-'Asqalani, vol. I, p. 563, biographical note no. 2987; *Al-Istai'âb fi Asmâ'il Ashab*, Ibn Abd al-Barr, vol. I, pp. 548-555; *Usud al-Ghâbah*, Ibn al-Athîr, vol. II, p. 271, biographical note no. 1800; *Tabaqât*, Ibn Sa'd, part 2, vol. II, p. 110; part 4, vol. I, p. 85; vol. IV, p. 55; part 7, vol. I, p. 70; *Tahzîb al-Asmâ' wa al-Lughât*, al-Nawâwî, part 1, vol. I, pp. 198-99, biographical note no. 182.

167. *Sunan al-Kubra*, al-Bayhaqi, vol. X, pp. 109-110; *Akhbâr al-Qudât*, al-Waki', vol. II, p. 118.

254. Whenever a judge is confronted with any problem he should deeply ponder upon it. If its solution is found in the *Kitābullāh* or in the *sunnah* of *Rasûlullāh*, then there is no need of any consultation with any person. If the solution is not found in the *Kitābullāh* or *sunnah* of *Rasûlullāh* , then he should consult the men of knowledge (*ahl al-'ilm*) and should not make haste in deciding the matter till he consults with such a person whose opinion, knowledge, and faith are creditworthy. If there is agreeement on any point, the judge should enforce his decision (based on such consensus).

255. If a judge consults a single person in any matter, it is sufficient.

It is so because if the judge is competent to exercise his own personal judgement and he decides the matter according to such personal judgement. it is permissible for him to do so. To consult is in view of the care and caution. If the judge is not competent to exercise his personal judgement, he is like an ordinary man (in the street). As it is sufficient for an ordinary man in the street to get *fatwa* from a *mufti* so it is sufficient for a judge to consult a single person. However, if he consults many persons, it is better to do so. As it is permissible for a judge to give decision according to his own personal judgement if he is able and competent to exercise it and if he consults another person so that his opinion may also be in conformity with his personal judgement, it is better do so. The same is the situation here. If he consults a number of *'ulamã*, it is much better as the truth will not remain beyond the circle of their consultation.

(Allah knows the best)

CHAPTER 10

Hikmah and Fasl al-Khitāb

256. *Imām Khassāf* (Allah's mercy be on him) has narrated the following statement of Hasan Basrí (Allah's mercy be on him):

"The *Qur'ānic* verse in which the words *fasl al-khitāb*[168] occur, those refer to the knowledge of administration of justice."[169]

There is conflict of opinion among the *'ulamā* regarding the meaning of the words *fasl al-khitāb*.

- ❖ One view is that the words *fasl al-khitāb* refer to the knowledge of administration of justice as stated above.

- ❖ The second view is that these words refer to the witnesses and the oaths.[170]

168. Al-Qur'ān, XXXVIII:20.

169. *Al-Durr al-Mansûr fi al-Tafsir bi'l-Ma'thûr*, al-Suyûtí, vol. V, p. 200; *Al-Jāmi' li Ahkām al-Qur'ān*, al-Qurtubí, vol. XV, p. 162; *Tafsir*, al-Tabarí, vol. XXIII, p. 139; *Mukhtasar Tafsír al-Tabarí*, Ibn Samadih al-Tajibik, vol. II, p. 171.

170. *Al-Durr al-Mansûr fi al-Tafsir bi'l-Ma'thûr*, al-Suyûtí, vol. V, p. 200; *Akhbār al-Qudāt*, al-Waki', vol II, p. 267; *Al-Jāmi' li Ahkām al-Qur'ān*, al-Qurtubí, vol. XV, p. 162.

❖ The third view is that these words refer to the words *amma ba'd.*[171]

❖ The fourth view is that these words refer to the knowledge of various forms of administration of justice.[172]

❖ The fifth view is that these words refer to the parties, but this view is weak. However, if the reference is to the deciding of the cases of the parties, then, it is a valid view.

257. Abû 'Abdur-Rahmân al-Sulâmi[173] (Allah's mercy be on him) narrated that when Hadrat Dâwûd (peace be upon him) was Divinely commanded to administer justice and when he could

---

171. *Al-Durr al-Mansûr fi al-Tafsir bi'l-Ma'thûr*, al-Suyûtî, vol. V, p. 200; *Al-Jâmi' li Ahkâm al-Qur'ân*, al-Qurtubi, vol. XV, p. 164; *Tafsîr*, al-Tabarí, vol. XXIII, p. 140.

172. *Al-Durr al-Mansûr fi al-Tafsir bi'l Ma'thûr*, al-Suyûtî, vol. V, p. 200; *Al-Jâmi' li Ahkâm al-Qur'ân*, al-Qurtubi, vol. XV, p. 164; *Tafsîr*, al-Tabarí, vol. XXIII, p. 140.

173. He was Abdullâh bin Habíb bin Rabi'ah al-Kûfi. He was a *qârí* and *'alim* of Kûfah. He was a pupil of Hadrat 'Uthmân Ghaní (Allah's pleasure be on him), Hadrat 'Alí (Allah's pleausre be on him), and Hadrat Ibn Mas'ûd (Allah's pleasure be on him). He heard *hadith* from them. He also heard *hadith* from Hadrat 'Umar Fârûq (Allah's pleasure be on him). He remained appointed as an instructor and teacher of the *'ulûm* of the Holy *Qur'ân* since the period of *caliphate* of Hadrat 'Uthmân Ghaní (Allah's pleasure be on him). He died in the year 73 A.H. It is also stated that his death took place during when Bishar bin Marwân was the governor of Irâq. Âsim is his pupil. Ibrâhím Nakha'i, Sa'íd bin Jubair, 'Alqamah bin Marthal, 'Atâ bin al-Sa'id, and Ismâ'il bin Abdur-Rahmân heard *hadith* from him. He was creditworthy (*thiqah*) and a man of great rank. See *Tazkarah al-Huffâz*, al-Zahabi, vol. I, p. 58, biographical note no. 43; *Taqrib al-Tahzíb*, al-'Asqalani, vol. I, p. 408, biographical note no. 250; *Ta'jil al-Manfa'ah bi Zawâ'id Rijâl al-A'immah al-Arba'ah*, p. 327, biographical note no. 1231; *Tabaqât*, Ibn Sa'd, vol. VI, pp. 49, 119, 120, 121, 126.

not do so, Allah, the Almighty said to him, "Demand witnesses from them and put them to take oath by the token of Allah."

This command was given to Hadrat Dãwûd (peace be upon him) after the raising up of the chain. The story of chain is well-known. The narration is that when Hadrat Dãwûd (peace be upon him) commanded to decide a case, a chain used to come down from heavens and the parties of the dispute used to go towards it. The chain used to come near to the party who had been truthful and the party used to catch it. If the party had been a liar, the chain went away from him and he could not catch hold of it. Thus, he used to decide cases on the basis of the said behaviour of the chain. Later on, the said chain was raised up.

The cause of withdrawal of the chain was that some people had begun to play fraud. It so happened that a man had deposited some dinars with another person as a credit. Later on, the person with whom the deposit was made refused to give back the said amount to the depositor on his demand. He was an old man and kept a staff with him. Both came to Hadrat Dãwûd (peace be upon him) with the dispute. The person with whom the deposit was kept doped an excuse that he made a hole in the staff and concealed the dinars in it. When the proceeding of the case started, the plaintiff stood near the chain and got hold the chain. After him, the defendant came forward and he said to the plaintiff, "Please take my staff in your hand so that I may catch the chain." The plaintiff took the staff in his hand and the defendant caught the chain and in this manner he proved truthful in his denial that he was not liable to pay anything to the plaintiff. Hadrat Dãwûd (peace be upon him) became perplexed. Thereafter, the Arch Angel Hadrat Jibrã'il (peace be upon him) came down and informed the prophet David (peace be upon him) of the occurrence. Consequently, the chain was raised up. In this manner, Hadrat Dãwûd (peace be upon him) remained unsuccessful to decide the said matter. Hence Allah, the Almighty commanded him to ask for the proof (witnesses) from the claimant and the oath from the respondent.

258. Hadrat Mujāhid[174] (Allah's mercy be on him) has stated that in the *Qur'ānic* verse "*yu'til hikmata man yasha'u*" the word "*hikmat*" does not mean "*nubūwwat*". Rather, it means the knowledge, the Holy *Qur'ān*, and the *fiqh*.[175]

❖   According to some *'ulamā*, the word *hikmat* refers to the

174. Mujāhid bin Jābar was popular with the name of Ibn Jubair. His surname was Abū al-Hujjāj al-Makhzumi al-Makki. He was *hāfiz*, *qāri*, and *mufassir* of *Qur'ān*. He was a slave of Sa'ib bin Abi al-Sa'id al-Makhzumi. He heard *hadith* from Hadrat Sa'd, Hadrat 'Ā'isha, Hadrat Abū Hurairah, Hadrat Umm Hāni, Hadrat Abdullāh bin 'Umar, and Hadrat Ibn 'Abbās (Allah's pleasure be on all of them). For a sufficient long time, he remained in the service of Hadrat Ibn 'Abbās and read the Holy *Qur'ān* from him. He is counted among those *tabi'in* whose depth of knowledge is well-known. Qitādah, al-Hakam bin 'Utaybah, 'Amr bin Dinār, Mansūr, al-A'mash, Ayyūb, and many other persons (Allah's mercy be on all of them) had transmitted hadith on his authority. He was an Imām of great rank, pious and abstinate *faqih*. He was Imām of *fiqh*, *tafsir*, and *hadith*. He died in *Makkah al-Mukarramah* in 103 AH.. The historians have given different dates of his death. See *Tabaqāt*, Ibn Khayyāt, p. 280; Tahzíb al-Asmā' wa al-Lughāt, al-Nawāwi, part I, vol. I, p. 82; *Tazkarah al-Huffāz*, al-Zahabi, vol. I, pp. 92-93, biographical note no. 83; *Mashahir 'Ulamā al-Amsār*, Ibn Habbān al-Basti, p. 590; *Mizān al-I'tidal*, al-Zahabi, al-Bajawi, p. 7072; *Mu'jam al-Udaba*, alYāqūt, vol. VI, p. 242, *Tahzib al-Tahzib*, al-'Asqalani, vol. X, p. 42; *Hilyah al-Auliya'*, Abū Nu'aim, vol. III, p. 279; *Khulasa Tazhib al-Kamal*, al-Khazraji, p. 315; *Sifah al-Safwah*, Ibn al-Jauzi, vol. II, p. 117; *Tabaqāt*, Ibn Sa'd, vol. V, p. 343; *Tabaqāt al-Mufassirin*, al-Suyuti, vol. II, p. 305; *Tabaqāt al-Huffāz*, al-Suyūtî, p. 35, biographical note no. 81; *Al-'Ibar wa Diwān al-Mubtada' wa 'l-Khabar al-Musamma bi Tarikh*, Ibn Khaldūn, p. 125.

175. *Al-Durr al-Mansūr fi al-Tafsir bi 'l-Ma'thūr*, al-Suyūtî, vol. I, p. 248; *Ma'alim al-Tanzil*, vol. I, p. 245; *Tafsir*, Ibn al-Kathir, vol. I, p. 322.

recitation of the Holy *Qur'ān*.[176]

❖ According to some other *'ulamā*, the word *hikmat* refers to the committing of the Holy *Qur'ān* to the memory by a person.

❖ According to still some others, the word *hikmat* refers to "*al-tafaqquh fi 'l-hakm*."

259. Hadrat 'Umar bin Abdul-'Azíz (Allah's mercy be on him) stated: "A judge must possess the following five attributes. If he lacks any one of them in him, then there will be a defect (*wasmah*) in him to that extent."

The words "*al-wasm*," "*al-fasm*," and "*al-qasm*" are synonyms but there is a difference in their meaning.

Al-wasm means: Ordinary breaking.

Al-fasm means: To break but a little more than ordinary breaking.

Al-qasm means: To break even more than that.

It is like the difference in the meaning of the words *al-qabs*," "*al-qabd*," and "*al-akhz*."

Al-qabs means: To hold an object with finger tips.

Al-qabd means: To hold an object with fingers.

Al-akhz means: To hold with full hand.

The five attributes mentioned by Hadrat 'Umar bin 'Abdul-'Azíz (Allah's mercy be on him) are as follows:

A judge should be—

1. a man of wisdom (*fahīm*);

---

176. *Al-Jāmi' li Ahkām al-Qur'ān*, al-Qurtubí, vol. III, p. 162; *Tafsir*, al-Tabari, vol. V, p. 553; *Tafsir*, al-Khazim, vol. I, p. 245.

2. a man of courage (*halim*);

3. a man of piety (*'afif*);

4. a man of knowledge (*'alim*); and

5. a man of solid personal judgement (*sā'ib*).

In some narrations a judge must be firm in his faith and asking others in seeking knowledge.[177]

So far as the four attributes of being a man of understanding (*al-fahm*), a man of forbearance (*al-hilm*), a man of piety (*al-'iffah*), and a man of firm personal judgement (*al-ra'iu as-sā'ib*) or firm in faith (*al-salābah fi'd-din*) are concerned those are essential for a judge so that he may not follow the lust of his self.

These are four attributes which we have mentioned.

The remaining fifth attribute is that a judge should be a man asking questions to seek knowledge. It is so because every man has not been given all the knowledge. Rather a few of it has been given to everyone. Hence a judge should increase his knowledge by asking questions to other persons. Therefore, it is necessary for him that he should be a seeker of knowledge from others.

(Allah knows the best)

---

177. *Musannaf*, Abd al-Razzāq, vol. VIII, p. 298, *hadith* No. 15286; *Akhbār al-Qudāt*, al-Waki', vol. I, p. 77; *Al-Bayān wa'l-Tabyin*, al-Jahiz, vol. II, p. 150; *Al-'Iqd al-Farid*, Ibn 'Abd Rabbihi, vol. I, p. 98; *Al-Tabaqāt al-Kubra*, Ibn Sa'd, vol. V, p. 272; *Sahih*, al-Bukhāri, kitāb al-ahkām, vol. IV, pp. 160-161; *Sunan al-Kubra*, Al-Bayhaqi, vol. X, pp. 110, 117; *Al-Mabsūt*, al-Sarakhsi, vol. XVI, p. 71.

Index